HANNIBAL LOKUMBE

BLACK LIVES IN THE DIASPORA:
PAST / PRESENT / FUTURE

BLACK LIVES IN THE DIASPORA:
PAST / PRESENT / FUTURE

EDITORIAL BOARD

Howard University
Clarence Lusane, Rubin Patterson, Nikki Taylor, Amy Yeboah Quarkume

Columbia University
Farah Jasmine Griffin, Frank Guridy, Josef Sorett

Black Lives in the Diaspora: Past / Present / Future is a book series that focuses on Black lives in a global diasporic context. Published in partnership with Howard University's College of Arts and Sciences and Columbia University's African American and African Diaspora Studies Department, it builds on Columbia University Press's publishing programs in history, sociology, religion, philosophy, and literature as well as African American and African Diaspora studies. The series showcases scholarship and writing that enriches our understanding of Black experiences in the past, present, and future with the goal of reaching beyond the academy to intervene in urgent national and international conversations about the experiences of people of African descent. The series anchors an exchange across two global educational institutions, both located in historical capitals of Black life and culture.

Laura E. Helton, *Scattered and Fugitive Things: How Black Collectors Created Archives and Remade History*

Sarah Phillips Casteel, *Black Lives Under Nazism: Making History Visible in Literature and Art*

Aïssatou Mbodj-Pouye, *An Address in Paris: Emplacement, Bureaucracy, and Belonging in Hostels for West African Migrants*

Vivaldi Jean-Marie, *An Ethos of Blackness: Rastafari Cosmology, Culture, and Consciousness*

Imani D. Owens, *Turn the World Upside Down: Empire and Unruly Forms of Black Folk Culture in the U.S. and Caribbean*

Gladys L. Mitchell-Walthour, *The Politics of Survival: Black Women Social Welfare Beneficiaries in Brazil and the United States*

James V. Koch and Omari S. Swinton, *Vital and Valuable: The Relevance of HBCUs to American Life and Education*

For a complete list of books in the series, please see the Columbia University Press website.

HANNIBAL LOKUMBE

SPIRITUAL SOUNDSCAPES OF MUSIC, LIFE, AND LIBERATION

**LAUREN COYLE ROSEN
AND HANNIBAL LOKUMBE**

Columbia University Press *New York*

Columbia University Press
Publishers Since 1893
New York   Chichester, West Sussex

Copyright © 2024 Lauren Coyle Rosen and Hannibal Lokumbe
All rights reserved

Library of Congress Cataloging-in-Publication Data
Names: Coyle Rosen, Lauren, author. | Lokumbe, Hannibal, 1948– author.
Title: Hannibal Lokumbe : spiritual soundscapes of music, life, and liberation / Lauren Coyle Rosen and Hannibal Lokumbe.
Description: [First edition]. | New York : Columbia University Press, 2024. | Includes bibliographical references.
Identifiers: LCCN 2024020929 | ISBN 9780231217859 (hardback) | ISBN 9780231217866 (trade paperback) | ISBN 9780231561938 (ebook)
Subjects: LCSH: Lokumbe, Hannibal, 1948– | Lokumbe, Hannibal, 1948– Religion. | Composers—United States—Biography. | African American composers—Biography. | Trumpet players—United States—Biography. | Jazz musicians—United States—Biography. | African American jazz musicians—Biography. | LCGFT: Biographies. Classification: LCC ML410.L8343 C8 2024 | DDC 780.89/96073 [B]—dc23/eng/20240508

Cover design: Milenda Nan Ok Lee
Cover photo: Randy Kerr

> *"The highest law is life.*
> *The highest life is knowledge.*
> *The highest knowledge is love."*
>
> —Hannibal Lokumbe

This work is dedicated to humanity.

CONTENTS

Introduction: Musical Alchemy and Spiritual Liberation 1

1 The Passages of Youth in Texas 12

2 New York City and the Jazz Years 44

3 Composing the Spiritatorios 93

4 *The Jonah People* and Becoming the Work 117

5 The Music Liberation Orchestra in Prisons and Schools 168

Conclusion: "Pure Mind Has No Time" 183

Coda: The Living Temples 201

After Coda: "The Shadow," poem by Hannibal Lokumbe, 1976 205

Acknowledgments 207
Notes 211
Bibliography 233

HANNIBAL LOKUMBE

INTRODUCTION
Musical Alchemy and Spiritual Liberation

When Hannibal Lokumbe was twenty, he found himself on the brink of death. He had a dangerously high fever in a freezing room in New York City, where he had recently arrived in pursuit of a life in jazz.

In November 1970, I was fighting with all of my might to stay alive in the jail cell room of the Greenwich Arms Hotel. I was too hungry to speak and too cold to die. My body was rife with fever," Hannibal recalled. "My immediate companions were the fleas living in my single wool army blanket and the murmurs of those languishing in the hallway outside the door of my room. From the unrelenting fever, I was forced to lie still upon my army cot and await my fate. In that freezing tomb, I was captured by the moans and cries of those but a few feet from me. From their moans and cries, I was inspired and found enough strength to play a few tones from my trumpet. Healing, life-saving tones they were, for when I started playing, their moans and cries would stop. A most unusual ensemble we became, one which proved to be one of the most influential of my life. When it became too painful for my fluid-filled lungs to continue to play, I returned my trumpet to its sack, laid upon my cot, and held it to my chest like a mother would hold a newborn baby. This, I did so that, if discovered lying dead, it would be told to my sacred mother that I kept my promise to her. The promise that I would keep my music close to me, no matter who, no matter what. In that massive, freezing concrete Greenwich ship, I made a promise to the members of our unique ensemble. . . . I promised that, if I lived, I would introduce them to the world.

Hannibal, now a prominent orchestral composer and jazz musician, reflected upon his always striving to fulfill this promise.

"In my compositions entitled *African Portraits*; *Can You Hear God Crying?*; *Healing Tones*; and *The Jonah People: A Legacy of Struggle and Triumph*, I find a certain peace in knowing that I kept my promise to them as well."

Throughout his life, Hannibal has stayed true to his covenant with the divine to give musical expression to the oppressed, marginalized, and suffering of the world. In Hannibal's experience, music is the ultimate source of vitality, healing, and spiritual liberation for humanity. Music can save people's lives, as it has Hannibal's on many occasions. Music is also a living consciousness of its own accord and is basically synonymous with life itself.

His whole life is one perpetual and ever-emergent musical composition, and this text is not separate from that overarching movement. This book is based on extensive conversations that Hannibal and I had over the course of three years (fall 2020 through fall 2023), and all of the conceptual and theoretical work has emerged in a truly collaborative, dialogical fashion. Any concept that I mobilize throughout the narrative has been generated through the discussions that we regularly had, virtually and in person, throughout the pandemic and beyond. His reflections and knowledge very much take precedence and center stage.

To this end, I have mobilized extensive quotes from him and from dialogues of our conversations. The cocreation of the text has been so thorough that Hannibal has joined as a coauthor, though the book is set in my voice.

The book follows Hannibal's creative and spiritual journeys over the course of his life and career. It foregrounds major moments from his youth in a segregated Texas in the 1950s and 1960s, his decades as a jazz trumpeter playing with many other great musicians and innovators in New York City and around the world, and his becoming a leading orchestral composer in recent decades. His spiritual life has been deeply interwoven with the broader tapestry of his life, especially following a dramatic spiritual awakening at the age of thirteen. Ever since that event, he has consciously lived in two worlds—one in the finite realm of things on earth and the other in spirit, in the formless world of the eternal.

His pathbreaking musical compositions—whether jazz, orchestral, oratorios, string quartets, or in other genres—are often centered on addressing the Black American experience in ways that chronicle as well as heal and liberate. His work also pays special tribute to the experiences of Africans and of Indigenous people who live on the lands now called the United States, while also expressing the suffering and liberation struggles of many others. One of his primary spirit guides is his great-grandmother, a Cherokee shaman who successfully fled the Trail of Tears. She, along with Hannibal's mother (who is now in spirit), plays a key role in guiding and inspiring his major works and life decisions. The ancestors and other spirits inform him at every turn as he proceeds through dreams, visions, waking communications, signs, and other modalities of transmission.

For Hannibal, sound is not solely tonal or aural. It also has feelings, textures, scents, colors, contours, and other spatial and sensorial dimensions. These spiritual soundscapes—a phrase used here to denote the multisensorial musical spaces and affective registers within which his co-creations with spirits take place—allow a reckoning with previous traumas or suffering, such as the Birmingham Church Bombing, the Vietnam War, or the Middle Passage of enslavement. Through working with the spirit guides to generate transcendent art, Hannibal offers his music as portals for healing, transmutation, or other transformations for humans in the present or future.

The following chapters explore Hannibal's journey of discovery and creation as he moves between worlds—the spiritual and the physical realms, the interior and exterior aspects of life. Hannibal coined the term "spiritatorio" to describe the ways in which his orchestral works are powered by spiritual inspiration and speak to the profound interrelations of science, spirituality, and humanity. He has concisely defined spiritatorio as "a genre of art which uses images, music, and text to evoke a profound intellectual and spiritual response."[1] He first used the term around 2015 to describe the oratorio *One Land, One River, One People*, in which he orchestrates and speaks to the interconnectedness of all humans and nature in physical existences (one land), in blood or life (one river), and in spirituality (one people).

Spiritatorio can apply to Hannibal's orchestral works writ large. Throughout his works, Hannibal seeks to reveal the interconnectedness of all persons and things, including the connectedness that lies beneath the seeming separation of spirit and matter, inner and outer social life, nature and humans, and one person from another. This interconnectedness and oneness of all people is something that Hannibal has felt and discovered throughout his life, beginning in his days of youth in Texas. He seeks to reveal this oneness, or remind people of it, through his musical arts of spiritual liberation. For Hannibal, everyone must come to discover within themselves their divine nature—that they have everything they need within them. Once they realize this, people can then recognize that the same is true for others. This inner work of self-knowledge and healing is a prerequisite for people's seeing and acknowledging this truth for others.

In offering this collaborative multisensorial ethnography of Hannibal's lifelong journey of musical creativity, liberation work, and spiritual practices, I seek to draw upon Hannibal's deep wisdom and philosophies in order to engage and expand recent work on soundscapes and affective archives, creativity and liberation art, and the importance of spiritual co-creation in pursuits of authentic justice. This brings the ethical, political, and aesthetic dimensions of musical soundscapes evermore powerfully into the realms of the spiritual. This approach also resonates with recent work that emphasizes embodied sensorial suites as sites of knowledge and knowledge production. Multisensorial spiritual experiences are a highly revelatory domain for bodily sensorial knowledge, and such spiritual experiences are central for understanding the embodied dimensions of language, discourse, and new media forms in music and in art, more generally.[2]

In the most distilled formulation, this book argues for the centrality of spiritual soundscapes for apprehending the ancestral, mystical, and multisensorial dimensions of Hannibal's creative journeys of music and life. By extension, it argues for the broader significance of spiritual soundscapes for expanding anthropological, philosophical, and other reckonings of artistic creativity, spiritual co-creation, consciousness, and the pursuits of true liberation and justice. Spiritual soundscapes are the multisensorial creative spaces through which Hannibal navigates his creative life and interfaces with various sources of spiritual inspiration and collaboration. The spiritual soundscapes of Hannibal's creative journeys entail a process of perpetual emergence in his own subjectivity, which is always unfolding and expanding, as it is entwined with dynamic networks and affective assemblages of ancestors and other spirits who interlace with his consciousness to co-create the art and to advance spiritual liberation and illumination.[3]

This formulation of spiritual soundscapes draws inspiration from multiple sources across music studies, anthropology, and social theory.[4] It also engages recent works on sonic worlds and affective spaces,[5] as well as various forms of cosmopolitics, theopolitics, and pluriversal politics.[6] This combination further expands the conceptual scope of soundscapes to encompass multiple mystical or sublime dimensions. It foregrounds the various ways in which spirits and ancestors—or forms of co-presences—are perpetually interlaced as co-creators with Hannibal's subjectivity. Hannibal co-creates with spirits beyond the confines of any religious rubric or system, as he does not subscribe to any formal institutional religious order.

In addition to my extensive conversations with Hannibal over the course of these two years, I draw upon materials from Hannibal's personal journals that he has kept over the past five decades and that he generously made available to me for this book. I also explore the social justice work he has done through the Music Liberation Orchestra, an organization he founded in the 1970s to teach and advocate for music education, genealogical research, and journal writing in prisons and schools. This work continues today.

By traversing Hannibal's creative journeys through spiritual soundscapes, we can understand music itself as a living thing, a spiritual consciousness, a potentially healing force, and a profound wellspring in the art of perpetual liberation. This journey also helps to reframe and expand our conscious understandings of art and subjectivity, including what it means to be human, to be connected to spirit, and to be free.

Born in Smithville, Texas, in 1948, Hannibal has devoted his life to creating and pursuing true music that is aligned with his soul purpose of spiritual liberation for all. He seeks to offer his creations to the world as nourishing meals or much-needed medicine for the pain and suffering that beset so much of the human experience.

"Like prayer, music can cover you, envelope you, and infuse your being with everlasting life," Hannibal said.

At all times, he co-creates with his cherished ancestors and other spirit guides, while receiving his musical and other creative assignments from the Everlasting, which he also calls the Creator (for the absolute being that many call God). Every act of playing or writing music is a form of deep spiritual communion and becoming one with the spirits.

"It is a becoming and a realization. You realize that you are the spirits, and they are you, and then you become the music," Hannibal said. "No one can truly write a piece, in a way that is real, unless they have become it. It is impossible."

For Hannibal, true or genuine music is that which flows from the soul and resonates with the harmonies of nature, creation, and the universe. It is deeply spiritual, and it is a force for healing and liberation from the forces of destruction or evil. In all of Hannibal's art, he helps people see or remember the inherent divinity within them. Hannibal contrasts true or genuine music with that which is destructive, mechanical, contrived, or stagnant. That type of music is not harmonious with his soul's purpose or his musical covenant with the Creator, and he does not participate in it in any way. As he wrote to me:

> My efforts as a musician have primarily been to affirm that humans are the miraculous replication of an eternal process. The concept of sin is but a creation of men who seek power by way of fear, thus creating the unending wars of greed and destruction. Sin is the result of not acknowledging both the mortal and the immortal of ourselves. We are all bound by the perfect principles of nature. It is a perfect principle, which exists in us all. The sunlight brings light into the temple that is the entire Earth. Its life-giving food not only feeds the lands deemed more sacred than others by the measured thinking of some beings. It covers the entirety of our divine home. All about us are the temples of life. The ocean, forest, land, and sky. It is in these living temples, and in the temples of ourselves, that we become The Everlasting.

Hannibal's remarkable career spans six decades. He started playing in local jazz clubs near Texas City after he got his first trumpet from his mother when he was thirteen. He formed his first jazz band, Marvin Peterson and The Soulmasters, early in high school. He was born Marvin Peterson, a name that he later changed. He received the name Hannibal in the 1970s from a Yoruba priest outside of a jazz club where he was playing. He got permission to publicly use the last name Lokumbe from his Cherokee shaman great-grandmother spirit guide, called Cora in her most recent life, after he completed a major orchestral work, *African Portraits*, in the 1990s.

The Soulmasters accompanied many legends who toured Texas, including T. Bone Walker, Lightnin' Hopkins, Jackie Wilson, Otis Redding, and Etta James. These artists and others would request The Soulmasters as their band of choice when they were in the region.

When Hannibal was twenty, his ancestral spirit guides gave him clear instructions to immediately leave Texas and head for New York City. He left that same day, drove there, and went straight to the legendary Village Vanguard. After a few fortuitous introductions, Hannibal soon joined the vibrant forces of the city's jazz scene and became an internationally known jazz trumpeter. He toured widely with his own jazz band The Sunrise Orchestra, releasing albums under the band's name and his own (Marvin Peterson, Hannibal Marvin Peterson, Hannibal, and, later, Hannibal Lokumbe). The Sunrise Orchestra included many prolific musicians, including among others Rahn Burton (piano), Cecil Brooks III (percussion), Andy McCloud (bass), and Diedre Murray (cello). Hannibal also played and recorded with many other jazz legends over the course of about twenty years, including Gil Evans, Roy Haynes, Cecil Taylor, Pharoah Sanders, Elvin Jones, Thad Jones, Mel Lewis, and Archie Shepp.

When Hannibal shifted course and started to compose for orchestras, he received major commissions. His oratorio, *African Portraits*, premiered in 1990 at Carnegie Hall with the American Composers Orchestra. It has since been performed around a hundred times in the United States and Europe. In 1995, the Chicago Symphony Orchestra under conductor Daniel Barenboim recorded it for commercial release. The piece is widely celebrated for its innovative coupling of jazz, blues, and spirituals into what many consider a classical orchestral composition. As Hannibal told me, "I know of no music that is more classical than jazz, than the music people call jazz." In *African Portraits*, Hannibal also foregrounds the powerful influences that African instruments and music have had, and continue to have, on so-called Western classical music.

Hannibal was recently composer-in-residence (2016–2019) with the Philadelphia Orchestra, where he premiered several major works, including *Can You Hear God Crying?* (2012); *One Land, One River, One People* (2015); *Crucifixion Resurrection: Nine Souls A-Traveling* (2017); and *Healing Tones* (2019). Music director and conductor Yannick Nézet-Séguin described Hannibal as "one of those stars, geniuses on the planet that just brings us all together in a very, very special way."[7]

Hannibal has composed numerous other commissioned choral and orchestral pieces over his career, including *Can You Hear God Crying?*; *Dear Mrs. Parks*; *God, Mississippi, and a Man Called Evers*; *Fannie Lou Hamer*; *Water Too High, Bones Too Low*; *In the Spirit of Being* (Hannibal referred to this piece as a musical memoir); *No Toussaint, No Purchase*; *Dr. King and the Crescent Moon*; *Gumbo à la Freedom*; *Trane's Legacy of Truth*; *One Heart Beating*; *John Brown and Blue*; *Dance Chief Crazy Horse, Dance*; *A Star for Anne*; *Flames of South Africa*; and *Children of the Fire*. He has written and starred in an autobiographical mini-opera, *Diary of an African American*, which was performed in cities across the United States, Europe, and Colombia. He has also published several volumes of poetry[8] and has received numerous awards and fellowships, including induction into the Harlem Jazz Hall of Fame.[9]

A journey through the entirety of the spiritual soundscapes of Hannibal's music and creative life would far exceed the bounds of a single book. In what lies ahead, I trace major movements in the arc of his life, interlaced with powerful formulations of his philosophies of music and nature, spirits and humans, and bondage and freedom. The final body chapter explores his decades-long work to bring music and other liberation work into prisons and schools through the Music Liberation Orchestra.

"It breaks my heart when I see how people are set upon from so many directions and what they have to face. And that all comes again from people not knowing that by virtue of their aura and their energy, their divinity, that they are not who others say they are. They're much more. They are more than the name by which people call them. A lot of that is in *The Jonah People* opera [in which the choir sings] 'We are not who you say we are.' We are more than the name you know."

Speaking of the perpetual expansion of human consciousness and self-knowledge, he added, "It's not just seeing, hearing, tasting, smelling, feeling. It's so much more than that, what people are and what people have to discover in themselves. Those senses are just a welcome mat to say come on in to discover these other places and these other abilities. People create spaces and places for people who do not know—or have not discovered—that they have these abilities within themselves. Everyone has them. I know of no shrine more sacred for creating than the human body."

His summation of much of his philosophy of religion, nature, and musical creativity is: "The true temples are us. We are the true temples. Humans are the true temples."

1

THE PASSAGES OF YOUTH IN TEXAS

One day, out of the blue, Hannibal read aloud the following passage to me. He had written it earlier that day in his journal, reflecting on the bounty of love and wisdom and sacred musical experience he had as a young boy, growing up in a racially segregated Texas in the 1950s:

> When my grandmother would hum alone in her tiny kitchen before the sunlight filled the house, I knew even as a young boy, that the tones coming from her gave her strength and protection from the people and the things which would violate the sanctity of her life. A talisman of sound her hums came to be. Often, they were brilliantly accompanied by a pan of sizzling bacon, a percolating pot of coffee, and a perfect fire of oak wood crackling and popping in the belly of her wood-burning stove. To awaken and witness so sacred a ritual was to learn to see with my ears, hear with my eyes and touch with my silence.

He shared a similar entry, titled "Talisman," dated February 11, 2022:

> Lately, my mind has been flooded with the imagery of my grandmother. Especially her times alone in the kitchen of her modest

home of tin and wood. Her seemingly placid state of grace while preparing breakfast was as nurturing to my psyche as were the first rays of sunlight filtering through the small doors and windows. The outline of her body moved in shadows upon the wall when she would get close to the flame in the glass oil lamp. The motion of her slim, strong, regal frame was a natural choreography of bliss and calm. Always she would sing or hum. The words in her songs touched my mind. The tones in her hums touched my soul. There is something Everlasting about the tones she summoned. They had the qualities of having never been born, and never will die, about them.

Often her hums were accompanied by the cooing of doves in the crepe myrtle just outside the kitchen window. Such moments, such richness of those visuals, sounds, motions, and sacredness experienced by my five-year-old presence, looms large in this composition. They are my guides, my source of clarity some sixty-eight years later.

To tell this story, her story, her father and his father's father's story, is to truly be reborn.

He attributes much of his ability to stay true to his covenant with the Creator—to use his musical gift for spiritual liberation—to the absolute love and profound wisdom he experienced firsthand through his mother (Lillian E. Peterson, 1916–2012), grandmother (Susie Burgess, 1887–1965), and grandfather (General Peterson Sr., 1888–1966).[1]

"For those who don't know that love, it is harder to survive the battles with the forces of destruction. Because I have known that love, though the journey has had its trials, I have been able to draw on that feeling and those memories to sustain me," Hannibal explained. "And they are always with me, my ancestors, when they were alive and after they transcended.

14 • THE PASSAGES OF YOUTH IN TEXAS

FIGURE 1.1 Hannibal with his "sacred mother," Lillian E. Peterson, near their apartment in Sanders Projects, Texas City, Texas.

Photograph courtesy of Hannibal Lokumbe (ca. 1965).

My mother especially. She is a part of me. I don't even have to call her. When she transcended, I did not lose any connection with her. In fact, we became a force, and I feel her even more fully as a spirit."

He also has navigated his career with the objectives and models that he learned as a child—how his family lived with selflessness, self-reliance, and without any preoccupation with riches or notoriety.

"I've never considered money or fame or fortune in my living art equation. That has never been a major factor in my life; that many people know my name or that I have more money than I know what to do with. I never factored that in," Hannibal said. "I do the work if I have two chickens in the pot, with carrots and corn, and I do it if I have one stone in the pot. Sometimes the soup with one stone is better for your system—all those minerals."

He follows his mother's and his grandmother's practices of cooking soup in layers and singing or humming as he stirs the pot.

"I think people take a risk eating things that people haven't sung to," he commented, laughing. The idea is that the heartfelt music purifies and blesses the food.

"I never paid attention to what went into the soup. I was more fascinated with what was in their eyes," he recalled. "Let me know how extraordinarily loved I was. And I wish every child, every human being, could have that. That's why I could survive what I have survived in society, when people hate me because of my skin and the texture of my hair. Many who didn't have that, it turned them into something they didn't want to be. When you don't have that primary love, it's easier to fall victim to hate. Loving requires a great deal more effort, strength, and courage, for sure."

Hannibal said one of the greatest feelings he has had is knowing that he is loved by people in his hometown of Smithville, Texas, where he was born (in 1948) and once again resides with his family: "People let me know every day, and usually it is strangers. A stranger will walk up to me."

Hannibal was born and raised in a racially segregated Texas. There were places marked as the white parts of town, where he was not supposed to go, whether by regulation or by his elders' not allowing it. His grandfather told him that he was forbidden from going in any establishment that said that Blacks had to pass through the back door and not the front.

"As a young boy, my grandfather made it clear that I was not to go in any place that told a person of Jonah that he could not enter the same way as whites. He told me that that would be begging and to stay away from such places."

Hannibal's mother, Ms. Lillian Peterson, was a fiercely loving woman with a degree in education. She was also a beautiful soul singer who toured the South. Ms. Peterson was the granddaughter of Silas Burgess, who escaped enslavement in Charleston, South Carolina, when he was fourteen years old. Silas had escaped with several older people but returned to get his half-brother, Hamlet (then around eight years old), who had been conceived from an enslaver's raping of Silas's mother. Another brother had been on the slave ship with Silas, but he perished in a fire caused by the enslaver's slamming a door and knocking over a kerosene lamp. After the enslaver (Burgess) falsely blamed Silas for his brother's death by fire on the plantation, Silas knew he had to flee as soon as possible.

Two of Hannibal's later orchestral works, *The Jonah People: A Legacy of Struggle and Triumph* and *African Portraits*, are direct tributes to Silas and to other ancestors who were enslaved. Silas Burgess ran all the way to Texas, where he worked on the railroad and saved enough money to buy 102 acres. After he paid for his land, he never worked for another person again. The family grew everything they needed on the farm. They even made candy. Silas raised fifteen children with his two wives, marrying again after his first wife died. He also founded the first Black church, Zion Hill Baptist, which also served as the first elementary school in Bastrop County, Texas.

"I always give thanks to the soul that my great-grandfather is to have experienced what he experienced and yet leave this Earth as a healer of people, all people," Hannibal said. "The [Texas] Secretary of State came to his funeral. They said there was a cloud of dust, so high from all the wagons that it was as far as you could see. It was just a trail of dust from all the people that came to his funeral. White, Black, Latino, everybody."

Hannibal is not only a part of the same spiritual continuum as his great-grandfather Silas, but he also grew up in the same area where he had lived and flourished.

Until Hannibal was five, he lived on his grandparents' farm in Upton, Texas. His best friend was the sky, which he described as "so generous, a different portrait every day."

He had no shoes. And no need for them.

There are two "box seats" that Hannibal names as the most important he has occupied in his life. One was his designated position under a wagon as his grandparents and other family members picked cotton in the unrelenting heat of the fields in Elgin, Texas. One day, his grandfather told him to wait beneath the shade of the wagon while the sun was scorching; Hannibal had just cut his finger picking cotton. The elders told him he would be the water boy. And he watched, listening to them sing with the most beautiful feeling in their voices that he has ever heard.

"I brought my grandfather the pail of water, and he threw it up in the air, and they kept singing," Hannibal recalled. "See, even in the 105-degree weather, they didn't need the water, because the music had brought them someplace else, to a place that was not of bondage."

He said this is like the monks who can control their body temperatures with their minds. His elders could control their body temperature with sound. The music they sang brought them someplace else, to soundscapes of spiritual freedom.

As a child, Hannibal had a beloved dog named Blue, who also taught him a great deal about spirit and freedom. Blue often would accompany him out to the railroad tracks where Hannibal would rest and reflect in reverie over the peaceful flow of Cedar Creek, which empties into the Colorado River. If he fell asleep on the tracks, Blue would hear the train coming and wake him up.

Years later, when Hannibal was first introduced to the trombone, he realized that it carried the sound of his dog, Blue.

"When I got introduced to the trombone, I said, 'That's Blue,'" he remembered.

I asked him if his surroundings carried multisensorial experiences for him, from as early back as he can remember, particularly tonalities, colors, and feelings.

"Yes, everything. Music was always in everything. I always heard it, felt it. Still do."

"What was the trumpet?"

"The sunrise," he replied. "I came to realize that the trumpet was just like the sunrise, and I would use the trumpet to play the sunrise."

Since Hannibal is a trumpet master, this was part of the genesis for the name of one of his jazz bands, the Sunrise Orchestra.

"The birds are flutes. The wind is strings," he continued.

To this day, Hannibal still goes to the tracks over the river, part of his grandmother's property that Hannibal now owns in part.

"That is where I go when I need to go to church," Hannibal stated.

He often goes to clear his head, meditate, and commune with the Everlasting. His grandfather taught him the healing powers of the river when he was a child. They would fish in complete silence. All sorrows or stresses would leave them. His grandfather instructed him, whenever he had troubles or worries, to always cross over some water when the soul needed healing. These moments of silent fishing are some of Hannibal's earliest memories of learning how to hear the music of nature even more deeply. He recalled them in his journal in April 2022:

THE RIVER

The river was always there, coming from everywhere, moving to everywhere. Once while checking the trout line with my grandfather, I turned and looked at him seated stoically behind me in the small wooden fishing boat. For the first time in our many fishing trips, I was captured by the placid look on his face. It was on that cool river morning that my five years of knowing understood how he could sit for hours in complete silence whenever we joined in the company of the river. In that gaze I learned that no words ever spoken could rival the soothing murmurs of the river. It was not a place for talking. At times, the wind would momentarily do a quick dance upon the surface of the water causing swirls of shapes and patterns to appear and fade in an instant upon the huge watery canvas. I would first look at them, then close my eyes. It was at that moment that I came to know that to see is to hear and to hear is to see. The few words which flowed from Grandfather's mouth were keepsakes. "Baby," he once said. "Whenever your soul is troubled, cross over some water." Then it became clear why he would at times go to the river without carrying his fishing poles or carry a can of dough bait to restock the stations on his trout line. While living in New York City, my water to cross was New York Harbor, by way of the Staten Island Ferry. In New Orleans it was the ferry to Algiers Point. In Smithville and Bastrop, it is the river called Colorado. A galaxy of pain, I was healed of by crossing those waters. Were that pain measurable in both soil and stone, then where those waters are now, would be dry land.

When Hannibal was five, he, his mother, and his older brother moved to Texas City to live with his mother and older brother. They had a place in the Sanders Projects, which Hannibal remembers as a beautiful village community where people truly helped and looked out for each other. He said the projects that he knew sadly are gone.

When Hannibal was thirteen, several very significant things happened, including fully realizing, on a conscious level, that he had been born a musician. He had always had musical gifts and sensibilities. For example, when he was a child, he would watch the flight of birds and hear it as music. He knew in his spirit that, one day, he would be able to write music to be played by orchestras. And this has proven to be true. It was in his thirteenth year that something fully formed within him regarding his soul's mission being music.

"I lived a thousand lifetimes at age thirteen."

The year was also marked by deep tragedy. His best friend in the projects, Eddie, died suddenly in a car accident. Eddie had asked him to come along to visit a friend in a nearby city; Hannibal had promised his mother that he would cut the grass and felt he could not go. He remembers that Eddie turned around to wave goodbye with both hands.

"I remember his waving like that because it was the only time he ever did it. I had a feeling, a strange feeling, about it," Hannibal said. "And that was the last time I saw him. He died later that day."

This was a profound loss for Hannibal, but Eddie's spirit has remained a part of him always. He recently wrote a musical version of a puddle that he and Eddie once saw together in his opera, *The Jonah People*. The projects were close to an oil refinery, and rain would leave oiled puddles on the ground. He and Eddie were walking once and chanced upon a crystal-clear puddle. They looked at it, and though they did not speak outwardly about it, Hannibal knew they had the same feeling. Hannibal said it was then that he really began to think about the justice of nature and about how, for example, the rain falls on anyone, no matter skin color, creed, or economic status.

"In that puddle, I saw everything," Hannibal said. "After that, I started listening to nature more and following nature more. Humans less. And I have never liked to follow humans. It's too confusing."

During his thirteenth year, he also shot a red cardinal, a tragic memory that has stayed with him throughout his life.

"It was so devastating to me when I shot that bird, the cardinal that was singing. It wasn't just sitting there. It was singing. And I'm always reminded that the Beast is always in close proximity, that the spirit of destruction is always in close proximity, and the only opposition to that is to try and make amends for what I destroyed. And that was a beautiful vessel of the sound," Hannibal remembered. "If I feel that way about a red cardinal, I can't imagine ever having anything close to the position my spirit is now in had I gone somewhere and killed humans, you know, in particular Vietnam. The monster would have prevailed and probably would still continue to prevail over my life because I struggle from time to time just from having destroyed that bird."

In his early twenties, Hannibal was able to avoid being forced to go to war in Vietnam. He was referred to a doctor who facilitated this by simply having him draw a flower and then saying he was not fit for military service. The doctor shared with Hannibal that it was a ploy he had used for many seeking to escape the tentacles of war.

There is now a commemorative mural of Hannibal that stretches across a brick building in the heart of Smithville. The mural features a red cardinal in his hair, next to his ear, signifying his shooting the bird and the haunting guidance the memory has provided.

In Hannibal's thirteenth year, he also received his first trumpet.

His first encounter with the instrument was with Mr. James A. Wilson, his school's music teacher and band leader. He was the man who would become Hannibal's musical master and someone Hannibal came to relate to as a father. Mr. Wilson passed to spirit in the spring of 2022. Hannibal almost instantly felt his loving and guiding presence from the ancestral realm.

FIGURE 1.2 Downtown Smithville, Texas. Commemorative glass and tile mural of Hannibal by master muralists Stefanie Distefano and Ali Denham. Commentary by Ted LeVieux. Commissioned by Jeri and Walter Winslett and David and Nena Marsh.

Photograph courtesy of Hannibal Lokumbe (2021).

Hannibal had never known his birth father, and he believes his father did not even know about him. He asked his mother once about his father, and she said, "He was the only man I ever really loved."

"That was all my mother had to say. After that, I didn't need to hear anything else about my father. If she had said something

FIGURE 1.3 Hannibal, after first receiving his trumpet from his mother, Lillian E. Peterson, at age 13, Booker T. Washington High School Band Hall.

Photograph courtesy of Hannibal Lokumbe (1961).

FIGURE 1.4 Hannibal with master teacher, Mr. James A. Wilson, Sugar Land, Texas.

Photograph by master cosmetologist and community activist Sumai Lokumbe (2019).

else, I would have had a lot of questions. But knowing that was enough for me."

With the powerful presence of his mother, Mr. Wilson, and other revered elders in his life, Hannibal said he did not experience the absence of his birth father as a great void. After Hannibal's mother transcended to spirit in January 2012, one of

Hannibal's relatives contacted his family to let him know whom his father was. Though his birth father had passed by that time, Hannibal has connected with his half-siblings.

Under the direction of Mr. Wilson, Hannibal's devotion to the trumpet quickly grew. It got to the point where Hannibal would walk by a music store every day after school and look at a particular trumpet with a price way out of reach. The store was more than a mile or so out of his way, but he regularly made the trip and would grab the promotional booklets of new trumpets.

One day, while eating lunch with some friends at school, Mr. Wilson came over and placed the trumpet on the table, opening its beautiful case to reveal the instrument inside.

"I remember thinking, 'This is so cruel of Mr. Wilson to do this.' And I had never known him to be cruel."

Then Mr. Wilson announced that it was for him. Hannibal's mother had purchased it as a surprise. Hannibal still remembers its exact price: $265.85. Ms. Peterson had asked Mr. Wilson to present it to Hannibal.

Hannibal remembers that moment so vividly, all of these years later. He even recalls what he was eating.

"String beans, smothered steak, with about a medium brown gravy, mashed potatoes, and cherry cobbler."

As soon as Mr. Wilson said the trumpet was for him, Hannibal grabbed it and, filled with exhilaration, stood on the table in the cafeteria and started playing it with his whole soul.

"And that was the end of the school day," Hannibal said, laughing. "The end for everyone. I walked down the hall, playing and playing, and people poured out of the classrooms into the hallway and followed me. I kept playing all the way home to see my mother, and a whole group of people from school followed me there."

He still recalls seeing his mother, sitting in a room with little natural light. Their electricity and water had been temporarily shut off since she had not had enough money to cover the bills. He said he suddenly became momentarily frustrated with her.

"I made a feeble attempt at scolding her," Hannibal said. "Mom, how could you spend so much money on a trumpet when we don't have lights or water?"

Hannibal said she simply looked at him with love and "that all-knowing look in her eyes."

"She smiled while looking into my soul and replied, 'You have great work to do, son, and you need a great instrument to do it with,'" he affirmed. "A week later her words coursed through my spirit as I played a trumpet solo in the Booker T. Washington school band during a football game. The power of the music caused the game to halt until the song ended. After the game, a long line of well-wishers entered our small three-room project apartment to congratulate my mother. She received them like the queen that she was. I retreated to a spot out of view. From there I wept at seeing my mother being showered with the love she so often showered upon others, and upon me."

He resolved to play and earn back the money she had spent on him. When he did—after he started playing in a club on weekends later in the year—he snuck the money under her pillow to surprise her.

"My mother gave me everything. I'll never be able to repay her for the sacrifices she made. All I can do is to try to be worthy of her sacrifices."

He couldn't put the instrument down. He played whenever he could, "morning, noon, and night." His trumpet would resound throughout the projects at all hours.

His mother gave him pantyhose to use as a mute and asked him to practice in the bathroom, so the sound would not be so loud.

He soon joined some friends to start his first band, Marvin Peterson and the Soulmasters. Hannibal was then going by his birth name, Marvin Peterson, since he had yet to receive what he considers to be his true names, Hannibal and Lokumbe.

Cleveland Gay joined the band as the trombone player. Cleveland and Hannibal had been best friends since second grade. He also, incidentally, was part of a musical family as the first cousin of Marvin Gaye.

FIGURE 1.5 Hannibal, then a junior in high school, at the helm of the mighty Soulmasters, who backed up the likes of Otis Redding, Etta James, T. Bone Walker, and Lightnin' Hopkins, ILA Hall, Galveston, Texas.

Photograph courtesy of Hannibal Lokumbe (1965).

Cleveland once told me that, when he and Hannibal first met in second grade, "our spirits merged, right away."

They remain close to this day. Cleveland recalled, in conversation, how he was playing his instrument more technically at first. "One day, Hannibal said to me, 'Just let your spirit roll.' And I did. And that changed everything for me, how I played. That was something he gave to me."

Later in his thirteenth year, Hannibal had a major spiritual awakening. It marked the moment when he began to consciously live in two worlds—the physical realm of Earth and the realm of spirit. This transition to clarity came after three weeks of lost consciousness.

One day, Hannibal agreed to have a showdown with the school bully in the yard outside the band hall after school. He had recently watched a professional wrestling match between Andre the Giant and Pepper Gomez. While the match tickets had been a surprise gift from his mother, who attended with him, he also took the occasion to study the techniques to use on the school bully. Things were moving in Hannibal's favor in the fight with the bully until he slipped and fell, with the heavy guy then falling on his head.

The blow knocked Hannibal out. He suffered from complete amnesia for three weeks, with his mother continuously praying over him.

He said that all he remembers are the hands and prayers of his mother and the music of one of John Coltrane's (1926–1967) albums, *Olé* (1961), which he recently had received as a gift from a neighbor and had been listening to on heavy repeat. He did not recognize his mother during this time, but he could sense a woman with the most beautiful voice speaking with unconditional love. And he could hear John Coltrane playing his saxophone.

"My mother and John Coltrane, they brought me back," he said. "See, my mother's love was so powerful, it helped to bring me back."

He said that where he went in the spirit realm—and where he still goes and co-resides—is supremely beautiful in many ways. Aspects of an eternal garden that is the spirit are difficult to leave at times. His mother's love and the music of John Coltrane, he believes, made his spirit want to return.

Following this period of amnesia, Hannibal's primary spirit guide came to him in a powerful visitation. This was Cora, his great-grandmother, the Cherokee shaman who escaped the Trail of Tears and the mother of Ms. Peterson's father. When Hannibal described the visitation to his mother, Ms. Peterson immediately told him that it was his great-grandmother Cora.

He has been in conscious connection with her, along with other close ancestors and additional divine spirit guides, ever since. They have co-resided with him in consciousness since he was thirteen.

"Did your mother know that the spirits were there with you?" I asked.

"Yes, she knew. It wasn't necessary to talk about it, though. We didn't speak about it."

When talking about the connection that he and his mother shared and share, and the connection he shares with his other spirit guides, he has spoken in terms of an umbilical cord.

"You know, the physical umbilical cord from mother to child is only one thing, though a very important thing," he said. "What people really need is the one that is not seen, as with most things."

He was referring to the cords of spiritual connection.

This spiritual connection has flowed through him, and all his music, as he has continued on his journey.

In a journal entry he penned during the composing of *The Jonah People*, Hannibal reflected upon this time of remembering the eternal garden and his reluctance to return to his human life on Earth. He also wrote about how he orchestrated the glories of the eternal garden and his hesitation to return to Earth in his oratorio *Healing Tones*, which premiered with the Philadelphia Orchestra in 2019. This entry is dated March 5, 2022:

> A breath from closing out The Last Supper [in *The Jonah People* opera], which in fact is the closing of act one. . . . The work is a constant source of nourishment for my life. Remarkable how biographical it is. Asase holds Silas' face in her hands exactly the way my mother held my face in her hands when healing me and restoring my memory, when due to an accident I suffered a three-week complete lapse of memory. It was during this lapse of memory that I came to know and love the true world of being. It is unrivaled in its beauty. I wrote of it in *Healing Tones*. The garden. The reluctance of the shaman to leave the eternal garden to return to the gravity of the Earth. The tones, their assemblage in this section of the composition is a clear representation of that alter world which has kept me whole for all of these years. Since that fateful accident.

Hannibal underwent another very significant spiritual trial and process of bearing witness when he was thirteen. This time through a slight, regal, and inspired elder—Ms. Sparks. She was a central object of great respect and even reverence among the youth in his community in Texas City, where she helped to save souls and heal people in the midst of brutal racist attacks on community members.

In vivid detail, Hannibal recalled in writing a series of transformative events where Ms. Sparks's guidance and actions served as a form of redemption and restoration. He wrote:

ORACLE

A PARTING OF THE SEA

The Sanders Projects in Texas City, Texas, where I grew up, were not the projects of Watts, Chicago, or other enclaves where violence and drugs were portrayed as being commonplace.

Children cursing in front of elders or spray painting on buildings was unheard of.

I can't recall one of the dozens of families living there having ever locked their doors, my mother as well. It was rare to see a family where the father was present. Those fathers that were, acted as a father to us all.

No one ever went hungry. No Christmas tree was without presents.

Ms. Sparks lived alone. It was known to all who dwelled in our project village that this elder was to be given the utmost respect. While playing, if one of us would curse and think that an elder heard us, we would call out an apology to that elder from where we stood.

If we thought Ms. Sparks heard us curse, we would run to her and say I am sorry. [. . .]

Our beautiful village did not go unscathed by the boiling racial turmoil of the sixties.

Texas Avenue was the demarcation line between the races and provided an imaginary line of safety for us. We knew, without being told, that it was the great divide and that to cross it meant putting your life at risk.

A group of young white teenagers started a gang called The Redcoats. They began a series of night rides to the projects. Their great contribution to the rebel cause was to drive by and throw battery acid on defenseless children. Some of the children were scarred permanently. The skin scarred could eventually be healed. To heal the scarring of our souls required a miracle. The kind of miracle our own eyes could behold. One we could smell and touch. One not given by way of a reading from an ancient text. One which could allow for a new beginning in our lives. And on a brutally hot Texas August night, that miracle came.

The getaway car driven by the gang had stalled after completing one of their missions. They desperately tried to restart their car which was now stationary only a yard from the projects. A cry of, "We got 'em," shattered the hot night air. When I reached the scene, the car was covered with bodies wielding chains, baseball bats and metal rods.

The sounds of metal against shattering glass and iron were not enough to drown out the screams of the souls now trapped inside of the battered car.

A man began pouring gasoline from a can upon the rear of the car.

It was at this moment that Ms. Sparks' frail, five-foot frame appeared as if it had descended from the sky. She began walking towards the car in complete silence. As she moved, a sea of people opened up before her creating a path to the side of the now demolished vehicle. She opened both doors and motioned to the five trapped beings to come with her. Not one in the massive chaotic crowd questioned her or objected in any way to her action.

The path created by her initial approach remained open and through it she took the five terrified young men with her to her tiny apartment. Moments after entering it, she lifted the shade covering her small kitchen window allowing a shaft of light to move from it out into the night and hopefully into us. All night she left it on. She would do the same on occasions such as the death of Medgar Evers, or on the tragic simultaneous death of my best friend, Eddie V., his mother, and his grandmother. She would also leave the light on overnight whenever a baby in the village was born.

Fifty yards from the divine light emanating from her window was the light made from the flames of a now incinerated car. Flames fueled by the dried, cracked, infested wood of racism, ignorance, and hatred.

The crowd quickly dispersed upon the arrival of fire trucks and police cars. The police rushed to the back door of Ms. Sparks' apartment. She stood stoically in the doorway not allowing them to enter. Eventually the five young men filed out of her back kitchen door, weeping and crying out in her direction a cacophony of "I am sorry, I am sorry, please forgive us ma'am, thank you for saving us."

In the projects, the only time you would see a policeman is when they came to arrest someone.

After that miraculous night, I began to notice the same policeman coming on a regular basis to Ms. Sparks' back door. He would always be holding a box or a bouquet of flowers.

It was later revealed that his son was one of the five souls Ms. Sparks kept from being burned alive.

His was not the only soul she saved that wretched night.

She saved us all.

That same immortal force so obvious in the small frame of Ms. Sparks was the same force I felt when Mrs. Rosa Parks entered the dining area of her Detroit condo to join in a circle of prayer and bless the meal we shared [in the early 2000s].

After dinner, the two of us sat for hours looking out of the huge plate-glass window of her living room.

In silence we watched as sheets of ice would drift slowly down the Detroit River like huge glass ships.

I wondered then, as I still do, how many of the jeweled bones its riverbed holds. Bones of those people of Jonah who, like Moses, died before reaching the promised land.

Mother Parks died before hearing the full production of the composition *Dear Mrs. Parks* that I composed in her honor.

I hummed excerpts of it to her and was the beneficiary of the light coming from her eyes.

The same light which came from the kitchen window of a soul who performed a much-needed miracle before our very eyes. One that we could touch, smell, see, and become.

These deep spiritual experiences, and many more, combined to drive a significant transformation in Hannibal's modes of being both in spirit and on Earth. The shifts naturally resounded throughout his music. Beyond his school's band hall, his career in the local music scene quickly took off.

A local musical prodigy, Hannibal was more than welcome on bandstands at thirteen soon after he got his first trumpet. His mother agreed to allow him to play clubs because, as she said to him, "I always knew that your mind was on the music."

He did not drink or smoke, and never has. In fact, it is against his principles and way of being. "As a Man of Jonah, in particular, I don't think the ancestors would be too happy if I were putting coins in that coffin," he said, referring to alcohol or drugs.

He often will feel a high from the beauty of the music and the spiritual connection.

"I always tell people, 'I never said I don't get high. I just have a different supplier,'" he said, laughing. By supplier, he meant the music, the ancestral spirits, and the Creator. "Drugs are so boring. People don't understand that the mind is designed to do those things naturally. It is just about realizing this, remembering this. I don't like anything that interferes with the miracle of thought."

Not long after the Soulmasters started playing local clubs on weekends, they developed a reputation for their mastery. Eventually, they became a top regional accompanying band that played with many great artists who came through the region, including Otis Redding, Etta James, Jackie Wilson, T-Bone Walker, and Lightnin' Hopkins.

T-Bone Walker and Lightnin' Hopkins especially took Hannibal under their wings, giving him sage advice and wisdom that has remained with him throughout his life.

One striking memory that Hannibal shared involves T-Bone Walker, the sacred fire in his eyes, his guitar playing, and his musical and verbal recognition of the sacred fire within Hannibal. He implored Hannibal never to lose that fire or to let anyone take it or diminish it, as the fire is life-sustaining.

"T-Bone started walking towards the stage and, as he was playing, he had this long cord, which afforded him the freedom to move about. The riffs that the Soulmasters were playing were as powerful as the notes coming from his guitar, and he acknowledged that by coming up and standing in front of the bandstand when we were playing. And he looked at us, and he looked at me, and in his eyes—and he began to play things that, like the words of the Marabout [a character in *The Jonah People* opera], things that only God would know, but humans have the ability to feel. And the joy and the life that that music brought into the people for whom he played, the *way* he played, with everything that he had. And all of the fame, the notoriety, and the money in the world, all of that could not equal the purity, the generosity, and the total giving of his soul. It could not, nothing could be comparable to what he gave to everyone in that room."

Hannibal recalled this moment and paused before continuing.

"And as I looked and I watched him, and how he moved—it's like he played as though it would be the last time he would ever play. So, we got the God of him, and when he came to the bandstand and the song ended, he looked at me, and he said, 'Baby boy, you got the *fire* in you. Don't ever, *don't ever* let go of the fire. The fire is what keeps us alive.' I said, 'Yes, sir.' And so, some many years later, writing a piece of music called *One Land, One River, One People* [for the Philadelphia Orchestra in 2015], I sat out beneath a pecan tree on a four-by-twelve-foot yellow bench that I and my son had made out of cedar, and I wrote what I experienced that night, which was a journey through a black hole. And I wrote it, every single note of it, and I wrote it for strings. Just for the strings. And there's fire. There's unrelenting, unending fire in that thirty-two-bar blugue [Hannibal's innovative fusion of blues and fugue sequences]. I relived that moment in those measures that I wrote, under a tree, on a table, unassisted by a piano, every note."

Hannibal then paused again, as though overcome with the feeling of the memory.

"It was a tribute to that experience, to that moment, to that gift. This sage, one of many, that because of the blindness that racism creates, he and others like him were never afforded the things of this world they so richly deserved. But in that blugue, I pay tribute to them, and there's nothing I have ever heard comparable to that blugue. But the fire is there, and the people felt it. They felt that fire. And so, I keep that charge, because that's what it was. He charged me with keeping him alive and keeping folks like him alive, and that their story is told by one that they gave the story to."

He also recalled how Lightnin' Hopkins used to teach him so much about the Delta blues musicians, including Robert

Johnson (born 1911 in Hazlehurst, Mississippi) and David "Honeyboy" Edwards (1915–2011; he would later play in Hannibal's orchestral piece, *African Portraits*).

"Lightnin' said, 'Baby boy, they don't really know how to explain how we do what we do. They have an idea of why we do what we do, but they can't explain how we do what we do,'" Hannibal recalled. "So now, my explanation of that lies in the Jonah People and in the fact that in us is that womb of the slave ship and all that occurred. From three wombs born. So that's how now I would explain to him, when they say they can't explain how we do what we do, but they have an idea of why we do what we do."

While he was playing with these musical legends in his teens, Hannibal had been forced to go to an integrated Texas City high school in 1965, during the period when schools were desegregated. It was for his last three years, tenth, eleventh, and twelfth grades. He graduated in 1967. He said integration was one of the worst experiences of his life. It was impossible to go back to his school, Booker T. Washington, because the city eventually shut it down as part of integration efforts.

"I just went into a shell. I was lonesome, homesick. And I had my first introduction to processed food. It was terrible. The white people looked upon us like we were some curiosity. And they were so shocked that we were so smart and knew so much. I think it truly shook them that it was a myth that they had been taught, that it was not actually true that the whites are smarter," Hannibal recalled. "The music saved me. It helped me endure it."

There was a white bandleader at the school, Mr. Renfro. When he first met Hannibal, he made a racist comment, saying Hannibal could not possibly be a trumpet player on account of the size of his lips.

"When Mr. Renfro said that to me, I could have just cancelled him in my mind right then and there, as I was taught to do with people who said such racist things. But I didn't because I could tell that it was not his essence, that it was not the truth, the God of him speaking."

Despite this initial encounter with Mr. Renfro, Hannibal went on to play solo trumpet in the high school band and was celebrated in great fashion at football games, including by white racist fans waving their huge Confederate flags and asking for "Pete's song." (People called him Pete in high school, short for his former last name, Peterson.)

"It takes a lot of pain and adjusting to live and thrive in such an environment. It can mess with your head. Very few teenagers have that experience, where they are reborn. I had that. Many of the students of color had not found their purpose for being. It can be very difficult facing that kind of social onslaught if you had yet to figure out your purpose in life. My purpose was the music, and I could always go to the music and decipher anything I needed to decipher, and that music deciphered a great deal of hatred," Hannibal said. "So, I could figure that stuff out and just leave it, and it would wash right off, like water on the back of a duck. But for young kids who didn't have that, they took it to heart. They didn't have a way to jettison that pain and insult out of their lives. You didn't have many alternatives; you either believed what the white people said, or you rebelled against it. And I rebelled against it."

Once, the high school band went to play the celebrated Rose Bowl in California. Mr. Renfro instructed band members to play the southern racist song "Dixie" as part of this widely celebrated performance. Hannibal and the three other men of Jonah in the band protested by refusing to play it. As they marched in sequence, Hannibal held the bell of his instrument to his lips, and the three other players displayed similar forms of protest.

But there was no real discussion of this protest after the performance. After the game, the band had a long bus ride home. The members of Jonah had brought sardines and crackers, so that they were not left hungry wherever they stopped. Many restaurants were still segregated and either refused to serve Blacks or required they enter through the back door.

The bus stopped at a restaurant on the way home, and Mr. Renfro and the band members all were very hungry. As they all filed into the restaurant to finally get something to eat, the manager signaled something to Mr. Renfro about how the students of color were required to enter through the back door and not use the front door (as they had just done). Mr. Renfro immediately ordered the entire band back on the bus, without any food.

Late in the evening, back on the bus, Mr. Renfro asked Hannibal to please come sit next to him. He was crying and apologized to Hannibal for asking them to play "Dixie."

"I will never play 'Dixie' again," Mr. Renfro said to Hannibal. And he did not.

"Mr. Renfro's children were the first people to call me 'sir.' He required it. And this was in a time when even grown men of Jonah were supposed to call white children sir," Hannibal explained.

Years later, during the 1990s, when Hannibal was doing a talk focused on the premiere of his *African Portraits* in San Antonio, Texas, Mr. Renfro attended. He told people that he knew Hannibal would be a success, but he did not understand just how successful. He also shared that he kept photographs of his family close to him on his desk and that, among these, were pictures of Hannibal, whom he considered a son.

Another profound experience from his last years of high school occurred when, walking home from his integrated school, he was brutally attacked by five white men who seemed intent on killing him. They asked what he thought he was doing in that part of town. Hannibal was able to fend them off, and while he was doing so, he rehearsed in his mind the music for a song, "Tenderly," that he was planning to play for his mother as a gift. With the help of three men of Jonah passing on a garbage truck, he broke away from those who were assaulting him. He focused on the music and made his way home.

"As I contemplated the music in my mind, I forgot about the beating," Hannibal said.

When he got home, his mother asked what had happened, but he never told her the truth about what happened that day. He knew it would be so upsetting and enraging for her. Instead, he focused on giving her the musical gift.

In a similar incident, this time with the Soulmasters, Hannibal thought he might be facing death when a belligerent, swaggering white cop stopped the band's car late at night. Hannibal was in the back, next to a bass drum, doing homework.

This would be the second most important box seat Hannibal ever occupied.

"I started running through everything my grandfather had taught me about how to survive a stop by a white cop. I also started mentally preparing for my possible death."

After the cop made some racist and otherwise harassing comments to the band, he ordered everyone out of the vehicle. The cop said that if it were true that they were a band returning from a show, then they should play music to prove it to him. So, they were forced to get their equipment out of the car, including the amplifier. They informed the cop that they could not plug it in because there were no electrical sockets. The cop then told them to plug the amplifier into the ground, which they did.

Hannibal said they all stood there with their instruments, and he was terrified, seeing the crazed-looking cop as his guns glinted in his holster.

Their singer, Little Clarence, was an excellent singer, but had a stutter. He always needed some time with the music before he would start singing.

In the moment, Hannibal said the spirit came to assist and started to flow through Little Clarence. He sang soulfully, without any warmup. Hannibal and the others looked at each other in disbelief, and then played to accompany him, almost forgetting entirely about the cop's menacing presence. After the cop fired his two pistols into the air, Little Clarence fell to the ground on one knee while singing passionately.

And then the cop let them go.

"The spirit came upon him and saved us," Hannibal reminisced. "He was still singing when we were miles down the road and the cop was gone. He had gone into a trance."

By the time Hannibal started at North Texas State University, he had been playing with some of the greatest musicians to come through the region and had established the Soulmasters as a leading act in jazz clubs. He said, upon reflection, that he went to college because he thought his mother really wanted that for him.

However, he was immediately put off by his teachers, particularly by his music professor, who was supposed to be a jazz expert.

"I went into his office, and he did not have a single person of Jonah on his walls. This is a so-called professor of jazz. He had photographs of all of these white people. None of Louis Armstrong (1901–1971), Dizzy Gillespie (1917–1991), Bird (Charlie Parker, 1920–1955), Duke Ellington (1899–1974), Billie Holiday (1915–1959). None of these great geniuses that actually in large part created the music that these other people were trying to play," he said. "And then he kept asking me about my trumpet-playing techniques. This guy was supposed to be my instructor!"

Hannibal quickly realized it was a total waste of his time to be studying music at the college. He lasted about a week at the university. "Seven days, which was seven years too many."

"I remember that they looked at me like I was an alien or something, because I wasn't impressed. I had played with people who they were studying," he remembered. "They sent me through hell there. I experienced hell. They wouldn't even let Black people rent a house in the city. You had to stay on campus. Even if you were a senior, you couldn't even rent a house in that town if you were Black."

He quickly resold his composition books, though he couldn't get full price for them, and slept in the forest. He credits the guidance of the ancestors with his swift decision to leave the university.

"If I didn't have the guidance of the ancestors, I probably would be in some plush office somewhere with all sorts of degrees."

He strongly felt that, if he had stayed, the mechanical musical indoctrination there could have threatened his musical creativity and his gift.

Years later, when he was returning to Smithville, Texas, from a trip to Oklahoma City (where he was working on a commission for a forthcoming piece in commemoration of schoolteacher and civil rights leader Clara Luper), he stopped by North Texas State University. He wrote about it in his journal in an entry dated November 22, 2021:

> The very sight of it made me uneasy. I could not help [but] think of how the institution tried to kill my soul. Rob it of its vast wealth and fill it with a bastion of European indoctrination. I hope to see my opinion of the place changing in this lifetime.

After leaving university in the late 1960s, Hannibal ended up getting a garage apartment in town through a guy he knew from a club, then working on the highway crew and playing music all the time. He had a great place and everything he needed. He was very comfortable.

However, one day the ancestors told him that it was time to leave Texas and go to New York City.

"And when they said to leave, they meant immediately. Now. Not tomorrow. Today," he said. "And I did. I packed some things into my car and headed north to New York City, with $50 to my name."

2

NEW YORK CITY AND THE JAZZ YEARS

Hannibal left Texas the day the ancestors said to go. He drove to New York City. It was 1970.

"I've always been that way," Hannibal said. "When the ancestors say to go, I go."

Hannibal always had the sense from the ancestors and from other musicians with whom he played, such as Lightnin' Hopkins (1912–1982) and T-Bone Walker (1910–1975), that at some point he would be called to leave Texas to pursue music in New York City. He just did not know the exact time that the spirits would instruct him to go. When the time suddenly arrived, he listened and followed their directive.

He had $50 to his name, was in the throes of an acute case of tonsilitis, and headed straight to the Village Vanguard, the epicenter of jazz that he had long dreamt of visiting in person. He parked at a White Castle fast-food joint across the street, went inside the club, walked straight to the bar, laid his head down, and fell asleep.

He was awakened by a kind man named Elton, the club's cook. He pushed a warm burger and fries toward him and asked him if he was hungry. Hannibal thankfully accepted the food, and after he had finished, Elton asked Hannibal where he was from and if he played, then told him to come back in the evening so he could be introduced to Thad Jones (1923–1986), as that Monday night the Thad Jones-Mel Lewis Orchestra would be playing.

When Hannibal arrived, Elton introduced them in the kitchen. Jones looked at Hannibal and said, "Why don't you join us at the bandstand tonight to play?" Hannibal, age twenty and having just arrived in the city, could hardly believe his good fortune. He gladly accepted.

When Thad Jones called Hannibal up to the stage, he introduced him as a special guest, Marvin Peterson (still his name at the time), the trumpeter from Texas. He asked, in his ear, in which key he knew how to play a certain piece.

"The song was Thad's ingenious arrangement of 'Summertime,'" Hannibal recalled, and in reply to the question, he said "It doesn't matter."

Hannibal could play it in any key. Any anxiety melted away when he started to play.

"Were you nervous, as this was completely unexpected, how he invited you up on stage that first night?" I asked.

"I was too much in shock to be nervous, standing on the stage next to such a brilliant mind and before so many brilliant musicians that I had studied when I was in high school."

After sleeping in the parking lot that night, he soon rented a room nearby at the Greenwich Arms Hotel, above the Village Gate nightclub. The $50 started to quickly dwindle, and he was struggling to pay for the room.

One evening, after playing, Hannibal was approached by a French woman in the finance industry who had a place nearby. She asked him if he would like to join her in her limo, saying something like, "I think you're really talented, and I would like to talk to you about your promising career."

"The way she said it, it gave me a bad feeling. It was like she was trying to sell me on something, like tires. I also remembered what T-Bone [Walker] told me. 'Baby boy, keep the home fire burning, and don't ever let anyone take it.'"

He listened to his inner feeling and his guidance and avoided her.

She appeared again the next week and asked him to leave with her. He declined, and then she offered him her penthouse apartment. She said he could stay there for free for a month while she was overseas and that no one would bother him.

He could sense her incredible loneliness, but he could also sense that things were off spiritually with her. He thanked her for the offer but again declined. This time she became angry and indignant with him, betraying another side of herself.

Hannibal eventually understood this to be the first major approach of Death coming at him through someone—this time a woman of great wealth—offering things that would have led to spiritual death. It was a bargain that could have cost him his musical gift and broken his covenant with the ancestors and the Creator. She was trying to buy him or something in him, and he instantly knew it was not right. He refused her offer, even though he only had $7 left in his pocket and he didn't know how he was going to continue to pay for his room. Hannibal said that this kind of approach by Death (the Beast) would become a recurring theme in his life. Many years later, in the 1990s, he would write journal passages that addressed Death and its attempts to overtake or infiltrate him. In one of them, he recalled how Death had first approached him through this rich French banker right after he got to New York. I asked him about this.

"What it would have cost me, had I accepted her offer?" he elaborated. "It would have been spiritual death. I felt that, and I knew that. I would have lost the music."

He went back to the Greenwich Arms Hotel, with its fleas and his solitary wool blanket. He prayed and gave thanks to the

Creator for his mother, Eddie, Cleveland Gay, the projects, his ancestors, his grandparents, his dog Blue, the music, food and water, his breath, and his life. He then went to sleep.

When he woke the next morning, he thought he might have been still dreaming. Outside, on the sidewalk, someone was joyfully calling, "Marvin! Marvin!"

Hannibal looked out. It was Joe Texidor (1941–2007), who played percussion in Rahsaan Roland Kirk's (1935–1977) band; he was telling him to come on the bus to go on tour with them. Hannibal had had no idea about the tour.

"None whatsoever," he recalled. "I was down to my last $7."

Hannibal gathered his few things, said a prayer of thanks, and joined them on the tour bus. On his way out, he left his $7 with a man who had escaped the brutal winter cold by sleeping on the floor inside the building's entryway.

"When you start new, it's important to start brand new," he said, explaining why he gifted his final $7. "And for me, brand new meant not having a single penny to my name."

"Did you just know that the band would provide for everything you needed on tour? Did you worry at all?"

"Well, I didn't worry. I was too sick to worry. It's like I was too cold to die. I was both sick and excited," he remembered. "And you know, you always know when someone comes and rescues you. It's a certain feeling you have. You have no fear."

Once on tour, he made money and had everything he needed. From then on, his musical presence in New York was set. He would go on many more tours, join the legendary band of Gil Evans (1912–1988) for many years, and start his own prominent jazz band, The Sunrise Orchestra.

"It was a remarkable laboratory for me because, at that time, I was touring extensively. And in between all of the social interruptions, I was full-fledged into the music," he said. "Usually, after we'd get through playing, I preferred playing in the small cities of countries like Germany. The Black Forest, I loved that. I didn't like the clamor of the cities."

Once, while in the Mediterranean region, he recalled swimming out into deep water and the tonalities he heard, things he had never heard before. They were so alluring and beautiful that he began to sink into their rhythms—and the water with them. He entered a form of trance.

"I was on tour, and I just decided I'd take a swim in the Mediterranean, and I was trying to—more and more, I heard this sound that was interesting to me. And I swam out too far. I was saved by a fisherman. He tapped me on the shoulder. I didn't realize how far I had gone out. But what made me come up was when I heard the sound, and I smiled, and I said, now I understand. I asked my grandfather once, 'What do you think the sound of the Earth rotating on its axis is?' I think I must've been about ten or something, or a little younger than that. I know we were in the field, and I asked him that question, and he looked at me, and he said, 'Well, all I can say is whatever is above is below.' That wisdom that comes from farming, from knowing, from being in touch with the Earth. That's the only way that so profound an answer can come," Hannibal said. "So, when I went down real deep, I heard this crackling sound. It was like a hum. And I smiled, and I said, 'Yeah, Grandpa, I see what you meant.' And I felt very confident that it was the same sound of the Earth rotating on its axis. And when I realized how far I had gone from shore, I felt a guy tap with the oar."

The fisherman brought Hannibal back to the surface—and likely saved his human life.

Although this sound experience almost brought him to his death, it was so transcendently beautiful that Hannibal referenced it in *Healing Tones* (which premiered in 2019 with the Philadelphia Orchestra), in the piece's eternal garden where the shaman goes in spirit. This sound of the rotation of the Earth, which Hannibal heard from the sea, is part of how he composed the moment. In the music, he wrote this aspect of the heavenly garden and its breathtaking beauty, which he had experienced floating out at sea decades prior.

Over his decades immersed in the jazz scene, Hannibal's work was voluminous and wide-ranging. He released many live and studio albums, both as bandleader and the featured trumpeter in others' bands, including groups led by Gil Evans, Roy Haynes (1925–present), Pharoah Sanders (1940–2022), Don Pullen (1941–1995), Elvin Jones (1927–2004), Eric Kloss (1949–present), Grachan Moncur III (1937–2022), Billy Hart (1940–present), Kip Hanrahan (1954–present), Frank Foster (1928–2011), Richard Davis (1930–2023), and Andrew Cyrille (1939–present).

He released early work under the name Marvin Peterson and, after he received the name Hannibal, under the monikers Hannibal Marvin Peterson, Hannibal Peterson, or often just Hannibal. In the early seventies, he formed Hannibal Marvin Peterson and the Sunrise Orchestra.

The albums are too numerous to list, but they include the following with Hannibal as the bandleader: *Marvin Peterson and The Soulmasters in Concert* (1968); *Children of the Fire* (1974); *Hannibal* (1975); *In Antibes* (1977); *In Berlin* (1977); *Naima* (1978); *The Light* (1978); *The Tribe* (1978); *Tribute* (1979); *The Universe Is Not for Sale* (1980); *The Angels of Atlanta* (1981); *Poem Song* (1981); *More Sightings* (1984); *Visions of a New World* (1989); *Kiss on the Bridge* (1990); *Crossing* (1991); and *One with the Wind* (1994).

In view of the vast range of Hannibal's works, I asked him if he would characterize them for me, or describe their arc. My knowledge, of course, has been informed by the remarkable work in music studies and free jazz studies—in, for example, the pathbreaking works of George Lewis, Paul Steinbeck, John Szwed, Michael Stephans, Howard Mandel, Maria Golia, Stephen Rush, Fred Moten, Henry Threadgill, William Parker, and many others.[1] With the depth and complexity of these works in view, I felt it important that Hannibal characterize his work in his own frame and words. He is of course a central innovator in his own right and often eschews conventional categories or labels. He also does not break his albums or later compositional pieces into phases, as some artists and many scholars do with bodies of musical work.

"When I think in terms of sequence of work, or when I think in terms of experiences, I think of the first album I made, which is *Marvin Peterson and the Soulmasters, Live at the Burning Bush*. Every once in awhile, I hear it, and it reminds me of what was ever-present in my life at that time. That was basically just figuring out how to get to New York City, how to leave the confines of an institution [North Texas State University], where I didn't see eye-to-eye with people on matters of creativity," Hannibal reflected. "I think the next album I was on was Roy Haynes's *Hip Ensemble* [1971]. That was my international introduction to musicians and to music lovers. Then, I did another album with Roy [Haynes] called *Senya* [1972]. Then, I think that's when I dropped *Children of the Fire* on them [1974]. That allowed me to say what I was feeling deep down inside about the ability of humans to decimate each other. When I did the *Angels of Atlanta* album [1981], that allowed me to no longer have a recurring nightmare about being—as Sister Toni Morrison said, she always felt like they were going to come and put her in a truck. I never had that sensation after I did *Angels of Atlanta*. It was around the time that it was clear to me that I had nothing to fear or no one to fear. I put everything I had into the music."

Hannibal then reflected on the broader significance and creative processes of his later albums. He shared that, if albums are not recorded in the first two takes, "it's all downhill." This fact means that it is crucial to assemble the right people in the band to record.

When I asked about whether he affixes certain specific labels within jazz or beyond to his studio albums earlier in life, he said that he will use categories as a shorthand, but they are not especially significant to him as a composer and musician.

"I find that people who come up with categories, they are seldom practitioners. I don't know any musician who called it free jazz, or who in fact called it jazz. It's just like rhythm and blues. I've never heard a musician say, 'I play rhythm and blues,'" he said. "A lot of people have made attempts to create different amalgamations of different music. But I don't see music in different forms. It's like planet Earth. I see it all as one. My first sight is not the division but is the whole. I just write and play what I hear. I don't say, 'It's this kind of music, or others. This category, or other categories.' A composer, Gunther Schuller [1925–2015], said to me, 'You've been doing what I've been trying to do all my life—integrate classical music into jazz.' I said, 'Well, if you're going to say that, you have to say gospel, too, and you have to also say African, because there are African drums in the music.' That's the problem with starting to name. Just say music."

Hannibal elaborated that he often uses the word jazz as a shorthand, only as it widely circulates, and people will have a sense of what he means when he uses it. He likened it to the way he uses the word God as a shorthand. He views albums as sound documents and written documents, bequeathed to the world and often providing spiritual nourishment or healing.

"I always saw albums as both a sound document and a word document to believe. In my case, I feel that making an album is like leaving a spiritual will for all of humanity to have and to hold, to hopefully benefit from. I've always seen them like that. They're very nourishing," he said. "On my wall when I was young, I had the Miles [Davis] (1926–1991) record *Milestone* [1958]. I really researched the word and its meaning. I really loved when the artist would write what they had in mind with each song in the liner notes on LPs. When I saw John Coltrane's (1926–1967) *A Love Supreme* [1965], it gave me spiritual nourishment—not only to hear the music, but to see the drawing. It's such a poetic form of creativity, albums, as opposed to now [with digital streaming]."

Although Hannibal enjoyed a rapid ascent in the New York jazz world after he arrived in 1970, it was not long before he was facing regular approaches of Death in various guises. This became a recurring theme throughout his life. Early in his career, Death seriously threatened him with an acute case of double pneumonia with severe complications. A doctor told him that he would not recover and would soon die.

"I thought to myself, 'If I'm going to die, I'm going to fly to Africa to die there,'" he recalled. "I wrote my mother a letter, which I interestingly did not actually send to her. I left it in my apartment. I then booked a ticket on the next flight to Africa, which was to Kenya. I would have gone anywhere in Africa. That just happened to be the next flight."

When he arrived, one miracle after another happened. When he walked off the plane, a man who was a complete stranger greeted him and said, "Welcome home, brother."

The man's name was David Murassi, and he asked Hannibal to come with him.

"Well, first, he took me out to the Serengeti, and he was talking to this man, and then he took me to the jeep and said, 'I'm going to take you to town.' And he said, 'I'm going to pick you up before sun-up.'"

David then took Hannibal to his home village the next day.

"So, the next day is when they greeted me. The chief was the first to greet me. And those my age said, 'Welcome, my brother.'

Those younger said, 'Welcome home, my father.' And those older than me said, 'Welcome home, my son.'"

The people in the community formed a circle around him, welcoming him.

"The medicine man looked at my tongue and had David take me to his hut, and then he made me some tea. I drank it, and the next day I was running with the kids," he recalled.

"And then you were cured?"

"Absolutely better."

Hannibal does not recall the exact length of his visit, but he was in Kenya a few weeks.

"They asked me to stay," he said. "When I was going to leave, they asked, 'Where are you going? This is your home.'"

The people in the village nourished Hannibal and performed healing ceremonies. It saved Hannibal's life after the doctor in New York had said he would die. Hannibal's experience with the Maasai people was one of the most beautiful things he had experienced in his life; a part of him wanted to stay with them and he was invited to do so. But Hannibal felt moved by his ancestors to return to New York City, no matter how brutal it would feel to return after having experienced this time with the Maasai. He felt he had a new directive and obligation to write the truth of the beauty and wisdom he had experienced into his music.

When he finally left, the villagers sent him with many farewell gifts, including an elephant hair bracelet, earrings, and a bundle of sticks with sulfur in them (a very valuable commodity because they helped to keep snakes away).

"I had to share what I had seen and learned with people back home, where my mother was, where the bones of my ancestors were. I knew I had to go back and write about it, and I did years later, in *African Portraits*," Hannibal said. "What I experienced was nothing like the indoctrination I had received about life in Africa, what I had seen portrayed in racist depictions in film, television, things people would say. I had to do my part to set things right."

The village chief gave him firm instructions before he left, telling Hannibal that he must not let his anger over the truth he had seen overtake him: "You must not let the anger rule you."

Hannibal was asked to use his new knowledge to help heal his brothers and sisters in the United States. Hannibal promised the chief that he would do so. A great deal of this experience would be poured into his first major orchestral work, *African Portraits*, which premiered at Carnegie Hall in 1990.

Hannibal incorporated violins as percussion in the *African Portraits* work—just one of the many influences that his time with the Maasai in the 1970s has had on his music.

"It's an ongoing saga of learning from my experience there—musically in particular," he said. "I would never have imagined that there are violins in a village compound in Africa. And I would never have imagined that those violins were played like drums. And that the drums were played like violins. I wouldn't have learned that in music 101."

Hannibal has not returned to Africa since that experience.

"The ancestors have made clear that the next time I go to Africa, I won't come back [to the United States]. So, I haven't been since then," Hannibal said, laughing. "I was going to Kenya to die, and instead I was reborn. The overture of *The Jonah People* opera captures this—facing and overcoming the fear of death, and being reborn. That is freedom. I don't remember the last time I didn't feel free. Things of this finite realm, yes, I deal with them. But in the higher sense, I am free. It gives me such pain that not everyone knows this freedom. There is so much suffering and pain. It brings me so much pain that people don't know the treasures they are and the freedom they can have—that they don't know their divinity."

More recently, during the composition of *The Jonah People*, the ancestors revealed to Hannibal that, if he continues to do the work, he will be able to return to the Door of No Return on Bunce Island (off of Sierra Leone), where his great-grandfather Silas Burgess was forced to pass into the horrors of the slave ship. The spirits have shown him that he will have the opportunity to crawl back through the door on his belly, on behalf of his ancestors, thereby enacting a healing or statement of resilience regarding what has happened to his ancestors and the Jonah People more broadly.

"Will you feel the same experience that they did?" I asked him.

"Of course," he replied. "Otherwise, it wouldn't be real."

He said this would be healing for the ancestors who were forced through that door. Yet it would not be only for them.

"I will go back through that door on behalf of every human who has been taken from their humanity and who seeks to return to it," he said.

When Hannibal returned to New York from Kenya in 1979, he went into an intense period of spiritual reckoning, reconciling what he had experienced with the falsehoods that he had been fed his whole life.

"It was brutal to all of a sudden come to the truth of things because that was always the most challenging quest for becoming free. The spiritual challenges are infinitely more difficult than the mental challenges."

He dealt with the fact that his people had been stolen from lives like those he had experienced among the Maasai. Hannibal did not leave his apartment for three weeks. As always, he had people appear around him to help. One of his neighbors realized he was struggling. She did not intrude or ask what was wrong, but left plates of food outside his door that he would periodically retrieve to eat. He eventually felt cleansed of his anger and able to reemerge into his New York life, but now with an even more intense fire and resolve to use his music for spiritual liberation and to help show people the truths he had seen.

Not long after Hannibal returned from Kenya, he unexpectedly experienced another moment of great spiritual liberation. It came by way of a stranger. While playing at the Blue Coronet Club in Brooklyn with master drummer Roy Haynes, he noticed a man in beautiful blue African-style clothes who he had never seen before. The man stood just outside the club every night for a week. Hannibal noticed him, but they never exchanged a word. On the seventh night, the man—who turned out to be a Yoruba priest—told him that the spirits sent him to give him his name: Hannibal. (At the time, he was still using his birth name, Marvin Peterson).

"He told me, 'Your name is Hannibal, and in time, you will see why that is your name,'" he recalled. "The man then left, and I never saw him again."

The name Hannibal immediately resonated with him.

"I never felt that Marvin was my name. When people would call my name, 'Marvin!' I wouldn't feel like they were calling me. It always felt strange," Hannibal said. "With Peterson, I felt that that was a slave name, a name passed down by those who enslaved my ancestors. I am so glad that I'm completely free of it."

He started using Hannibal almost immediately, especially after his mother embraced it. She told him, without hesitating, "I think Hannibal is a beautiful name."

With her blessing, he started using it as his name—sometimes without the Peterson or the Marvin Peterson after it—even though he was well-known as Marvin Peterson. Receiving his true name felt liberating and revitalizing. He was not concerned about losing the recognition he had gained under his birth name, since feeling at home with his name was far more important.

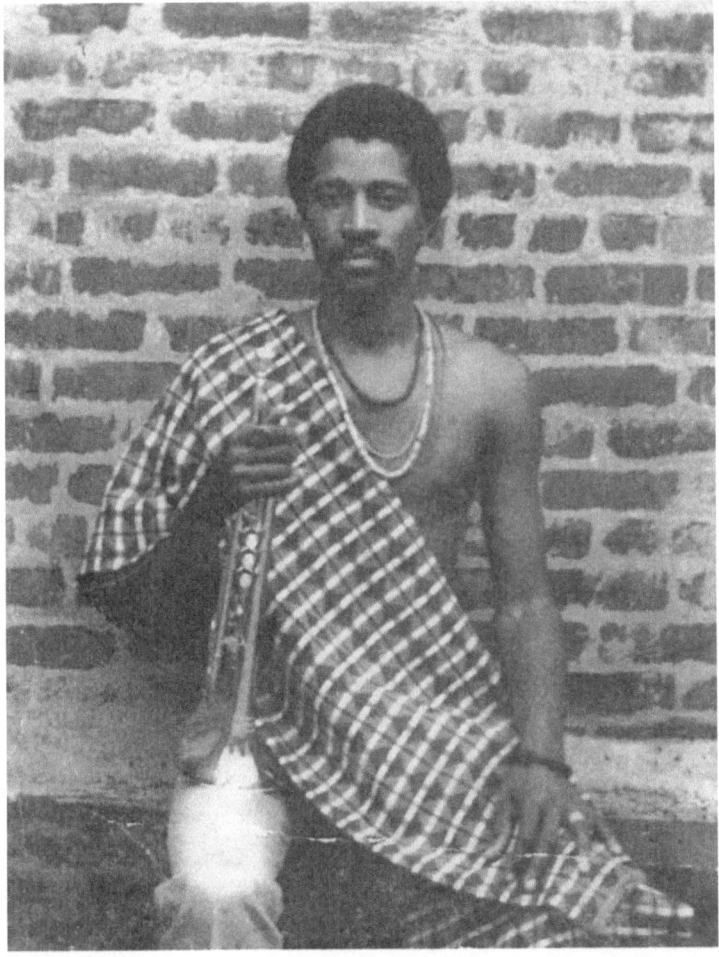

FIGURE 2.1 *Metamorphosis*, the musician after being given and receiving the name Hannibal, New York City.

Photograph courtesy of Hannibal Lokumbe (ca. 1985).

He would receive Lokumbe years later, from his greatgrandmother spirit guide, Cora.

I asked Hannibal whether he had come to a deeper meaning of the name Hannibal, as the Yoruba priest said he would in time.

"It's the erasure of a stain, of a mental and a physical stain. A mental and physical brand," he said, referring to how the name had been passed down from those who had enslaved or attempted to enslave his ancestors. "Some people say, 'My grandfather's name was Johnson, and I'm proud of that name.' And I always say, 'Well, you're still a long way from the truth. And the truth of the tree is the root. What was the root of your grandfather's tree? It sure wasn't Johnson.'"

He said that those who relate to the names passed down by enslavers have not yet experienced the liberation that comes with throwing off such a stain.

"You can't tell me that they know what it feels like to be liberated. They accept the limb of the tree as being the root of the tree. Without the root, the limb wouldn't exist," he said. "Whenever you seek to find the root of things—the root is the essence of things—that's when you will find monumental challenges."

"This is true of music, too? When you seek the root or the essence?"

"It's true of everything and of anything. Because there are powers that would not like you to be free—that force and those people who serve the force that is not true, the force that does not serve the truth," Hannibal replied. "America is suffering deeply from that. I mean more and more and more, it becomes pervasive. It's hard for people to deal with the truth. And people who are afraid to deal with the truth are the greatest allies of the despot, and all that ever comes from that is chaos and destruction."

He shared that, after playing at the Blue Coronet Club and hearing a magisterial drum solo by Roy Haynes the week he received the name Hannibal, he came to see "music as one of the natural wonders of the world, like gravity and the pyramids."

NEW YORK CITY AND THE JAZZ YEARS • 59

Over the course of Hannibal's decades of playing and touring in jazz bands, one of his closest friends and collaborators was Gil Evans. The great pianist and arranger, along with many others, helped to innovate and expand styles dubbed cool jazz, free jazz, modal jazz, and jazz fusion.[2]

FIGURE 2.2 *Bliss*, Gil Evans and Hannibal lighting up the Village Vanguard, New York City.

Photograph courtesy of Hannibal Lokumbe (ca. 1980s).

Hannibal first met Evans when the great bassist Richard Davis (1930–2023) invited him to a recording session that Evans was doing with his band. Hannibal thought he would go to listen. But once there, Evans invited him to sit in and play without any rehearsal. Hannibal did so, and a collaboration with Evans continued for years.

He and Evans shared a deep connection. They would just know when to call each other and what music to play together.

"With Gil, I could talk about anything and everything. We would talk and talk, and 90 percent of it was not about music, because there was no need," Hannibal said, adding that the music flowed from their souls. It was understood without the need for spoken conversation.

Earlier, Miles Davis had played for many years with Evans. Davis credited Evans with teaching him a great deal and said Evans was his best friend in his autobiography.[3] Davis was also deeply spiritual and felt those who had been close to him and crossed to spirit were still inside of him, a part of him. He also related to music as being spiritual and a lifeforce that resonated through the world beyond the time of its playing or recording.[4]

As Davis was also a trumpet master, I once asked Hannibal if it would be correct to say that he succeeded Davis in Evans's band. His reply, in short, was no—and his answer was illuminating.

"No one could ever, or as in my case, should ever want to succeed Miles. Gil and I had our own personal, as well as musical, relationship. He had a deep appreciation and love for my way of playing the instrument. 'Hannibal, please play more solos. I could listen to you all day,' he often said to me," Hannibal shared. "I preferred to listen more than I chose to play. I learned a great deal more that way. Still do. Listening sharpens the ears and develops sound sequencing. As well, it helps tremendously in the art of building mutual respect and intellectual stamina—two items so obviously missing in the repertoire of most politicians."

On another occasion, Hannibal shared that Miles had dedicated a song, "Hannibal," to him, adding that "I love the live concert version of it where the great alto saxophonist Kenny Garrett (b. 1960) plays an earth-shattering solo."[5]

Evans's two children, Miles Evans (b. 1965, named after Miles Davis) and Noah Evans (b. 1964)—both musicians today—remember Hannibal as like another dad because of all the time they spent with him in New York and when they joined tours. (They were very young at the time).[6] They shared with me how warm Hannibal was and how he show love to them, take them places, teach them things, and help take care of them like they were his children. Miles Evans particularly remembers going swimming with Hannibal at the local YMCA. Hannibal had spent a great deal of time at Gil Evans's place.

All three of them—Miles Evans, Noah Evans, and Hannibal—also recalled how extraordinarily humble Gil Evans was. He never acted as though he was better than any other person in the world. They shared how he always chose to give money to those who were asking for it at eye level, never looking down on their outstretched hand. Instead, he always crouched down with kindness, gratitude, and love in his eyes.

While this book was underway, Miles Evans wrote a message to Hannibal, Noah, Evans and me one evening about "Aurorean Roar," a song Miles Evans was about to release. A little later, Hannibal told me that he had sent a short note replying to Miles Evans, reminiscing about his times playing with Gil Evans.

"Yeah, I sent Miles a little note about his father. I was telling him how one night about two o'clock Gil called me over, and he was roasting a turkey, and we sat up till the sun came up, eating turkey, and yeah. What a special moment that was. Every moment with Gil was special, more than special. Like these beautiful clouds passing overhead in these mountains."

When I spoke with Noah Evans and Miles Evans, I asked if they heard the musical harmonies through nature as Hannibal does. They replied that, for both of them, everything is music.

"You are music then, as Hannibal is music?"

They both replied yes.

Another major influence on Hannibal's later orchestral compositions was the drumming of Roy Haynes, another ingenious innovator of what many call free jazz. Hannibal learned a tremendous amount from Haynes and played in his band much longer than he might have if he had not been gaining so much vital musical information and wisdom from the experience. Hannibal would often position himself as close as he could to the drums when they played together.

"Master drummers, Roy included, have the ability to play patterns that would affect you physically and that were used just as medicine is used in Africa and other places," Hannibal said. "People knew this in ancient times."

"Jerry Lee Lewis (1935–2022) once introduced Buddy Rich (1917–1987) as the greatest drummer in the world. I got a chance to correct him," he recalled. "There is a massive difference between beating the drums and playing the drums. The greatest influence on my orchestrations came from my years playing with the master drummer, Roy Haynes."

Hannibal would often join Roy Haynes's band on the Jazz Mobile bandstand, an outdoor concert trailer that traveled through Harlem. This mobile stage would have a piano, amplifier, and everything else they needed on it.

"They would hook the trailer up to a truck, and we'd go right in the neighborhoods and play. I was so happy to be in Harlem, the real Harlem. There would be little kids running around, people who would never come downtown to a jazz club. And we would play. And I'll never forget after it was over, we'd ride a trailer back to where we were parked. And I'll never forget, as long as I live, we were crossing over this bridge and the sun was just setting and we had played like it would be the last time we ever played."

Hannibal then paused before continuing.

"I'll never forget that one moment, because nobody was talking. We were too exhausted to talk. There was nothing that needed to be said. There's nothing that could have been said. And I'll never forget, I turned, and I looked at Roy. He turned and looked at me at the same time. And what we said to each other in that look said everything," Hannibal said. "That's why I went to New York City. That's why you go anywhere, you know?"

"And when you left, it was because that was gone for you?"

"Yeah. But that time with Roy was unbelievable, man. It was unbelievable. I mean, I played the full range of that instrument, and that's rare. That's very rare to be able to say that, for a musician to say that they played the full range of their instrument. Well, on that day, I played the full range of my instrument, and Roy played the full range of those drums. People were spellbound, man."

"And that full range probably means some things that people don't hear, right?" I asked.

"Right. The fact is that the full range of an instrument means everything possible. So, it ranges past the impossible. Anything else in addition you would say would just be a replication of what, in some form, of what you already played."

Hannibal said that when they played the totality of their instruments, the sun and the air around them responded. The people responded. Everyone felt it. It was as though the sonic alchemy had converted or transmuted the matter all around it, the nature and the people.

"Usually, after we finished playing, we'd be talking about where we were going to go eat or something. Some words. But there were no words. There were no words."

"It just didn't feel right?"

"There was no need."

But among Hannibal's many musical influences, the single greatest is John Coltrane. Hannibal has had a love and devotion for Coltrane's spirit and music throughout his life. Even though Coltrane played saxophone, Hannibal credits Coltrane as his single greatest musical influence. Though the *New York Times* published a story that said Hannibal studied directly with Coltrane, he passed in 1967 at the age of forty before Hannibal arrived in New York City.[7]

"Even though I never met Trane in the flesh, I never felt as though I didn't know him," he said. "I've never picked up the trumpet and not felt the presence of Trane, or of Louis Armstrong [1901–1971]."

Hannibal often invokes Coltrane's legendary 1965 *A Love Supreme* album as a triumph of the human spirit and a testimony to the spiritual liberation and healing power of music that remains true to the Creator. After all Coltrane had been through—all of the pain and suffering and addiction that he navigated—he broke free and wrote *A Love Supreme*, a year after he had released his purifying album *Crescent*.[8]

For their medicinal power, it is to *A Love Supreme* and *Crescent* that Hannibal will often turn. He recommends them to others when they are depleted or navigating something difficult.

"Please take a dose of *Crescent*," he once wrote me. I was exhausted, though I had not mentioned anything to Hannibal about it. He said he was moved by the spirit to send the suggestion. I followed the advice, and *Crescent* instantly elevated my energy and spirits.

I once asked if he could hear the difference in Coltrane's playing between when Coltrane was struggling and when he had broken free of the struggle.

"No, the feeling, his sound, was always the same. The soul is the soul," Hannibal replied.

He said that when people play from the truth of their life and their soul—rather than from a space of untruth and destruction—the authenticity and the divinity of the sound always come through. He also gave as an example Charlie Parker Jr. (nicknamed Bird) (1920–1955), the saxophonist who was one of jazz's greatest innovators. Along with Dizzy Gillespie (1917–1993), Charlie Parker directly taught and played with Miles Davis and many other jazz legends. He passed in 1955, long before Hannibal got to New York, and the two never met.

"If you take another of these gods, Bird, if you look at everything that he went through with his body, with the drugs, with all of the pain that he lived through as a Man of Jonah in this country, his sound is true and pure every time because he never gave in to the Beast. And his sound is his true sound, pure, every time, because he never gave in to the Beast. He never let the Beast touch his musical gift."

Hannibal did get to know Dizzy Gillespie, a kind, brilliant, generous soul. Hannibal often recalls a conversation he had with him during his sixtieth birthday party.

"I'll never forget what Dizz said to me that night. He said, 'Hannibal, I'm playing things now on this instrument that I've never played before.' He was discovering new things in the music. And I said, 'Dizz, how can you say that, after all you have done for the music?'" Hannibal recalled. "And he said to me, 'You'll see what I mean, Hannibal. You just have to live long enough, and you'll see.' And I have to say, at seventy-three, I'm now playing things on the trumpet I never have, going places in the music I never have. I now know what he meant."

Hannibal was returning to playing trumpet daily for the first time in years.

"I am so excited about playing. The inner ear continues to expand," he said. "I am playing my trumpet, and I've been feeling that secondary consciousness of the sound—like knowing what's going to come with the sound before it happens."

"Is this part of what you mean when you say you can see around the corner, as a jazz musician?" I asked.

"Yeah, that's what Charlie Parker was known for. Him, Dizz, they changed sound. And you can hear it."

Hannibal has some moving insights concerning the intense collaboration, and eventual parting, between Miles Davis and John Coltrane.

"This is only known in certain circles, but Miles and Trane were like Dizz and Bird. They needed each other. They stayed connected, even when they no longer were playing together. They were still a part of each other," Hannibal said. "When Trane saw a different path, he had to travel that path. Miles knew that, being the brilliant light that he is. He knew that. You have to follow what you hear."

Although Hannibal and Miles only ever exchanged a few words, Hannibal received word from mutual friends that Miles thought Hannibal's work was very beautiful. Once, while Hannibal was staring into space backstage before a show, Miles stopped and asked him, "What are you looking at?"

"The universe," Hannibal replied. Miles looked him up and down and left.

When Coltrane was nearing the end of his life, he stopped playing the saxophone. It was confusing to so many who knew him, Hannibal said, as he was someone who never wanted to put down his instrument. Like so many of the masters, most days he would practice throughout the day.

"See, what happened is that he no longer needed to play. He had reached a point of mastery with the music where he had escaped the gravitational pull. He had reached that place. And when you escape the gravitational pull, it's, 'See ya!' He bought a telescope, and he spent his days contemplating astronomy, physics, and the universe."

The great jazz double bassist Jimmy Garrison (1934–1976), who played for years with Coltrane, once related to Hannibal that soon before he passed Coltrane said he was interested in moving into composing for orchestras.

In gratitude to all Coltrane has given, and continues to give from the spirit, Hannibal published a poem in his memory, "Trane's Love Supreme." He dedicated it to his good friend Max Roach, a master jazz drummer and fellow liberation fighter.

TRANE'S LOVE SUPREME
(FOR MAX ROACH [1924–2007])

What a magnificent love he is
A sound of great splendor and light
That heals our broken souls
A force he is
Now supreme in time
At peace with what he did
With his vision of God

Chorus:
Great love that heals my soul
Thank you John for your Love Supreme
Pure sound from God you made
A sound of resurrection
So we thank you Trane
For your vision of
God.[9]

"I love Max. I miss him," Hannibal said one day after I brought up this poem. "But he's always with me."

He and Max became closer in the late eighties and nineties. They had started to talk about doing some joint liberation work, and the conversations got deep.

"Max and I often spoke of collaborating on liberation work. We became extremely close. He is the reason I had the word Liberation engraved on my trumpet. I trembled upon hearing of his passing."

Though Roach died in 2007, they last saw each other in the early nineties at the Abyssinian Baptist Church in New York City. Roach had come to see Hannibal perform part of his autobiographical mini-opera *Diary of an African American*. After the performance, they were talking and Hannibal recalls Roach telling him, "I'll always be with you, even if we're not physically together."

Hannibal said it seemed at the time as if they both knew it would be the last time they would speak in person. Roach, like all the other master musicians and spirit people Hannibal has known, is still with him and is a part of all his works. He often appears to Hannibal in his dreams.

All of the people who have been close musical companions remain a part of Hannibal, even—and perhaps especially—those who are now in spirit.

Hannibal also has deep relationships with those musicians in the orchestras who have performed pieces that he composed.

By way of example, Hannibal explained that "the musicians in the Philadelphia Symphony Orchestra are as dedicated to music as the masters of blues and jazz I have had the privilege of playing with. Many from the orchestra accompanied me into the concrete bowels of prisons and shelters where their playing liberated many a souls locked in a constant cycle of despair."

Much of the mastery of music has to do with the blood and soul the musicians put into their work. The blood can be literal or metaphorical. Hannibal literally bled on the altar—or the bandstand or stage—the first night he played at Carnegie Hall in New York City. This was on March 12, 1974.

He had really started to make his way in the jazz scene when the legendary pianist Cecil Taylor (1929–2018) invited him to play with him. Hannibal had just undergone an essential procedure for his acute tonsilitis. The doctor had told him that any playing of his trumpet whatsoever was off-limits for about two months.

"I thought to myself, okay, I know the doctor said I can't even touch my trumpet. But I have this show set up with Cecil Taylor. And I've dreamt of playing at Carnegie Hall my entire life," he recalled. "And so, I got onstage, and played with everything I had, as I do every time I play. Soon after I started, blood started coming out of my horn. Then, it was going all over the altar, including on this new, gorgeous piano they had on stage. I remember thinking to myself, 'Well, if this is my time, at least I'll go on the altar. And what better place than Carnegie Hall, where I always wanted to play?'"

Hannibal finished the set despite splattering blood from his horn. At the end of the show, someone at Carnegie Hall looked at him, looked at the blood on the piano strings, and told Hannibal that it was a really nice piano that he had bled on.

"I told him, 'Well, I guess you'll have to get a new piano,'" Hannibal said, laughing. "Man, talk about sacrifices for the music, life on the line. I was ready to die if had to, to play that night."

I asked him if his mother had been at Carnegie Hall that night.

"No, thank God, she probably would have come up there to get me herself. And my mother wouldn't have listened to anybody.

She wouldn't have cared who anyone was, Cecil Taylor or anybody else. She would've said, 'My baby!' She would have come on stage to get me herself."

Although laughing while recounting this story, Hannibal was serious in saying that a stage or a bandstand is an altar. Hannibal pours libations in gratitude to the ancestors and other spirits who have co-created the musical works before his jazz and orchestral ceremonies. (They are not performances, as "performances are for entertainers," as he once clarified for me.) Bandstands are sacred places where people journey into other spaces or soundscapes. No one should desecrate them by bringing anger or anything else up on them.

"It's understood, with almost everyone I've ever played with, that everyone is dealing with something. You don't bring that to the bandstand. You bring your *life*, you bring everything you have, but not whatever you happen to be going through at that time in anger. When people play angry, it sounds different, and it feels different," Hannibal said. "To bring anger to the altar is disrespectful to the music; it's disrespectful to the rest of the band, and it's disrespectful to the people who are there to hear the music. It's very selfish to play angry."

Hannibal said he only played angry once. It was in Vienna after he had lost a pair of new shoes that he was convinced had been stolen.

"I allowed myself to succumb to the anger, and I brought that to the bandstand. And it was immediately clear in what I played. It sounded totally different. It was off. The other guys in the band were looking at me like, 'What's the problem?'" he said. "That was the last time I did that. I never took my anger up there again."

One day, I shared a striking photograph of the exterior of Club Baron in Harlem, not knowing anything about its significance for Hannibal's journey.

"My anointing took place here," he replied. Later, in writing, he explained:

Rahsaan Roland Kirk took me there one glorious night to meet the drum master, Art Blakey [1919–1990], to possibly join his brilliant band, The Jazz Messengers. They were playing at the club that night. During a break, Rahsaan introduced us. Art looked at me long and thoroughly. "Want to come up and play a tune?" his deep raspy voice floated towards me. Although stunned by the offer, I immediately replied, "I would love to."

The place was packed and responded with excited applause when, from the bandstand, Art glowingly introduced me. Before the applause died down, Art took his throne behind his drums, and whispered to me, "You know "'Round Midnight?"

"Yes, sir," I immediately responded.

He instantly struck his floor tom, which was the start of a thunderous drumroll. It sent chills through my body—hearing his mastery live, as opposed to experiencing it on many of his albums I had studied so intensely as a teenager.

After my solo, the audience erupted in a continuous frenzied applause, cheering.

I poured everything into that solo. All of the trying moments in the freezing cold army cot with the flea-infested wool blanket, the cries, the feces, and the urine-scented halls of the Greenwich Arms Hotel—all of this burst forth from my life. The not knowing—or caring—if I would have died alone in that jail-sized room created a force which came screaming out of me into the appreciative souls of those living in what was still the land scented with the fragrance of [James] Baldwin [1924–1987], [Billie] Holiday, [Marcus] Garvey [1887–1940], Zora [Neale Hurston] [1891–1960], [Art] Tatum [1909–1956], and Dizz.

Climbing the stairs to the bandstand was master trumpeter Freddie Hubbard [1938–2008], with his trumpet in hand. To add spice to the moment, Art announced on the microphone in a provoking gesture, "Well, Freddie, I told you one day one of these young guys was going to cut your a–." The expression on Freddie's face made it clear that he did not appreciate the joke. A joke it was, for no one could play the trumpet better than Freddie Hubbard. I can't recall the title of the song we played, but I clearly remember that the power of it had many in the audience standing atop the tables applauding.

As the room light brightened, I immediately recognized the faces of master trumpeter Lee Morgan [1938–1972], Donald Byrd [1932–2013], Thad Jones [1923–1986], Ornette Coleman [1930–2015], and many more masters present, showering me with their approval.

It was a year later when speaking with master trombonist, Dick Griffin [1939–present], about that fateful night that he clearly explained what occurred.

"It was your blessing, your anointment, your acceptance into the family," he solemnly said.

He continued with the same tone.

"None of the cats knew you were playing, they just showed up. It always happens like that."

After this remarkable recollection, Hannibal sent another message, with a link to Ornette Coleman's playing:

He was one of many giants present at the club that night to welcome me into the family. Ornette started the Loft Jazz Movement in lower Manhattan. After he opened his space on Prince Street, then came the Loft's master drummer, Rashied Ali [1933–2009], Sam Rivers [1923–2011], Charlie Mingus [1922–1979], and others.

Ornette's Loft was more of an international cultural center. There I met prominent painters from Nigeria, China and Japan. The Nigerian painter was in fact a chief. In that space, it was commonplace to meet architects, scientists, astronomers, novelists, dancers, and chefs. And there was always music being created which you would never ever hear at the so-called established jazz clubs and festivals.

Ornette was one of the most advanced thinkers of this century. He, like Kepler, saw the singularity of creativity. How the rivers of all forms of art flowed into the one ocean of creativity. His contributions to music are parallel to those of Robert Johnson [1911–1938], Marian Anderson [1897–1993], Louis Armstrong, Charlie Parker, and Miles Davis.

Often, while shooting pool on his magnificent loft pool table, he would say, 'Brother Hannibal, you don't just play the notes. You become the notes.'

His orchestral composition, *The Skies of America*, remains one of the major healing injections I receive when it is time, like Chief Crazy Horse [ca. 1842–1877], to pitch my tent, alone upon the prayerful prairie.[10]

In reflecting upon the ways in which so many geniuses are forgotten due to deep racism and the spiritual decay of much of American society, he returned to the third womb—the slave ship—and all of the remarkable things that the Jonah People have done. Much has been forgotten or erased from collective memory.

"All these geniuses have died, and many people don't even know about them. It's like in sports. If segregation hadn't existed, then the most coveted sports record in human history, the home run king, would have been held by a Black man [such as Joshua Gibson (1911–1947)] a hundred years ago. So, you think of all of the ones that could easily do that, not easily do it, but who could hold that position, but who haven't, but because they weren't allowed! Incredible," he said. "But the music—there's this outgrowth, outpouring of music from wherever we were taken. So yeah, Ornette, there are a thousand images that I have imprinted in my mind and soul about Ornette Coleman that you won't see in a book. You'll never see them in a book."

Among other things, the extraordinary and indispensable music that so many great artists of Jonah generated and perpetually expanded gave birth, in many ways, to genres like rock and roll. These are so often erroneously cast as "white," as the people that many credit with inventing rock and roll, such as Elvis Presley (1935–1977), are white. This has occurred even as people like John Lennon (1940–1980), David Bowie (1947–2016), and Mick Jagger (1943–present) directly credit Black American artists as being their musical inspiration and, through their records, their greatest teachers.

One of the great innovators many artists do credit is James Brown (1933–2006).

"I would say James Brown's soul is the mirror image of John Coltrane's saxophone. That's what I would say about James Brown," Hannibal said one day, after I had asked him.

"Charlie Parker, so many of these brilliant Black artists, they transformed sound. They illuminated new dimensions of sound, possibilities of sound. So, for someone to come along and make so profound a statement, you know, Miles to Jimmy Hendrix, it's just really something to behold. It really is something to witness," Hannibal said. "It's like witnessing creation. When Lightnin' [Hopkins] would play, you could see this transformation in people."

On one of Evans's albums, Hannibal ended up singing Jimmy Hendrix's (1942–1970) songs for Evans's arrangement. Evans and

Hendrix had planned a collaboration of jazz versions of Hendrix's songs. However, Hendrix tragically passed before it could be recorded. Evans asked Hannibal to sing in Hendrix's stead.

"I initially was not inclined to do this, because I did not ever consider myself a singer, but I never wanted to say no to Gil," Hannibal recalled. "Gil told me that I was one of the best singers that he had ever heard, and I never knew Gil to tell a lie. He also told me, 'Hannibal, you have the stories of your life to tell, and you're a great storyteller.' And once I heard his reasoning, I thought, 'Alright, he's right, I have my stories to tell in the singing. I have my feeling.' So, I did it. I sang on those pieces. I realized that Jimmy Hendrix, like Billie Holiday, was a great storyteller."

One of Hannibal's great musical presences in human form was Duke Ellington (1899–1974). He met him once when they crossed paths in Central Park.

"Duke was so serene, like a beautiful lake," he said. "We spoke about nature, mostly."

Hannibal knew John Lennon a bit, crossing paths with him in the Village in the seventies, before Lennon was murdered across the street from Central Park in 1980. Lennon would ask Hannibal about the great legends that Hannibal had played with when he was younger, such as Lightnin' Hopkins and T-Bone Walker.

Walker, born in Linden, Texas, in 1910, innovated the electric blues along with styles called jump blues and West Coast blues. He was extraordinarily prolific (as was Hopkins), and many, including Hannibal, credit him as the first to record an electric guitar. Walker brought together jazz and blues, and he fashioned a style that has had a very large influence on guitar-playing across genres.

Listening to Walker, Hopkins, and other blues legends in Liverpool—where their recordings had reached local disc jockeys—led Lennon to want to play guitar in the first place. He shared the significance of such influences on many occasions in interviews, though these are sometimes overlooked.

One day I mentioned I had read that, in early January 2022, all pre-1923 music would come into the public domain.[11] Hannibal told me that much of the music by the people of Jonah has been stolen by white musicians, managers, and record companies, or had been released under agreements that were entirely unjust and unfavorable to the original artists.

Hannibal was skeptical that this could actually set anything right, given the gravity and brutality of everything that has happened to artists of Jonah.[12]

"The opulence those ill-gained royalties provided to many over the decades erases any sense of relief or justice which might come from newly implemented unlicensed domain status," he said. "In many ways, this perpetual dilemma is much like that of reparations for the Jonah People. How could five hundred years of moral indignation be monetarily compensated? What action could reasonably abate so grievous a spiritual tragedy, as five hundred years of human bondage? The answer, I am sure, will not come from the species who created the dilemma, but from the Creator of the species."

During the decades Hannibal spent fully immersed in the jazz scene with these great musical masters, he came to realize—and more fully become—what he always was but had not fully remembered or discovered. And those forms of becoming, and the consciousness of them, take people to a new place. This new space, this new mode of being, never leaves. People might try to run from that place, to run from the revelations about the truth of what they have become and what they have realized they always have been. But running, ultimately, does not actually work because, as Hannibal said, "you can't leave what you are."

One night in the 1970s, while Hannibal was playing a show in Harlem, something inexpressibly powerful came over him: new dimensions of becoming music, or music's passing through him, or emerging from within him. Whatever it was, and however it moved, his soul and existence as a human became even more merged, one, identical—"there is not a word," Hannibal said—with the music. He realized this union—that always was—on an even deeper level of consciousness, his perpetual becoming *with* the music and always expanding *with* the music *as* music himself.

He shared a photograph of him as he played in the New York City days. He said the image visually captures the experience he was trying to express in words.

I asked him if he would like to share any more about the experience of becoming the music, or whether it was simply beyond words.

In affirming the ineffability, he started to excitedly walk around and whistle. He then paused and said, in oracular fashion, "What is the saying? Seek and ye shall find? I think it's more like seek and ye shall discover. Because to find means that what is found doesn't necessarily have to have been there. To discover means it was there, just not discovered. I'm a believer that everything is within us, and it's just a matter of discovering it and not running from it. People are taught to fear what is within them."

Hannibal has also undergone profound processes of spiritual recognition and expansion throughout the course of his everyday life.

He once crossed paths with a mirrored reflection of his soul in a passerby on a subway in the eighties in New York City. They exchanged no words, but they locked eyes while on the train. Hannibal had an instantaneous knowing that it was Silas Burgess's mother, Hannibal's great-great-grandmother, who had fled the plantation at some point in that life. The family history

FIGURE 2.3 *Becoming the Music*, Hannibal, the New York City jazz years.
Photograph courtesy of Hannibal Lokumbe (in the 1980s).

that has been passed down to Hannibal and his relatives does not have an account of what happened to her. Hannibal composed her life and journey, as far as he knows it, as the figure of Asase in *The Jonah People*.

"I saw her on the subway," Hannibal recalled. "I knew it was her, her spirit. I had never had that experience before, of looking into someone's eyes and seeing a mirror of myself in that way. We didn't speak, but I knew she felt exactly the same thing I did. I went into a sort of trance. I was frozen. By the time I got off at my stop and shook myself from the trance, the train was gone. I was filled with regret that I didn't speak to her, but I couldn't move when I saw her."

After this encounter, Hannibal headed straight to practice with Evans and his band. Evans would usually greet him with a jovial line about merriment, but he could immediately sense something was wrong, that Hannibal had been shaken. Instead, he calmly welcomed him.

Another significant passage in becoming the work happened when Hannibal was composing *Children of the Fire*, an album released on the Sunrise label in 1974. He was in his mid-twenties, and this was the first time he had ever composed for strings. He wrote the piece on a piano for a suite to be recorded with an orchestra.

"It was around the time when everyone in New York was starting to get electric pianos, so that they could have more space in their studios or their places," he explained. "So, a manager for a pop band offered me an upright piano for $50. I paid $125 to move it. And I sat down, and this music came. I then went on a tuna fish diet to save money to have it recorded."

The piece is a tribute to children and others who had fled napalm bombings during the Vietnam War. He had seen coverage of it on television, which immediately electrified him with a sense of recognition.

"I was charged. I leapt to my feet. I realized I *was* them. I realized we were the same. I realized I *was* Dr. Phuc," Hannibal said, referring to Dr. Kim Phúc Phan Thị (b. 1963), once known as the nine-year-old "The Girl in the Picture" in the iconic and notorious photograph of children fleeing in terror from a bombing outside of their village in South Vietnam. Now living in Canada, she is a philanthropist and UNESCO Goodwill Ambassador.

In 2019, Hannibal had the opportunity to perform *Children of the Fire* at a church in Philadelphia with Dr. Phuc present. When his trumpet solo came, he invited her to stand, and he played his healing music all around her person. I was present at

FIGURE 2.4 *The Healing*, Hannibal plays healing tones upon the body of the woman who is known as "the girl in the picture," Dr. Kim Phúc Phan Thị, at the Philadelphia Cathedral.

Photograph by Abdul R. Sulayman / Studio Forty (2019).

this performance. The entire church felt charged as people witnessed this homage and healing.

"I played those healing tones on behalf of my ancestors," he said, sometime later. "When I wrote that music, I asked the Creator for that young girl to one day hear the music I wrote. I never thought to ask that I could be present when she heard it."

He explained to me how, in the process of writing *Children of the Fire* in the early 1970s, the Creator revealed to him the entire event, "every excruciating note," so that he could become the work and it would be true. He said that he wept profusely when writing it.

"When I wrote *Children of the Fire*, I came undone many a time," he said. "And so, at the cathedral [in Philadelphia in 2019], that's what I was letting her know when I covered her body in sound."

"And that's why the music came through as it did? Because you had made the journey yourself?"

"There you go. How on Earth could you see something like that and not become it?" he asked. "But you know, when I saw her, when I saw the image of that child, I didn't hear her crying with my eyes, but I did with my soul. And I saw. And I heard with my eyes, you know? You can see with your ears and you can hear with your eyes."

Through these multisensorial journeys, Hannibal comes to realizations of the essence of the work. And he becomes the work.

Once he realizes that he *is* the work the Creator has given him, there is no option but to do the work, even in the face of great challenges or hurdles that other people or musicians themselves try to place on the paths of creativity.

"If I don't flow, I die," Hannibal said. "I must do the work. I must always be moving."

Often Hannibal will have been doing the work, sometimes on a spiritual level, without even realizing it. Or he will not notice until, later, certain things that his spirit had been creating toward a certain work come into focus.

"It's just like jazz," Hannibal said. "You don't necessarily know the destination, but you move as the spirit moves."

"Yes, you taught me such a powerful lesson about improvisation and moving by the soul's knowing, a profound lesson about that," I said.

Earlier he had pointed out the body language signs, things that I had been doing with my hands subconsciously while speaking with him in his Smithville studio. By bringing these to my attention, he helped me see how my body did things based on knowledge or in concert with a deeper soul source or repository, even though I didn't consciously realize I was doing so.

"You were doing it, but you didn't know it," he said. "It is the same with jazz."

He was referring to the ways in which the music flows from the soul, in connection with the ancestors and the creator. It does not need to be thought or written in advance. In fact, part of the great genius of what people call jazz is the way the masters improvise, letting their spirits flow, without prior knowledge or even discussion with the other players about where the music will go. There may be three notes, three chords, or a well-known foundational melody that serve as the points of departure or reference, but then the musicians bring forth the music organically in real time, fusing and diverging and interplaying with each other as they proceed.

"As long as you have the beginning and the end as a reference point, a foundation, to bring people back, you can take them anywhere you want throughout the piece. You can take them off into outer space like Trane did [with] *Interstellar*," Hannibal once explained, referring to the experimental, ingenious, universe-traversing album that John Coltrane created late in his career.

This journeying through music—through what I am calling spiritual soundscapes—is at once an act of liberation for the person playing the music and an invitation to others to ride with them into its soundscapes. True music offers medicine to those who hear it and otherwise imbibe or bear witness to it through any other perceptual portals or affective capacities.

Hannibal explained that the modes of spiritual liberation through music—or writing or the creative arts in general—are epitomized by what he calls the New Beings (as expressed by the character Marabout in his most recently completed opera, *The Jonah People*). The New Beings are the people of Jonah. They are those and the descendants of those who have passed through three wombs: that of the Creator, a mother, and the slave ship. By virtue of their not having acquiesced to the demands or tactics of the Beast, and through their suffering and overcoming all the horrific racism and systemic oppression that people have tried to throw at them, they have emerged as exemplars of the New Beings. They are doing the authentic work of perpetual spiritual liberation for themselves and others, and they are generating some of the most sublime musical and other artistic creations.

"They not only were free, but what they played gave people a kind of blueprint as to how to be free in the mind and in the spirit. That's one of the seldom mentioned gifts that the New Beings gave to the world. It's like, they laid it out, and you could hear it," Hannibal said. "You could read it, as in the case of Ralph Ellison, but in the music, you could hear it."

Part of the freedom that the New Beings offer in music is the altering of thought patterns and consciousness. The healing music can cut straight through stagnant or destructive thoughts, depression, suffering, or the various limitations of measured thinking. He said that people are always talking about the so-called Mozart effect, how playing music to infants is supposed to make them more intelligent as they develop. What Hannibal is describing with the great jazz innovators is the same, with added dimensions of freeing the minds and spirits of listeners, which the New Beings are able to do on account of all that they and their people have been through.

"Trane said that music affects the mind, the thought patterns," he said.

He also said that many of the legends of the profound music that people call jazz resented, and still resent, the word jazz. Hannibal uses it as a shorthand, as people will have a general idea of the kind of music he means when he is speaking and because it is now common parlance.

"I use the word jazz for people to know what I'm talking about, but it's a word that I honestly wish did not exist," Hannibal said.

"Ornette [Coleman] and Duke [Ellington] and a lot of them, they resented the word jazz because they didn't create it. They didn't create that word. That was a word that was given. And Miles [Davis], too, he despised that word. And Rahsaan, he despised it," Hannibal explained. "That's what was great about the Art Ensemble of Chicago. They called it great Black music. Man, Lester Bowie [1941–1999], Joseph Jarman [1937–2019]. That's some other stuff. But you know, Chicago has that kind of power. The South also has a certain kind of power. Mississippi. Mississippi has that blues power. Texas has that blues power, too, but it is not as noted as the Mississippi blues power, but we had some people here. One of them was called Gray Ghost [Roosevelt Thomas "Grey Ghost" Williams, 1903–1996], piano player, and he and a group of pianists in Houston developed this unique style, unheard anywhere else in the world of playing the piano . . . from Texas, and he's from around here. He and my mother were friends."

Hannibal has often had to confront racist or other offensive questions in the world of classical music and symphony halls, where people are constantly referencing and asking him about the same famous white composers, many of whom are from prior centuries and some of whom never even visited the United States. These invocations are all the more problematic because people so often fail to even mention the great Black American musical geniuses in these questions and remarks.

I once asked Hannibal about how he related to the musical scores of composers like Stravinsky (1882–1971), Bach (1685–1750), or Beethoven (1770–1827).

"If I look at them, it's just to check them out, to see what was going on with them. I never study them. I study Duke [Ellington]. And I learned far more from Duke's eyes and from our walk in that park than I ever did from the scores of those other composers that people are constantly referencing," he quickly replied. "One of the things that I've had to become very good at discerning is the difference between outright racism and well-cloaked racism, especially in my field. . . . What I saw as a cultural equivalent to [outright racism] is the Mozart [1756–1791] effect, the intent being to say that listening to Mozart would increase your intellectual acumen, in a land of [Duke] Ellington, [Charlie] Parker, and [John] Coltrane, where you're not also mentioning the Ellington effect. Needless to say, I not only fought against that but did not fall victim to that well-cloaked narrative called the Mozart effect. If you can't mention the Ellington effect, then you should not mention any effect."

Hannibal frequently notes the constant attacks, or attempted attacks, that besiege artists who serve true spiritual liberation—and how this is especially so for liberating art that is created by the New Beings called the Jonah People.

While Hannibal is composing, he often deals with attacks from negativity in the form of other people. Once, while working on *John Brown and Blue* (it would later premiere at Carnegie Hall with a recording released in 1999), someone who was then close to him had muttered something about physically attacking him in the ribcage with a knife.

Rather than remaining stuck in his fear and shock, he pushed through and continued to move forward to write the piece at the piano. In fact, he slept underneath it.

"I had one of the best sleeps of my life."

He then arose and completed the powerful piece in tribute to the freedom fighter John Brown. He had initially been reluctant to compose the piece, since he did not often compose for the piano.

Judith Arron (1942–1998), an open and magnanimous visionary who was then the executive director of Carnegie Hall, was a dear friend of Hannibal's. She told him that she wanted him to have seven days each year to feature all of the music of these lands, and elsewhere, in a series of events that he would curate for Carnegie Hall.

"I asked her, 'You mean, if I want to bring over some musicians from the Ituri forest [in the heart of Africa], I can do that?' And she said, 'Hannibal, you can bring anyone you'd like, as long as they're on the planet Earth.'"

When she asked him to compose the piece about John Brown (1800–1859), Hannibal told her he would have to think about it.

"I told her that I was truthfully intimidated by the piano and all that it required," he said, laughing. "So, then, she sent me a $5,000 check for the piece. How was I going to refuse a $5,000 check for this, being that I was two months behind on my rent? In other words, I was divinely coerced. And then the music started pouring into my mind, and I wrote it. And it was selected to be performed and recorded at Carnegie Hall. I'm so proud of that piece for so many reasons."

At the end of the sheet music, which has been published with a CD and book by Boosey & Hawkes and Carnegie Hall, there is a notation to slam the piano shut.[13]

"That sound is to signify the hanging of John Brown, 'the dropping the trap door,'" Hannibal explained.

Tragically, Judith Aaron died of cancer toward the end of the twentieth century before the annual collaboration with Hannibal could come to fruition.

"She treated me like I was Beethoven," Hannibal said.

During the composing of *John Brown and Blue*, Hannibal constantly dealt with spiritual attacks or attempted interferences with the completion of the work. This is an unrelenting and recurring theme throughout his life.

"There's nothing you can do to stop it from coming. It's like a great song. It just keeps coming," Hannibal said.

One of Hannibal's refrains for dealing with spiritual attacks of destruction is: "Keep moving. Always keep moving. Doing the work with a pure heart is the best protection. We're only really safe when we're doing our work."

Hannibal avoids wasting a lot of time in conversations that would detract from doing the work of the music, or that would pull him into exchanging words with someone who is coming at him from a place of negativity, by a technique he calls, "giving them the Louie."

By this, he refers to deploying Louis Armstrong's approach of smiling at people, saying little or nothing—basically wishing people well without engaging—and then walking away and returning to the work.

"I'm trying to get people to understand the perfection, the yin and yang, of the Louie, to see the perfection and the great philosophical importance of the Louie. People thought he was just smiling. That's some powerful, deep protection, that smile. And it's a nice way of asking people to leave you alone,"

Hannibal elaborated. "Also, this is a response to a lot of Louis Armstrong's critics, who would criticize him for smiling in the way of an Uncle Tom. They were missing the point. Then, the whole music industry was controlled by white people, as much of it continues to be. What was he supposed to do? Pull out a gun? He didn't have a lot of options. His handling things the way he did made it possible for a lot of other people to do their work, to serve their purpose. He made it possible for Miles [Davis] to say, 'kiss my ass.' Pop's smile was a potent weapon against the racist venom he faced on a daily basis."

Hannibal noted that the greatest dangers come when people succumb to the pressures of the Beast, when they give into the forces of destruction, usually in exchange for some illusory promises of wealth, power, or fame.

"When money is the main reason people make music, it makes it so much easier for the Beast to infiltrate them, to take the gift that the Creator gave them and turn around and use that gift to destroy people."

Hannibal has continually worked to honor his covenant with the Creator, but that does not stop Death or the Beast from trying to approach him.

The music has brought him untold gifts as well, though the spiritual and physical dangers are always in his mind.

He once was playing a benefit for a friend's philanthropic cause in the late eighties. For the fundraiser, he wrote a piece in honor of James Baldwin entitled *The Fire Next Time*, an homage to Baldwin's collection of the same name. To Hannibal's surprise, Baldwin showed up to the New York City premiere of the piece.

"I saw *African Portraits* in James Baldwin's eyes," Hannibal said. This was before Hannibal had started composing that major work.

Another time, Hannibal's poetry brought him into a soulful meeting with Toni Morrison (1931–2019). Someone from *The Amsterdam News* (newspaper) had read Hannibal's poetry collection, *The Ripest of My Fruits*, and asked him if he had ever met Morrison. Hannibal had not. The journalist arranged their meeting in New York.

Morrison gave Hannibal a book about windows. She told him that reading his poetry gave her the sensation of looking outward and inward, akin to passing a gaze through windows. She also shared with Hannibal that she always had this feeling that, as in the time of Nazi Germany, someone was going to come and force her into a truck for writing with the truth and power that she did.

"She knew that an artist's pen is mightier than the sword. We had been talking about the Holocaust. I had been telling her about the string quartet piece I was planning to write in honor of Anne Frank [1929–1945]. And we had been talking about racism and things," Hannibal said. "I always have this feeling myself, that the truck could come at any moment and take me away. It's not so much a fear. It's an awareness."

In contemplating his true direction and purpose, Hannibal began to feel pulled away from playing jazz in the mid-to-late 1980s. He explained the change by recalling earlier conversations he had had with three musical legends.

The first was with Nina Simone (1933–2003), who had seen him play one night in Paris at the New Morning Club. The next day, the two of them were talking, and she told him that he could not keep playing the way he did.

"You're giving them too much," Simone said to him. "Never give them everything."

Not long after she said this, another veteran jazz musician came over to their table, looking very depleted, as though to affirm her comment, though this musician had not heard their prior conversation.

"What did she mean by that?" I asked.

"Every time I would play, I would play with everything I had. I can't not play that way. And it was exhausting me, draining me," he said.

He also realized he wanted to spend more time with his family. He had sought advice from a revered elder, Charles Mingus (1922–1979), one day over lunch.

"When I shared with Mingus my concerns, he said, between bites, 'Why don't you start writing more?' And that's what I in fact did," Hannibal remembered. "I was tired of being on the road all the time, tired of playing the clubs. I was tired. I knew it was not sustainable. I did not want to be one of those people who turned seventy and never even got to know his children. It was an all-consuming life."

Hannibal also added that what Davis had once said was true—that a lot of the jazz scene was too much like a plantation.

"A few rich white guys basically ran the jazz music industry," Hannibal stated.

With the brutality of these economic structures also comes a threat to the spiritual integrity of the music. He no longer wanted to be a part of it.

"When I finally stopped playing those so-called established jazz clubs, I felt like I did when I got my name Hannibal. It was a shedding. I felt reborn, and I felt free. I was free of all that."

Hannibal's spiritual purposes writing and playing were not aligned with the purposes and intents of club owners, prominent managers, or record labels. At one point in the eighties, Hannibal's manager was Sid Bernstein (1918–2013), the legendary industry figure credited with (among other things) helping to bring awareness of The Beatles to the United States. However,

Hannibal walked away from that relationship, feeling that their purposes did not align.

"I never sought fame or fortune through my music, and just like the people singing that music in the indigo fields and in the tobacco fields, they didn't sing it to make money. And yet look how much money was made off of it. They sang that music to stay alive," Hannibal said. "When you make music purely to make money, then you make enemies of humans, and it does not show them what lies beyond their own limited imagination."

He then paused before adding, "So many fields, so many fortunes, so many souls. That's one of the names of the scenes in the [*Jonah People*] opera."

Recalling the end of his heavy jazz touring days, Hannibal spoke about how something was missing and his exhaustion. It was no longer a source of great spiritual nourishment—as it once was.

"I'd be touring Europe playing almost every night for four weeks straight. I would just look at my trumpet, and it would start playing," he said, laughing.

This perpetual devotion to the instrument generated a sound that many came to recognize as his.

Hannibal once shared how much it meant to him when he heard that Charles Mingus had said, "Hannibal has his own sound."

I asked him if he recalled the time frame.

"It was after I released *Children of The Fire*, I believe," he replied. "Navigating my way through the miraculous trumpet garden created by [King] Oliver [1881–1938], [Buddy] Bolden [1877–1931], Armstrong, [Kenny] Dorham [1924–1972], and Davis, while establishing a sound uniquely my own was of major concern. To especially have Mingus, Gil, and others whom I greatly admired validate the uniqueness of my own sound, was more than important to me: it was essential."

Later in the 1980s, following those earlier conversations with Mingus and Simone—and another with Evans—about his desire to turn away from touring, Hannibal moved toward the next segment of his musical journey. This shift would become a decades-long devotion to composing for orchestras, string quartets, pianos, and choirs. He would innovate by fusing and interlacing genres of music that usually were seen as separate—classical with jazz, soul, blues, and spirituals. He would also bring African musical influences directly to the forefront in the pieces he fashioned. He continues this orchestral work to this day.

Yet his love for jazz, and his existence as a jazz musician, have not dissolved or vanished. He still regularly plays his trumpet, though he almost never agrees to play clubs anymore, because playing his trumpet is "the best medicine I know, for myself."

"Even though I'm no longer living that life, I'll always be a jazz musician. I can't not be. It's in my spirit and blood. For me, life is one long jazz composition."

3

COMPOSING THE SPIRITATORIOS

In 1990, Hannibal attained another significant aspect of spiritual freedom in another change in his name. When he finished writing his widely celebrated and genre-defying *African Portraits*—his first large-scale composition for a symphony—his great-grandmother Cora, the Cherokee shaman, gave him permission to publicly use the name Lokumbe. She had previously revealed the name to him in spirit by drawing it in the sand, but he had not yet had permission to use it in public. He learned from his spirit guides that it means "the spirit that lives in the wind."[1]

He was thrilled to use it in both his personal and professional lives and quickly got rid of Peterson. He legally changed his last name to Lokumbe, which he said released a significant weight by throwing off the name passed down from those who had enslaved his ancestors. He wanted nothing further to do with it.

In *African Portraits*, Hannibal orchestrated a musical expression of four hundred years of the African American experience, including his ancestors stolen from Africa, the horrors of the Middle Passage, enslavement in the United States, and the fight for freedom and liberation by African Americans (for whom, along with other African diasporans, he now uses the term the

Jonah People). Hannibal said that, in many ways, *African Portraits* presaged and prefigured his recently completed *The Jonah People* opera. He brought strong elements of jazz, blues, and spirituals—the greatest musical achievements of the United States, as Hannibal says—into the orchestral works that are conventionally called classical. He also brought African instruments and musical influences to the forefront of the piece, featuring a West African kora player, blues and gospel singers, three choruses, and a jazz quartet. Unlike many composers, Hannibal wrote both the libretto and the music (as he does with all of his pieces).

In many performances of *African Portraits*, including its 1990 premiere and the 1995 album by the Chicago Symphony Orchestra under the baton of Daniel Barenboim, Hannibal had the honor of including David "Honeyboy" Edwards (1915–2011), a legendary blues guitarist from the Mississippi Delta. In both performances, he played a piece while everyone on stage sat in respectful silence.

"The entire Chicago Symphony Orchestra hearing pure Americana," he said. "Sometimes I think of that, and it's just like, wow."

I asked Hannibal how he first approached Edwards, then probably in his eighties and living in Chicago, about playing in *African Portraits*.

"I think it was the American Composers Orchestra, because we did it with them first, and they asked what blues guitarist [he had in mind] and somebody had told me about Honeyboy, and they contacted his agent," Hannibal replied. "When I saw his hands, you could look at his hands, and his hands alone told a million stories before he even placed them on the guitar. His hands spoke what was in his eyes. And when he sang and played, it was a gift of gifts."

"Was it always a spiritual experience when he played?"

"It was more than that. Whatever perfect could be, that's what it was. And when I saw him and heard him play, I think I had a smile on my face for a week. It was the same feeling I had when I met Mrs. [Rosa] Parks [1913–2005]. It's a very powerful thing to be in the presence of someone who has become what they do. They are without a doubt what they do. There's no separation."

"And it was the same with Mrs. Parks?"

"Yes."

Hannibal would meet Parks some years later and compose a work in her honor, *Dear Mrs. Parks*. Before its premiere, he was able to show her the score and libretto and go through it all, word by word, note by note.

Following the performances of *African Portraits*, some considered it a counterintuitive innovation that Edwards played on stage while the entire orchestra listened in silence.

For Hannibal, this made perfect sense. Why continue to keep the greatest musical innovations and styles that have come from America out of the so-called classical world and its symphony halls? He said that of course famous composers like Beethoven, Mozart, and Bach wrote great works, but that was in Europe centuries ago. They had never set foot in this land. Hannibal is adamant that it would make no sense to just imitate them and what they were doing and ignore the greatest musical achievements and geniuses of the American musical tradition, ones who gave us the blues, jazz, soul, and spirituals.

"If Bach were alive, he wouldn't just stay stuck doing the same thing. He would expand, keep moving; he wouldn't just stay where he was in the eighteenth century," Hannibal said.

In an interview that Hannibal gave around the time of the premiere of *African Portraits* in 1990, he said, "If Mozart were alive today, I know he'd be hanging out in Harlem."

When I mentioned this wonderfully direct comment, Hannibal quickly specified, "The old Harlem. Not the Harlem now, which is like Madison Avenue."

Hannibal recalled how, the last time he was in Harlem, he knew he would never return. Among other things, he was deeply disturbed by the racial gentrification and the commercialization of the neighborhood.

"The place had been transformed. The Harlem I knew was gone. It was Whole Foods, Starbucks. White people jogging. It was completely different, not the place I had known and loved," he said. "Bill Clinton was the last nail in the coffin, putting his office on 125th Street."

African Portraits first premiered on November 11, 1990, at Carnegie Hall under a joint commission from the Baltimore Symphony Orchestra and the American Composers Orchestra. The date was also Hannibal's birthday. His mother and Mr. Wilson, his childhood musical master, were seated in the front row for the premiere—a deep source of joy for Hannibal. The work was widely recognized as a major innovation and statement; it has been performed around a hundred times in the United States and Europe.

With the celebration of the work came discontent from people who did not like what he was doing. Hannibal said he received multiple death threats following the premiere of the piece. He said these threats came by phone and, laughing, that they were "great compliments."

"Sometimes I would even thank them. I would ask them sometimes, 'What in the piece upset you?' And they would generally say that I was showing white people in a negative light or as evil. I said, 'But the people who lynched my people, you can't say they're nice, can you? Because if you say they're nice and you beat my great-grandmother with a whip, I'd hate to see your definition of mean.'"

In a journal from around the time of the completion of *African Portraits*, Hannibal wrote:

> Much of the heart, that is known as humanity, beats in an agonizing
> Rhythm. A rhythm that gives no basis upon which
> The music of peace and mercy can be played.
> All that I can do, I will do, to see that the
> Brilliant harmonies of freedom, love, and justice will
> Fall upon the ears of those who
> Are deaf from lack of it. When I think
> Of the majesty and the beauty of this great, great heart,
> I have no other choice but to do so.
> This is my purpose for being and the main objective of my music.

Giving musical expression to human suffering—and seeking to do the work of helping to transmute it through the liberation of musical healing—continued to be the driving force of Hannibal's music and his life.

The flourishing of *African Portraits* marked a lasting turn toward composing full time, rather than touring around the globe. Hannibal found himself supported at all turns in this new phase of his creations.

"With the success of *African Portraits*, commissions, and the support of Carole Haas Gravagno [b. 1942], I was able to transition from a life on the road to a more productive state of creativity," he reflected.

It was at a performance of *African Portraits* that Hannibal first met Gravagno, who became one of his most significant supporters throughout the many years of his composing career. She has been a foremost patron and close friend of Hannibal over the subsequent decades.

"After the Philadelphia Orchestra performance at the Academy, I noticed behind the stage a noble-looking woman who, in many ways, reminded me of Mrs. Sparks. With her was another joyful and kind-looking woman by the name of Carole Gravagno (now, Carole Haas Gravagno). She had a condo on Rittenhouse Square, which eventually served as a place for respite over the many years of traveling and working in Philadelphia. *One Land, One River, One People, Can You Hear God Crying?*, *Healing Tones*, and a number of other works were fully developed in that space, which I came to call the Nest," Hannibal reflected. "Heartbreaking though it was when Carole sold the Nest, I have been fortunate to continue to enjoy her support of my work and purpose. As an example of her growing faith in my work, I looked up one day from my desk at my studio in Smithville, Texas, and there was a tractor-trailer with a huge sign of a piano on it. After greeting the driver and assuring him that I was in fact the person on his manifest, they began to unload the very piano on which I composed these pieces in the Nest in Philadelphia over so many years. It fits now like a dream in my studio."

With the success of *African Portraits* and the support of key figures such as Gravagno, as well as the support of several other commissions, Hannibal had fully launched the composing phase of his life's journey. Soon after the premiere of *African Portraits*, Hannibal embarked on another orchestral composition, *Dance Chief Crazy Horse, Dance*. In preparation for this work, he traveled to the Lakota community that had been Chief Crazy Horse's (c. 1840–1877) home when he was leading the Oglala band in the wars against the U.S. government in the nineteenth century. The federal policy was to support white American settlers as they brutally encroached upon the Lakota's land, people, and ways of life.

The Lakota elders granted Hannibal permission to write the piece but also gave him so much more.

"I was so grateful that I went to get permission, and I was given more than I ever could have imagined being given. Extraordinary

FIGURE 3.1 Hannibal with two visionaries, conductor Yannick Nézet-Séguin and artist Martin Payton. Nézet-Séguin had just received Einstein's Rattle, made by Payton and used in the world premiere of Hannibal's *One Land, One River, One People* with the Philadelphia Orchestra. Backstage at Verizon Hall, Philadelphia.

Photograph by Sumai Lokumbe (2015).

FIGURE 3.2 Hannibal with music and artistic director of the Philadelphia Orchestra, Yannick Nézet-Séguin, and soloists Karen Slack, Rodrick Dixon, and Funmike Lagoke, during rehearsals for the premiere of *Healing Tones* with the Philadelphia Orchestra.

Photograph courtesy of the Philadelphia Orchestra (2019).

how that happens. It's a bit like the miracle called life and death. In fact, they are closely interwoven. They are perfect companions. One could not do without the other, when you think about it."

The elders took him to a sweat lodge for a purification ceremony, a longstanding Lakota cultural tradition. Through it, Hannibal came to see various spiritual aspects of things he had been carrying inside—some unbeknownst to him—which he depicted in a drawing in his journal that he kept during his visit. After the lodge ceremony, he felt clearer and more fortified for the composition work he faced. He was getting ready to ask the work to reveal its essence to him, as he always does with his pieces, so that he can realize and become the work.

A medicine man from the community asked Hannibal if he had room to build a sweat lodge in New York (where Hannibal then lived) for purification. Hannibal said that he did not, as space was so scarce in the city.

The medicine man replied, "Then leave immediately."

After all this, Chief Crazy Horse's spirit guided him in writing the piece. While with the Lakota in Pine Ridge, a healer told him to look up. Hannibal did, and there was a perfect cloud formation of a man on a horse, which represented the blessing and presence of Chief Crazy Horse.

"They gave me the nickname 'firewalker,' because whenever I would tend the stones of the fire, you could smell my boots burning," Hannibal said. "Initially, when I got there, I knew I not only did not have the right to go in the sweat lodge, but I wasn't ready to go in, so they let me tend to the stones."

When Hannibal was preparing to leave the Lakota, the group asked him to stay, saying that they had a home for him there. Hannibal said he had to return home to his family and write the piece. The Lakota healer gave him some stones to build his own sweat lodge. He did follow the Lakota medicine man's advice to immediately leave New York City and left for Texas as soon as he felt he could, three weeks later.

"I was dying slowly in New York City, and I didn't even realize it," Hannibal said. "Also, all around me, people were dying. And I realized that the New York that I was living in during the early nineties had ceased to be the New York I sought when I left Texas in 1970. By that point, people had become so fascinated with riches, with their fancy apartments and cars. The scene became full of people locked in gilded lives of luxury."

Feeling again spiritual liberation, Hannibal soon relocated to Texas, which he decided would be his base for the rest of his life. He lived for two years in Austin in the mid-nineties before moving back to Smithville, the town where he was born. He bought the home that his mother, Ms. Peterson, used to clean.

"Was she glad you got the place?" I asked.

"Yes, she was. In fact, she stayed there with us for a while, after she had a stroke. We took care of her in that house," he recalled.

Hannibal later bought a former gas station in Smithville to serve as his studio. Its attendant, decades earlier in segregated Texas, had told Hannibal that he could not use the bathroom because of his skin color. When he bought the place, he happily demolished the station's old bathroom and installed his own floorplan. The building serves as his sacred studio space when he is composing, close to his home in the nearby town of Bastrop where he lives with his family.

Around the same time Hannibal moved back to Texas, he started a long span of composing residencies at arts centers in New Orleans, including years at the Contemporary Arts Center. He commuted between his studio in New Orleans and his home in Smithville. For many years, people in New Orleans would ask him if he could stay another year with his residencies, and he would agree. This continued until Hurricane Katrina, which forced him to rush out of the city.

"I left the city, physically," Hannibal said. "But I will never actually leave the city. My spirit will always be there."

He has held residencies in New Orleans since Katrina, including one at the Ashé Cultural Arts Center, but he has not regularly composed there recently. In the late 1990s and early 2000s, Hannibal met the renowned artist John T. Scott (1940–2007) at Ashé. A mutual friend, the photographer Eric Waters

FIGURE 3.3 Hannibal with "his brother from another mother and consummate genius," John T. Scott, at Ashé Cultural Arts Center, New Orleans, Louisiana.

Photograph by renowned visual historian of New Orleans, Eric Waters (ca. 2000).

(b. 1946), told Hannibal that he and John seemed like twins and that they must meet each other.

"When John and I first met, it's like we were already connected. We *were* already connected. I don't even think we greeted each other," Hannibal said, explaining that they went straight into conversation of their works.

He said that their most profound conversations were held in silence. They could have whole discussions about things without speaking. Hannibal said Scott remains a part of him and everything he does, even as he resides fully in spirit now, having passed over in September of 2007.

"John and I are spiritual reflections of each other," Hannibal once said to me, speaking of their deep and instantaneous connection.

Scott devoted his entire being to his work. Hannibal often remembered, in speaking with me, how Scott would say, "You know, Brother Hannibal, there might be people whose art is better than mine, but no one is going to outwork me."

Hannibal said he never saw Scott when he was not working. Not once. Even during meals, he would be working or, at the very least, discussing work. For example, during Hannibal's farewell dinner before he was about to leave New Orleans and reside in Texas full time, Scott was at work. While at the dinner table, he had been making a sketch of Toussaint and Josephine, which he gave to Hannibal at the end of the meal.

Scott looked up at Hannibal and said, "You're never going to leave New Orleans."

Hannibal said that Scott was right. "New Orleans is a part of me, spiritually," Hannibal said.

One of Scott's closest students, the celebrated artist Steve Prince, now often works with Hannibal on his musical pieces, including creating artwork for Hannibal's opera *The Jonah People*: A Legacy of Struggle and Triumph.

Prince also created art for Hannibal's oratorio *Crucifixion Resurrection*, designing the banners that are reverently carried in silence during the Walk of Love that precedes the musical portion of the piece. The banners represent and commemorate the Charleston nine—or "the nine saints" as Hannibal reminds people—who died in a horrific mass shooting carried out on

FIGURE 3.4 *Thinking About a Griot*, drawing of Hannibal by brilliant artist Steve Prince in Nashville, Tennessee (2023).

June 17, 2015, by a white supremacist at Mother Emanuel African Methodist Episcopal Church in Charleston, South Carolina.

Hannibal has Scott's photograph not far from his piano in his Smithville studio. It sits alongside photos of his family, mother, and other cherished ancestors. He greets all of them every morning with gratitude, love, and a kiss.[2]

Around the same time he became close to Scott, Hannibal met two other artists in New Orleans who remain very close friends—Martin Payton (b. 1948), a metal sculptor whose work is inspired by jazz improvisation, and Ron Bechet (b. 1956), an artist and professor at Xavier University of Louisiana, where Scott also taught for forty years.[3]

Hannibal said that all three artists are among the most generous spirit people he has known.

"John, Martin, and Ron, they saved me many times when I was composing the piece on Medgar Evers [1925–1963], and many other times, too," he said. "I would be going through something with the music, and they would just know. I hadn't said anything to them, but one of them would show up and say, 'Let's go get some shrimp for lunch.' That sort of thing. It was so special."

Hannibal said his experiences in New Orleans were like a cultural renaissance for him, his version of the Harlem Renaissance that had its fullest expression long before Hannibal moved to New York. But he had brushes with echoes of that milieu while residing in New York.

Hannibal knew Paul Robeson's (1898–1976) son, Paul Robeson, Jr. (1927–2014), who lived near Hannibal's place and who often spoke of the honorific medal his father had received while in the Soviet Union. Robeson told Hannibal about how there were no requirements for nonwhite people to enter through back doors or use separate bathrooms in the USSR.[4]

And life in New York included a year living in the same apartment building as Ralph Ellison (1914–1994).

"Ellison played a bit of trumpet, in fact. We spoke often about how the converging mass of Black geniuses in Harlem caused white people to lose their minds with fear and with awe," Hannibal recalled. "[We] had many fertile conversations while doing laundry at the laundromat. In particular, my interest was of the Harlem Renaissance: Zora [Neale Hurston] [1891–1960], [James] Baldwin [1924–1987], [Duke] Ellington [1899–1974], et al. His face lit up as he spoke of it. His description of it only added to my longstanding sense of having missed taking part in it."[5]

"When I moved to New Orleans and met Tootie [Montana] [1922–2005], John [T. Scott] [1940-2007], Martin [Payton] [b. 1948], Eric Waters [b. 1946], Ron Bechet [b. 1956], Mrs. Leah Chase [1923–2019] [co-owner and chef of legendary Dooky Chase's restaurant], and many others, it was immediately clear that I was part of what I call the New Orleans Renaissance," Hannibal continued. "For almost six years, I thrived in the absolute cultural splendor of it. Took a storm named Katrina to make me leave. My heart and soul, however, still remain."

In August 2001, in the midst of composing in New Orleans, Hannibal wrote in his journal of the nourishing divine light that guides him through the crucibles of his life on Earth. In an entry dated August 1, 2001, he wrote:

> God puts this light before me. It is clear in its purpose and grows in its luminosity in spite of my shame and my folly. A light that guides my worn and tattered vessel through the high winds and black howling seas. The sharp rocks cut at my belly as I roll and rise and then drop again. Yes, but I still see the light that forms a deep and lasting mercy. It and only it gives me the full measure of peace upon this uncertain sea of man. Towards this, I now move and pray that I will continue to be found worthy of its sight.

In 2002, Hannibal published his second collection of poetry, *Love Poems to God*. He dedicated it to Mrs. Mamie Till-Mobley (1921–2003) and her late son, Emmett Till (1941–1955).

FIGURE 3.5 *Bond of a Lifetime*, Mrs. Mamie Till-Mobley, mother of Emmett Till, with Hannibal, in Kokomo, Mississippi.

Photograph by Eric Waters (2002).

Mrs. Till was a confidante and great source of inspiration to Hannibal while she was in human form and continues to be so from spirit.

He told Mrs. Till that he was given the assignment to publish *Love Poems to God* in an effort to raise money to relocate the sacred bones of her slain son to a suitable grave site, one that did not sit atop a sewer system where rain made it difficult to even visit his grave. Emmett Till, a fourteen-year-old boy, was brutally abducted, killed, and thrown into a river in 1955 by a gang of white men after he supposedly offended a white woman in her family's grocery store. Recently, the woman—Carolyn Bryant Donham (1934–2023)—admitted that she fabricated parts of her testimony in the trial at which prosecutors charged her husband and his half-brother with the murder. An all-white jury infamously acquitted the two men.[6]

Mrs. Till also introduced Hannibal to Mrs. Rosa Parks (1913–2005), which coincided with an assignment Hannibal had received to compose his oratorio *Dear Mrs. Parks*.

"It began with a conversation we had about that misunderstanding of people thinking that Mrs. Parks refused to give up her seat [on the bus] because she was physically tired, as opposed to her not giving up her seat because she was spiritually tired," explained Hannibal. "And that fatigue in particular was her thinking about what had happened to Emmett Till. That's why she refused to get up. That's what inspired her. All of the tragedies that had been burning through the lives of our people. That was the catalyst."

He started having conversations with Mrs. Parks and her best friend and caretaker, Elaine Steele. He was even able to go over the libretto and the music score with Mrs. Parks soon before she passed, though she was not able to hear the actual piece in her human form before transcending.

In fact, to his knowledge, Hannibal reading the piece to Mrs. Parks is the last image taken of her, as Elaine had taken photos of the two of them.

"What did she say as you read the piece to her?" I asked.

"It was a kind of glow. We just mostly sat quietly watching the ice sheets float down the Detroit River. Yeah. It was really powerful."

Mrs. Parks will still visit him in dreams, as do so many others.

"Sometimes people like that, they come by way of a sunlight in a dream. They could be the sunlight in a dream. Sometimes, they would be a raindrop."

"How can you tell who they are?"

"I get a feeling.

FIGURE 3.6 *Spiritual Warrior*, Hannibal with the legendary Mrs. Rosa Parks, sharing the piece he had written in tribute to her, *Dear Mrs. Parks*, Detroit, Michigan.

Photograph courtesy of Hannibal Lokumbe (2004).

COMPOSING THE SPIRITATORIOS • III

While composing *The Jonah People*, Hannibal would often recollect his relationship with Mrs. Till, including the strength and wisdom he continued to receive from her spiritual presence. In one journal entry, dated May 3, 2022, he wrote:

> I recall many conversations with Mrs. Till as though they were currently unfolding. One in particular involved my apologizing to her for not being present in the protest marches, sit-ins, and other civil rights actions. She smiled that all-knowing smile and said, "Well, Hannibal, I am sure there will be plenty opportunities for you to participate in. Evil never dies. Just keep creating your music. That is the best protest you could ever make." As usual, her wisdom prevails for the efforts by many to destroy the people of Jonah are incessant and increasing. The Civil War, World War, and Human War will never end. And neither will the efforts of those who seek to end them. This is why what I am creating now takes everything I have and more to do. I must endure the brutal isolation and inner suffering, the brutal spiritual attacks. My ride into the jaws of evil is no less than that which the gallant Freedom Riders faced in 1964 Alabama. My segregated lunch counter is this one hundred square foot sanctuary where often I fall upon its floor in abject pain and elation.
>
> It was not my fate to cross the Edmund Pettis Bridge in the company of that shining knight, John Lewis (1940–2020), and the other noble disciples of freedom, yet the sounds of their cries from the billy clubs against their skulls, the distinct hooves of horses mounted by cowards, swirl inside of me, waiting to find themselves upon my score paper today when I began composing the battle scene for the Haitian Revolution. Alone under the watchful eye of those who love me, I now mount a protest, a revolution of the highest order. One that will allow voices from the grave to be heard. One that will bring healing to a people long suffering in a world, which without them, would not exist.

As he was composing a major oratorio, Hannibal also completed his next volume of poems in 2003. *Trilogy, Freedom Dance Cycle* speaks to the murders of James Earl Chaney (1943–1964), Andrew Goodman (1943–1964), and Michael Schwerner (1939–6194), three civil rights activists who were helping African Americans vote in Mississippi in 1964 as a part of Freedom Summer (also known as the Mississippi Summer Project). This grassroots effort aimed to draw attention to the violence that African Americans in Mississippi faced when exercising their constitutional rights. Hannibal's volume was not published until 2014, eleven years after it was written, after he found it in a box from his New Orleans studio that had been packed during the tumult of Hurricane Katrina in August of 2005. He wrote in the beginning of the poetry collection that something he witnessed at prison in Philadelphia compelled him to publish it after these years. He left that something he had witnessed undisclosed and unspecified.

Mrs. Till was a major source of spiritual sustenance while he wrote these poetry volumes and the major oratorio *God, Mississippi, and a Man Called Evers*, which honors Medgar Wiley Evers (1925–1963) and was written during a residency in New Orleans. Evers was the trailblazing civil rights activist and first field secretary of the NAACP, murdered by a white supremacist at his Mississippi home in 1963.[7]

The piece premiered with the New Jersey Symphony Orchestra. During its composition, Hannibal visited Medgar Evers's home, which has been maintained like a museum, with furniture and other items where they were on the night of his murder. He strongly felt Evers's presence and had felt a deep connection to Evers since he was a teenager, when Hannibal arrived home from school to find his mother sobbing about his murder. From that time forward, Hannibal has had a spiritual connection with Evers.

COMPOSING THE SPIRITATORIOS • 113

FIGURE 3.7 *Sweet Glorious Peace*, Hannibal, New Orleans, Louisiana.
Photograph courtesy of Hannibal Lokumbe (2001).

"I really felt his presence in the home, when I visited as part of the research for the piece. And the ancestors were there, everyone was there. They showed me everything, so much of what had happened."

FIGURE 3.8 *Bamboula Magic*, drum circle, Congo Square, New Orleans, Louisiana. In the photograph, Naomi DeBerry.

Photograph by New Orleanian poet Kelly Harris-DeBerry (ca. 2009).

A major component of Hannibal's piece was Evers's triumphing over the Beast when it tried to manipulate him into giving in to the forces of destruction. The Beast pointed out to him all of the horrors being done by white racists to the people of Jonah.

"The fact is that you are alive, you have survived, and you are not a killer. You have not yielded to the Beast. That's the powerful thing about Medgar. There's a section in the composition where Medgar confronts the Beast, because Medgar was an expert killer. He was in Normandy [in the war]. The Beast was saying, 'Man, you've got to be out of your mind. You let these white people treat you like that, and you're a professional killer.' Go down to the capitol with your M1. . . . And he said, 'No.' Then appeared an angel, who said to Medgar, 'I'm going to grant you any wish you desire because you denied the Beast.' Medgar replies, 'My wish is that my children would be grown and see me as I now am.' And the spirit says, 'That has already been done.'"

Hannibal said that, many years later, Evers's family did reopen his grave and his body had not decomposed in the slightest. Evers's wish had been granted: his grown children saw him as he looked before he was killed.

I asked Hannibal if Evers's confrontation with the Beast could be found in any books about Evers's life and struggles.

"No, that's information you get from the spirits," he said.

"And in many ways, that is some of the most important information, right? How to avoid capitulating to the manipulation of the destructive forces, even in such trying circumstances?"

"That's right."

In the composition, God, Mississippi, and a Man Called Evers, Hannibal includes in the libretto a pivotal figure, a spirit guide named Ruth who materializes in the flesh to help Medgar Evers do his liberation work when he was in human form. Ruth's spirit also visited Hannibal while he was writing the opera for Evers. I asked Hannibal if there is anything he would like me to write regarding Ruth's spiritual guidance for the piece.

"Before I wrote about Ruth, I was getting these very strong feelings about how many women of Jonah have been raped, and killed, and forgotten, so Ruth is the spiritual representation of all the women who suffered such a fate. And my mentioning of Ruth and that entire sequence is my recognition of all of the women who met such fate. And it would be criminal of me not to do so," Hannibal said. "Just like the whispers in the [*Jonah People*] opera in the Middle Passage scene—that pays homage to all the people who perished in the ocean during that voyage. And it would be criminal of me not to do so, and it would be criminal of society not to do so. They didn't just go away. They're still somewhere, because their aura can't be destroyed, so they have to be somewhere.... They're everywhere. That's why it says [in the libretto to *The Jonah People*], 'their spirits still roam the skies.'"

In the early 2000s, when Hannibal was still commuting regularly to New Orleans, he returned to his land near Smithville in a town called Rosanky, where he often goes to spiritually recharge or to meditate, pray, and rest. It is the same forest where the Creator would (in 2012) reveal to him the Jonah People as a moniker and symbol.

While he was lying on ground there, he had a vision of spirits—the bodies of people of Jonah—all flying eastward across the sky toward Africa, toward home.

"Their bodies were so many that they covered the sky, they blotted out the sun," he said. "And I went home and went to sleep, and I saw them."

When I asked if he knew any of the spirits, he said: "I knew all of them because they are me. The name didn't matter. That's why they revealed themselves to me, because they knew I would know we're the same.... Just like in the Jonah People symbol. It depicts how the people who perished still are connected to those who survived. That's eternal connection."

The Jonah People symbol captures the threshold between the dead and the living, the continuous connection between those who have passed to spirit and those who are walking the Earth in human form. The perpetual connection and co-creation with the ancestors have brought him his most recent assignment from the Creator—the composition of his first fully staged opera, *The Jonah People: A Legacy of Struggle and Triumph*. The creative process of this opera would bring him into a more profound experience of becoming the art, becoming one with the Work, than he had ever experienced.

4

THE JONAH PEOPLE AND BECOMING THE WORK

As Hannibal and I spoke over the first couple of years for the book, he was fully immersed in his composition, *The Jonah People*: A Legacy of Struggle and Triumph. This opera premiered with the Nashville Symphony in April 2023. Many of the multifaceted dimensions of his composition and spiritual co-creation processes came into view for me as I witnessed his composing and had ongoing conversations with him about his creative journey along the way.

The composing process involved traversing many spiritual soundscapes, which included visiting spaces in the past (for example, in his previous lives or his ancestors' lives), and experiencing or reexperiencing—or realizing and becoming—what he was composing.

The Jonah People tells the story of his great-grandfather, Silas Burgess, and others who were enslaved and fought for freedom in the United States. It commemorates liberation triumphs while acknowledging ongoing struggles among the enslaved and their descendants, including the tremendous contributions of ingenious musical and other artistic innovations, as well as powerful movements for true racial and social justice.

As part of the work, Hannibal shares a new name—the Jonah People—for people known as Black or African American, or as African diasporans. He received this directly from the Creator when he was alone one night, lying upon a table he had made, praying and meditating in the pinewoods on his family's land in Rosanky, Texas.

With his spirit lifted to the sky, feeling merged as one with the stars of the Milky Way, Hannibal shared, "I asked the Creator, what do you call us? And the Creator said, 'You're like Jonah, except rather than being followed by swallows, your ship was followed by sharks.' You must seek, you must ask for such things to be revealed."

This spiritual revelation of the Jonah People moniker came around 2012 when he was composing his spiritatorio, *Can You Hear God Crying?* The work is a tribute to his great-grandfather, Silas Burgess. Around the same time, he also had a powerful visitation from his mother who offered to him guidance that saved his life.

"All I know is that you can never get too far from the grace of the spirits, you can never get too far away. That's as dangerous a thing as you can do. To get too far from the spirits. I was sleeping out there for a week, and my mother came to me in a dream and said, 'Go home today.' And I went home, and the next day when I went out to my tent, a tree had fallen, and where my bed and sleeping mat were, where my body would lie, there was a branch of a tree that had fallen, about three inches in diameter, and it had impaled itself right where my head would lie," he recalled. "The tree crushed the tent, but right where my body would have been, I would've been impaled by a branch that was buried some 8 inches into the ground. So, I say, you've got to stay close to the ancestors. It was the spirit of my mother who saved my life, yet again.

When you do the work, you'll always have what you need. Mom would always say, 'The Lord will never take you into a place and not bring you out of that place. And when you come out, you will not be the same.'"

Through the revelation from the Creator in Rosanky, Hannibal understood that the Jonah People are born of three wombs: the womb of the Creator, of a mother, and of the slave ship. He said that much of the power of the Jonah People's spirit comes from triumphing over all that has been done to them and all of the attacks that continue to be leveled at them. Those who undergo the horrors and the arduous struggles of enslavement and ongoing racial liberation struggles—and do not succumb to the evil of what has been and continues to be done to them—have given birth to some of the most ingenious work across all fields and ways of life.

In time, Hannibal came to understand that the Jonah People was given to him as a name to share with others and that he would write an expansive opera about it. He now regularly uses the Jonah People—or people of Jonah, man or male of Jonah, woman or female of Jonah, or children of Jonah—in place of Black or African American.

"You see, when you've gone through what the Jonah People have gone through, and you do not give in to the Beast, to the forces of destruction, you already have what you need. You have that connection to the divine that is within you and from there you can create magnificent things," he said. "There is no need to go to the Egyptian temples to train and initiate in the mysteries and all of that, if you have survived the passages of the third womb and refuse to give in to the Beast."

Hannibal also received, by spiritual revelation from the Creator, the Jonah People symbol. He now often wears it on t-shirts, has it imprinted on his musical composition sheets, and places it on objects that are around him. The symbol has become a central part of his life and the message of his work, especially in *The Jonah People* opera. He seeks to share the symbol with people as a reminder and activation symbol of consciousness for all to know the truth of the Jonah People, including that of the divine within the Jonah People. All of this is part of his broader efforts to remind people of—or to help awaken people's consciousnesses to—the divine power that resides within all people.[1]

The Jonah People symbol represents the third womb, which is the slave ship, and also a door or threshold between the two worlds, one inhabited by the Jonah People who have crossed over (the ancestors) and that of the Jonah People who continue to walk the Earth as humans. The symbol's two marks represent the males and females of Jonah. The marks above the ship represent those who survived the Middle Passage and those below represent the spirits who perished in the horrors of slave ships. The parts above also represent those Jonah People who are alive today, while the linear forms below the ship represent ancestors after their crossing over to spirit.

"The connection of the Jonah People is continuous and eternal," Hannibal said. "People have but to realize and remember this if they have not done so already. The ancestors are always with us. We never walk alone."

When Hannibal and I began regular conversations for this book in the fall of 2020, he had completed much of the libretto and was really starting to settle into composing the piece. He also was in the midst of becoming the work itself and communing more deeply with the spirits of the work and with the ultimate Creator. The co-creative composing process served as a womb, or a space of gestation, both for the opera and for his spirit.

Hannibal worked on the overture for the first couple of months. He often explained to me the transmutational properties of the different components and the intent behind the elements of what he was doing. In his composing, he was imprinting, or encoding, his intent in the musical movements. The overture was both a celebratory announcement of the magnificence of the Jonah People and an opening into the next parts of the opera, which cover the brutal ripping of people from their homes and families in Africa to be placed aboard ships that carried them to the enslavers' auction blocks in the so-called New World.

The overture intones the horrors of what is to come in the opera and, at the same time, offers a healing portal for people to enter through. People at once are offered access to the horror and to the transcending of it.

"True healing can only happen with the truth. For this opera to be worthy of its purpose, it must convey the truth of the atrocities as they happened. At the same time, I have interwoven cords of sounds and light that can hold people in the space of the music, so that they might be healed as they listen. Or at least, I am offering that to them. The opera puts the meal on the table, a meal of reckoning and healing. Whether people eat it is up to them," Hannibal explained. "My task is to put it on the table for the people."

At the beginning of the opera, Hannibal has two spirits—a male and a female, played by two children—walk around the stage in silence, sprinkling sand to signify the opening of a sacred space. Hannibal shared with me that this is reminiscent of the pouch that his great-grandmother Cora, the Cherokee shaman, used for her sacred medicine. The pouch was an essential element of a sacred ceremony that she performed and that he experienced many years ago. He rendered this experience in a poem called, "Great Grandma's Gris Gris":

It's something that I saw
when the day became the night
when the stars did their dance
upon the blue face of the sky.
The small things ran for cover
in the thickets and groves.
Sulfur floated above a well-made fire,
a sword whipped through the air.
From beneath her robe
a sash of herbs appeared
wolves began to wail
and the beast became uneasy.
The young man began to writhe and groan
as the saplings holding him to the table came undone.
Upon his chest
Great grandma quickly climbed.
She spoke to his ancient soul
in words not found on tablet or stone.
Powers of the then and now
pulled the beast from its place.
Out of the young man's mouth
the thing of death flew.
The sword became a fire
that sutured his ruptured soul
now lying beneath Great Grandma's
blanket of birch, sage, and mint.
Between the full moon
and the tall-pointed top pines,
the beast was seen moving with great speed
towards yet another vessel of marrow and bone, soon to be
in desperate need
of Great-Grandma's Gris Gris.

Hannibal has witnessed and participated in many healing ceremonies. This is but an example, captured in his powerful and evocative poem.

Although Hannibal does not explicitly say this in the program or libretto, the two spirits—and the stage directions for them—are homages and invocations to the sanctifying presence of Cora, and all of the ancestors, particularly the great ancestors of the Jonah People.

During the overture, a choir representing the spirits of the ancestors sings consolations, including "I will never leave you" in whispers.

Hannibal said that the choir's words are an acknowledgment of the constant presence of the ancestors. It is also an affirmation for people who might be trepidatious about opening fully to the demanding and healing force of the journey that lies ahead in the opera. No one walks alone. The ancestors will always be there, just on the other side of the proverbial veil of consciousness between humans and spirits.

When Hannibal was starting to embark upon the Middle Passage portion of the piece, he was having very intense dreams and visions. These would often come in the middle of the night, which would suddenly awaken him. These came after he had asked to be shown the essence of the work. He was shown and, he said, spiritually traveled back to the slave ship that his great-grandfather Silas was on.

"I'm starting to see their eyes, their faces. I'm starting to see the other people on the ship, smell the smells. And I hear the cries and moans, and I feel it all. I have to go through this because otherwise I could not write it. It has to be real."

One particularly harrowing passage was when Hannibal wrote the orchestration of the slave-trading ship's white captain as he read a letter to his wife. He had to go to a place in which the force of evil that had brutally oppressed his ancestors was expressed.

At one moment in the Middle Passage, during Veil II of the opera, the Marabout—a figure in the opera—triumphantly rises and praises the Creator of life. A woman then holds a baby up toward the sky. Even in this hell, an enslaved person was able to give birth on the ship.

"You see, in this moment, we have the principle of perpetual life. They can try to kill the Jonah People, and people were dying on that ship, or jumping to their death, or being thrown off the ship to their death. But their spirits do not die. They are all connected eternally. And the Jonah People, as a people, continue to live on and create and procreate. This is one moment in which the piece shows the remarkable strength of the Jonah People."

Hannibal explained how he had orchestrated a cord of light, love, and sound that connects all beings at this moment. It invites all those witnessing the opera to open to the resonance of interconnectedness and oneness that this cord offered and demonstrated. He sought to show how, even in the midst of this horrific experience on a slave ship during the Middle Passage, those enslaved did experience the divine within and around them and continued to procreate, generate, and venerate the principle of life. This truth of everlasting life—eternal life that is ultimately indestructible by mortal or finite things—supersedes all else. When this divine connection is made conscious through, say, music and imagery, it can help transmute the pain and suffering that occurs within the earthly realm. This is an example of the essence of Hannibal's musical alchemy. It also sometimes works for people, even if only on a subconscious level, with respect to their waking minds. That is, it can remain active and transformational if people's spirits are open to receiving the transmutation of pain and suffering, even if their conscious waking ego minds do not process it as such.

As the mother raises to the sky, and to the Creator, the newborn baby on the ship, the juxtaposed imagery offers a portal into the sonic alchemy of the opera. There is the purity, beauty, and joy of the divine cord of the newborn baby while concurrently chains bind the ship's enslaved humans. In the opera, Hannibal orchestrates the Marabout's calling forth the light cord that is, as Hannibal put it, connected "to the placenta of God, to feed us again the food of eternal life."

In this movement, Hannibal both composes stark separations—and the violence of these separations—and works to suture or show the enduring and unbreakable connection of the divine essence that runs through the higher truth. Here, between interior and exterior worlds, humans and the divine, humans and nature (on the ship encompassed by the ocean, thunder, lightning, sky), and within humans themselves. In this scene, Hannibal powerfully portrays, encodes, and imparts all of this with sound, imagery, text, and the movements of the piece's elements. In so doing, Hannibal invites people into a deep spiritual reckoning that is also a space where profound spiritual liberation and healing can occur.

One day, in the midst of composing this part, Hannibal said he wanted to read from the journal entry he had made earlier that day.

"I want to share this with you. I actually wrote some in my journal today, as opposed to all over my manuscript," he said. He then read:

> Moved so well on the work the past few days and can see the completion of the first half. Patrick Dailey, the Marabout, will sing his proclamation alone. His accompaniment will be the sound of the chains on his wrists. When he enters, everything, including the sound of the movement of the ship, stops. It is as though the entire world stops in order to behold the power of his words.

He is not pleading but passing on the eternal message of freedom—a message, a power, an energy, a force—which predates humanity. A natural order which governs all things and is present in all nations and has been, continues to be, and will always be spoken in every language, in every land. At the conclusion of the Marabout's text, he turns. The chains drop from his wrists. He disappears into the black ether, out from the confines of the wooden womb of hell as did Moses, Fannie Lou Hamer (1917–1977), Christ, the Buddha, Chief Crazy Horse, and all of the spirit people who could not resist the everlasting call of spiritual emancipation.

Spirit people is a designation that Hannibal uses to refer to those who do the work of spiritual liberation.

Hannibal added that he was thinking about putting the text of this journal entry in the program for the opera. He wanted the audience to clearly see the connections of the Jonah People to all of these great spiritual leaders throughout the ages and comprehend the deeper meanings of this moment in the opera.

He also emphasized how the Marabout was addressing the whole universe with this proclamation, accompanied only by the sound of the chains, as he prophesies the birth of the New Being, born of three wombs—the Creator, the mother, and the slave ship.

"I speak not just to you, on the Earth, but wherever you might exist. . . . I now declare to the immortal seed free of these chains. Freed from our collective fear, a new courage will prevail from our shattered lives and broken spirits. A new joy will come. And from this, our womb of horror, a new being will be born from whose spirit and soul will come a force that will heal nations and reveal to them the true face of heaven,'" the Marabout says.

Throughout the composition, Hannibal would become completely drained. He said the entire process "takes more than a lot."

Sometimes, he would get so exhausted and overwhelmed with the music and spiritual information coming into his mind—at times making its way into his piano or composition pages—that he would have to stop entirely. He would become entirely still and silent for hours, sometimes even for a day or more, so that he could recalibrate and resume the process.

"I've never done work that has required so much, including sheer physical exhaustion, than composing. When I was young, before I left for New York, I spent some time doing work on a highway. That was nothing compared to this work of composing."

All of the information that comes to him and through him drains him, and that sometimes requires his complete attention. But the work of composing is akin to playing. As he hears the music and works through it, he is also playing the music. At times, it is as if he is playing a show full throttle. The process is just as all-encompassing.

"I have this certain kind of sense that comes with being faithful to the request. It's a very powerful feeling. I can't say it's like mixed emotions, but it definitely is a very steady hum that I'm getting ready to share with the world, a story that has been passed down to me for hundreds of years," he said. "You know, during the auction, the choir has this line; they say, 'When can we have rest? When will this hell be done?' They're singing that behind the auctioneer, as he's auctioning off the people."

Of course, there are moments of great euphoria and enervating lows of profound sadness. There is a perpetual vacillation.

"And I'm grateful for all of it. Even the lows, that's part of it. The suffering is important. I am grateful to have been found worthy of being given something for which I will gladly suffer. Great beauty may be created from great suffering. Just look at what people call jazz, or look at the blues."

The journey of suffering has been a great creative ally of Hannibal's throughout his life, though difficult to endure at times.

During *The Jonah People* composition process, he endured frequent nose bleeds from the sheer intensity of the musical consciousness and energies coming through him in the process. When I asked Hannibal for his sense of the significance of the nose bleeds, he replied, "With birth comes blood."

For Hannibal, composing is a form of giving birth, and he feels his life to be on the line every time he embarks on the journey. His ancestors and spirit guides help to nourish and protect him through these especially stressful and vulnerable times.

"I would not even attempt such an undertaking if I were alone or thought I were alone in the process. It would be impossible to do the work alone, without the Creator and the spirits."

In the end, the trials of suffering allow for deeper expansion in the creative process and for spiritual evolution. It is all about what one does with the suffering—whether one allows it to overtake them, or if a person meets the opportunities for growth, spiritual expansion, and creative transmutation that suffering offers.

"Learning and understanding how to suffer, and how to do the work to move through it, these are of great importance. I have too much work to do to sit in the suffering, and that's how I like it. Often, if I'm feeling depressed or down, when I turn to listen to the ancestors, they quickly will remind me that I'm feeling that way because I'm allowing myself to focus too much on myself. And I'm grateful when they remind me of that because it's true," he said. "So much for Freud and psychoanalysis. There's no time for such things. No time and no need, when you devote your life to doing the work."

In a journal entry dated December 14, 2021, Hannibal wrote of the healing he found through communing with nature, his greatest teacher and his greatest temple beyond the inner sanctuary of his soul. He wrote:

While walking upon the pristine sand yesterday, beneath the whispering blue sky of slowly moving white puffs of clouds, it was obvious the healing I was receiving. My spirit was one with the splendor of all that my eyes beheld. The sky in all of its reverence did not require that I cover my head or my shoulders, as is required by the Vatican, to walk within its halls. The wind and coconut trees did not require of me a passport, visa, or bank statement. The Healing Tones of the incessant waves did not demand to know, or care to know, if I professed allegiance to any religion, in order that they continued to vibrate inside of me as they crashed against the rocks and sandy shore.

Life is in us and before us. How we live it creates the place called heaven or hell.

He recalled many times when people attacked him or his work, and how he has striven to see the gifts that are buried within such negative expressions or actions.

"They reaffirmed my lessons and my experiences about suffering, which are miraculous in the lives of the Jonah People. They make breathtakingly clear the fact that suffering can become your ally and not your foe. The people sitting on the verandas of the plantations drinking mint juleps, their suffering was an invisible kind of suffering that would have them be suffering and not even know it," Hannibal said.

This invisible suffering can be even more pernicious than conscious, open suffering, since people can so easily be blind to it, or to its depth and magnitude while they carry their own.

"Like fighters always say, shadowboxing is one thing, being in a real fight is another. It's for everyone to deal with their suffering and their pain, in their own way."

When Hannibal is moving through the morass of suffering, he is usually silent with others about it.

"Often, when I suffer, the only entities that know about it are myself, my God, and the ancestors. They're the only ones. And they quickly remind me that there's too much work to be done to relish for a second too long in my suffering."

At one point in the summer of 2021, Hannibal had been writing for a week or so straight and doing little to nothing else, aside from necessarily daily routines. He was going deep into Veil III of the opera, aiming to complete it as soon as possible, which required tuning out any and all distractions, including his own mind and voice. He often has to isolate himself in his studio when he goes deep into a phase of composing a piece.

"I'm just trying to bear down on this, and I'm just chomping at the bit on the piece, man. I've been writing like, man, wow," he explained.

Referring to these intense periods of writing, I asked him what it is like when he goes into this kind of zone, without his normal daily routines.

"Are the ancestors working with you most of the time, throughout the day?"

"Yeah, and it's a funny thing, I never feel alone. When you do the work, they don't allow you to feel alone. Or at least, they don't allow me to feel alone. But I've been, for the most part, isolated in this studio. I've been doing my exercise. Every day, I take like an eight-, nine-, ten-mile bike ride," Hannibal said. "I've started doing my pushups and getting ready for the tower."

He was referring to his planned climbing of the water tower in Smithville, where he would play his song "Hymn for the World" in front of a gathering of people from the community. He had dubbed the event Tin Man. Then, there would be a procession to a local restaurant, where a celebration would continue with a with a jazz band from New Orleans playing throughout the evening. He had been training for weeks after receiving the okay from the city manager and even had a wonderful trainer practicing going up the tower with him in a harness to ensure safety.

Hannibal received this particular mission from Fannie Lou Hamer—in spirit—along with other ancestors. He followed their instruction. In so doing, he realized that he had conquered his fear of heights, and he had had the opportunity to play "Hymn for the World" from the highest point in his hometown.

Writing to me about "Hymn for the World," Hannibal once shared: "From the sky it all came and from the sky it will come and to the sky it shall all return."

He elaborated, in parentheticals, on the meaning of a couple of passages from the hymn: "The Earth is the mother of us all (mortals), our Father the endless sky (Eternal Being)."

Often, in everyday conversation, he invokes words from the end of this hymn, "Hatred requires so little, love the greater test."

"I wish people could have this song," Hannibal once said, adding that the hymn was for all people, not just those of one nation, team, or community. "Rather than national anthems or pledges of allegiance or other things that speak to the separateness of people, I wish people could have this, which is for all the people in the world."

Fannie Lou Hamer (1917–1977) had first come to Hannibal by way of a dream, when he was fourteen years old. She was pushing a wheelbarrow full of notes, which were flowing out of it with a beautiful melody. Hannibal asked her, in the dream, where she got the song, and she told him, "You wrote it." Later in life, he did write a piece based on the music she brought to his awareness in the dream state.

Hannibal followed Hamer and the instructions of other ancestors about the Tin Man event. Later, many people in town shared with him that this event had inspired them to face—and work on overcoming—their own fears about various things. It also helped heal people from anger. As Hannibal often says, "Anger and fear are twins. They go together."

Hannibal shared that much of the intent behind his opera, *The Jonah People*, had to do with retrieving a sense of home for people who had been ripped and stolen from their native lands.

"Home is where there is peace. But to get to that place, people must go through so much. There is a shedding that must be done. That's a lot of what this opera is about. . . . In the opening scene of the opera, Rodrick [Dixon, a tenor who will sing in the Griot role] will have a suit on. The suit doesn't allow the wind to do its thing. It's a very impractical thing to wear, something tight like that. And then, on the stage he will take that off and have the kente [traditional Asante cloth from present-day Ghana] or an indigo cloth. Freer. This is symbolic of the shedding and going back home."

In composing *The Jonah People*, Hannibal of course wrestled a great deal with anger over the atrocities of what happened and what continues to happen to the Jonah People. Hannibal said that he constantly had to work to avoid writing from a place of anger.

"It's like not bringing anger to the bandstand. It's disrespectful to the gift of the music to write from anger. You can feel angry about everything that has been done to you and your ancestors; you can feel a very justifiable anger. But you don't compose the music that heals from a place of anger, because it doesn't work that way."

Hannibal also said he received straightforward instructions from the Creator about not composing this piece from anger. His climbing Tin Man to release his fear of heights may have had a larger purpose: to spiritually clear anger or other fear-based energy or emotion.

"They just gave me the instructions, and I followed them. I accepted the instructions, and only later did I even remember that my greatest fear was a fear of heights," he noted. "The Creator has made clear to me that if I write this piece from a place of anger, then I'm on my own."

Through the entire process of composing *The Jonah People*, Hannibal said he sought to offer a healing water for the people.

"The music, visuals, text, and all offerings of my creation, *The Jonah People*, are meant to be living water that will flow into every crack, crevice, stream, river, and ocean of pain to have ever existed, that is currently existing, and that will yet exist in the lives of the people of Jonah."

The Creator gave him the allegorical symbolism of the Jonah People, as it would resonate most widely and deeply. Other than Christianity, many had their religion stolen, erased, or forbidden.

"Christianity was what the Jonah People were allowed to have, and, for all of its flaws and corruptions with the way humans misuse the messages of Jesus, it has been critical for the survival and the flourishing of the Jonah People," he said. "As I always tell the children, there would be no civil rights movement without the Black churches. It was the only place that people of color could really gather in that kind of way, and it fed their spirits. And just listen to the glorious spirituals that came from that."

He said that the vast majority of the Jonah People will resonate with the Christian touchstone of Jonah, rather than other iconography, and see the higher truth of the message that is beyond any single religion.

"The Creator gave me the term, the Jonah People, because out of every 1,000 people of Jonah, 999 will adhere to that name, that principle. That allegory is in our muscles. It's in our bones, like a drum, it is in our muscles and in our bones. So, when I think of how perfect the Creator is to give me that kind of information, to have it, to help change, and to work toward the liberation of a people who were imprisoned by the same book in the hands of mercenaries and killers. Isn't that something?"

I asked why Hannibal prefers not to speak while eating, whether it is spiritual for him. I noticed that he did not like to speak and eat a meal at the same time.

"You know, food, like music, was one of the things they couldn't take from us. Around food, we were able to restore ourselves, just like around church. And you've got to remember that the food that was given to us wasn't the same food given to the white man who held the whip in his hand," he said. "That whip is symbolic of many things. It's not just a whip. Like he says, I spell it out real clear [in the opera], where Henri says to his wife, 'With my whip, I will control his body. With my name and my God, I will control his soul.' So, when you think about it, what's so remarkable about the Jonah People as being the New Being is when you think of what they have had to do to survive what was against them, in every aspect—food, finances, art, culture, everything, has been a fight."

The figure of Henri in the opera is symbolic of the white enslaver, with surname Burgess, who purchased Silas Burgess and his brother and mother (Asase) from the auction block in Charleston, South Carolina. He then forcibly took them to the Burgess Plantation, where they remained until they ultimately escaped. Hannibal set the opera in Haiti, so he gave Henri and some others French names. He said that he wanted to pay homage to the Jonah People in Haiti, which he said is one of the most maligned and misunderstood countries, with its religious beliefs and its impoverishment, and it is also a place where the enslaved triumphed in revolts and in a legendary revolution against the enslavers. Hannibal wanted to pay tribute to all of this in the opera and to remind those Jonah People in Haiti that they are always on his mind and that the Jonah People are one.

The auction scene is pregnant with many layers of meaning. Hannibal is orchestrating what actually happened to his direct ancestors in South Carolina, but set in Haiti as a tribute to the Jonah People there. Henri (Burgess) was about to purchase Asase without her children. In fierce determination, she writhed on the ground "with the sacred fire of the Creator," as Hannibal said to me. She spoke with her eyes and her body and her soul, in a way that the soul of Henri understood. Asase was asking that he purchase all of them. She touched the tip of his boot and looked at Henri (Burgess). Without saying a word, Henri then gestured to the seller at the auction that he would purchase all three.

Asase had connected to Henri's (Burgess's) soul, and with the fierce determination of the divine within her, she succeeded in convincing this man—in the midst of one of the most craven of acts—to at the very least allow her to remain with her children. And all of this exchanged without the language of the human tongue.

"She spoke to him with the language of the soul," Hannibal said. "And he responded to it."

Hannibal said that within the pages of this music, where his great-great-grandmother—Asase in the opera—is being sold, he was simultaneously orchestrating the sounds of hell and paradise. In the musical composition and its spiritual counterpoints, he referenced a vision he had while playing at the Village Vanguard in the seventies or eighties with his band, The Sunrise Orchestra.

"It's going to be a replication of what I saw one night when I was playing in the Village Vanguard. It was real dark, and I saw these two plumes of smoke, white and black, intertwine, in the far back of the room. They started at the floor, and then moved up and spread out through the room."

"They were spirits?"

"Yeah, they were the perfect replication of matter and antimatter. It was beyond good or bad. Good or bad would be such an inaccurate description of it. It was life, you know? But there were parts of it, it's what I'm going to write," he said. "So, while great-great-grandmother is saying, 'No,' and the spirits are saying, 'You cannot destroy me. My God is within me,' you're going to hear the attempt to destroy her. You'll hear it. And I'm going to have the musicians, I'm going to bring them, even with notes, which they're familiar with, I'm going to use the notes in a way that's going to take them to a place they've never been before in sound."

Another time while composing the opera, Hannibal's mother came to him in a dream to reveal, in sounds, an illumined path that led to the place where she and other ancestors now reside. This came at one of the many times when Hannibal was feeling burdened by the sheer physical demands of the composition.

"In a way, I want to put the physical phenomenon of life behind me. In this piece, I feel I'm shown these musical pathways that are showing me attributes of life that have nothing to do with the skin or the bones—and certainly not with the physical markers of race, gender, and belief," he said. "Mama brought me some tones that were clearly pathways that were lit up, to where she and others now abide."

Hannibal reflected in his journal, after writing the music of Asase's lament, in an entry dated November 7, 2021:

> Finally, but finally, completed the full orchestration for Asase's lament. The most challenging music I have ever written. The melody is extremely simplistic in its structure which allows the text to be dominant. The mystery lies in the chords and their transition from one to the next. The completion of these ten pages is well worth the cost of creating them. Before leaving the studio last

night, I began writing a haunting flute solo which will act as the set up to Asase's entrance into the sugarcane field. A strong, strong desire to rest today.

As he composed this scene, Hannibal wrote the poem "Asase's Prayer" that he added to the opera's libretto. In it, Asase speaks to the Creator while writhing on the ground, touching the boot of the man who would purchase her:

ASASE'S PRAYER

Kunanamui [God in Kpelle], thank you for gathering up the stars and making of them a path for my soul to travel and to see what my eyes are now too filled with the dust of this world to see. Upon this ground which holds the weeping blood of children and the feet of those now complete strangers to your love, you have chosen to enter my temporal skin and crawl with me and guide me to your Eternal vision.

To follow you is to become you
To follow you is to become you
To follow you is to become you.

Hannibal later had these translated to Asase's language, Kpelle—the same language Hannibal heard his mother speak in her final hours on Earth—and added the Kpelle name for God, Kunanamui, at the beginning. The prayer was sung in the opera.

The last night that Hannibal's mother was conscious in human form, she spoke with him and imparted a gift that Hannibal said is indestructible.

"I was the last person my mother recognized. When she was dying, my mother said, 'Reet, you're my top rock,'" Hannibal recalled, adding that his mother affectionately called him Reet. Some others in his family did as well. "That was all I needed to hear for the rest of my life. I didn't need anything else. This woman who has helped so many."

Before his mother finally left her body, Hannibal heard her speaking in a language he had never heard, though he would remember the sound of what she was saying. Years later, in a church in Philadelphia, he recognized the language being spoken there as the same tongue he had heard his mother speak. He asked people in the church and learned it was Kpelle, spoken by people in present-day Liberia and Sierra Leone. Some of Hannibal's ancestors are Kpelle.

"At four in the morning, I heard her conversing in this language. I'm convinced that her grandfather's mother who ran away—Asase in the [*Jonah People*] opera—came to get her, to hook her up. Why? Because I remember words. I'm a musician. I remember sounds, especially when they're new and interesting to me. I remember her saying sounds that, in Kpelle, mean, 'My name is?' It had the sound of a question," he recalled. "Now, in the opera, I not only get to tell the story of my great-great-grandmother, but I get to tell it in her tongue. When she's crawling on the ground, being beaten, the first word out of her mouth is *Kunanamui*, which is God in Kpelle."

The stage direction in the libretto, following Asase's prayer, reads: "Henri's [Burgess's] wife looks at him. Henri [Burgess] acknowledges her gaze, turns toward the auctioneer and raises four fingers suggesting 400 dollars for the two boys to which the auctioneer bangs the gavel and points it toward Henri in acceptance of his offer. The boys run to their mother sobbing. The three embrace."

The libretto then turns to the next lines of dialogue, in which Asase says: "Where now am I to go on this endless journey of pain? My fate but a fading ember before me as I am now given to traverse the shadows of this world."

As the lights go down, a soprano then sings "The Four Tones of Salvation."

Soon after, the scene shifts to Asase, Silas, and other enslaved people cutting sugar cane with a percussive rhythm. Another enslaved woman, Fatiman, speaks powerfully to revitalize the people around her. She is named in honor of the legendary Haitian vodou priestess, or mambo, Cécile Fatiman, who played a key role in the 1791 Bois Caïman ceremony that helped ignite the Haitian Revolution.[2]

In the libretto, Fatiman states: "It will not be long, my daughter. We are not alone or forgotten by the God of life. It will not be long before the blood of freedom will run red in the fields, rivers and streams. Soon it will run red in the cups of those who sip away, without care, the blood of our lives."

While Hannibal was working on this orchestration, he reflected in his journal (notated December 4, 2021, 2:35 P.M., studio):

> The issue of the trombone as being a voice of strength glowing from the hills to strengthen and reassure the spirit of Asase and others toiling away in the cane fields, cottonfields, rice fields, tobacco fields, has just been resolved. The trombone continued to remind me that it and only it was the sound most possessive of the tonal qualities of both male and female as certainly I do not wish to imply that the voice of divine power is singularly male or female. The absolute proof of this can be realized by simply looking at the contours of the river which is both linear and serpentine. This trombone pattern is kabuki-like in its majestic simplicity of moving half note tones. It and the sound of machetes are the only accompaniment to Mama Fatiman's lamentations proclamation.

Hannibal's stage directions then indicate, in part: "The power of Fatiman's words have summoned new life into the body and spirits of the enslaved. Through the power of the music, they are once again unified and made aware of their connection to the Creator."

They then sing a piece, "Red Coffee," with the choir.

She sings: "Is it sweet enough / Your ebony drink / Black gold in your porcelain cup."

The song ends with the choir singing: "Can you taste my fire / Can you taste my blood / Can you taste my dreams / Can you taste my LIFE."

Hannibal wrote in his journal about the trials of composing the Red Coffee sequence on December 17, 2021:

> After a considerable amount of mental rambling, the entire structure of Red Coffee came pushing its way to me like a herd of wild stallions. Notes, lighting sequence and tones almost caused a couple of my circuit breakers to trip. Uncanny how it all pulls me to a kind of forced fast. I continue, however, to make every attempt to feed the meat, bones, and blood of me.
>
> Moving on Red Coffee now with pristine clarity. Water, water drank my fill of it today. Trying desperately to reverse my sleeping hours. So challenging to sleep during the daylight hours.
>
> From about 11 P.M. until 6 A.M., it is so still. Traffic is almost nonexistent. To open the window is always to be greeted by a cool breeze rushing up from the river.

At another trying juncture in the composition process, Hannibal wrote in his journal of a visitation from his mother (dated January 6, 2022):

> Two nights ago, Mom came to me. We were at Schermerhorn Hall in Nashville. It was the opening night of the opera. An usher was

assisting the two of us in finding her a seat that would allow her to exit freely and come upon the stage immediately after the opera had finished. I informed the attendant that Mom was going to come upon the stage and share some words at the end. Mom never spoke a word during her visit. She was regal. Her eyes, her presence, her movement spoke clearly. She came to warn me and to assure me that the work would be completed. And that I had the power to determine how much suffering would be required to complete it.

While Hannibal was composing Veil III, he read his poignant journal entry to me (dated to August 1, 2021) about his mother's spiritual visitation a few days beforehand and how it nourished him and fed his composition:

> Mom's spirit appeared some days ago. The sight of her remarkable presence replenished my worn-out body and gave renewed strength to my ever-expanding mind. She stood resplendent in an Oriental-style dress of multicolored shades of plum, ivory, and blue. The dress had sleeves and ended just above her knees. A few vertical ivory-colored beads reached the start of a small, raised collar. She stood still and silent in front of what seemed to be a cluster of distant stars, clouds, and light. The presence of her body gave joy to my flesh and bones. The content of her eyes gave solace and healing to my soul. . . . Slowly finding my way back to the opera, to Veil III where great-great-grandmother [Asase in the opera] crawls on her belly to touch the right boot of slaveowner Burgess, [called] Henri in the opera. This she does in an effort to keep from being separated from her two sons, one whose given slave name is Silas Burgess, who in fact is my great-grandfather. In the opera, he is Boukman.[3] As she crawls toward Henri, the French sugarcane plantation master who has just purchased her, she is beaten with a whip by the assistant auctioneer. Each time he strikes her, he looks at Henri as if to receive instructions, for

obviously, the bite of the whip is visibly destroying the flesh he now owns. Henri looks on in silence and in complete awe, for never in his privileged so-called civilized life has he witnessed such an act of unbridled courage as was crawling on the ground towards him. This act did not only challenge his safely concocted Catholic indoctrination: it made him question its validity. Moving towards him was something he could not find in his Bible or in the other holy grails of literature, which lined the gilded walls of his massive library. This was not God conveniently tucked away in the pages of a book. This was not Jesus hanging on the cross of those who had the power to write history as they saw fit. Moving towards him on the ground was the same fire which consumed the flesh of his heroine, Joan of Arc. Crawling towards him was his own cross, his own crucifixion, his own chance for resurrection, for salvation. God was not moving *at* him but *for* him as well. To his mind, such things were foreign. To his soul, there were lingering signs of familiarity. For when her pilgrimage ended and she reached out and touched the tip of his right boot, he immediately raised four fingers in the direction of the auctioneer and purchased her two sons, who were then allowed to run to her bleeding aid.

After reading me this entry, he was silent for some time. Then, as an afterthought, he added: "Can't play God. People play God. Can't play God. Wouldn't know God if they saw God."

Embedded in this sequence of Asase crawling with divine fire is a form of spiritual power that is deeply poignant and revelatory, as it shows the speaking of embodied memories and of the soul. The entry directly speaks, in clear and forceful fashion, about the distinctions and interplay among subconscious body-soul memories and conscious-mind memories and how they pertain to knowledge.

In *The Jonah People*, the enslaver Henri has a soul recognition of the significance, meaning, and power of Asase's touching the tip of his boot. She is pleading, fiercely and without words, that he not brutally separate her from her children. When Henri then raises four fingers, he seems to fuse, in an instant, the soul's knowing with the conscious mind's knowing—through an almost unthought signifying language with his hand—that he will purchase these kin together.

Hannibal's rendering conveys a slaveowner's soul-level recognition of Asase's wordless pleading, an aspect of the scene that would remain hidden or almost imperceptible if it were not for Hannibal's insights into the intricate significance and symbolism of this sequence.

As his journal entries and other commentaries reveal, this horrifying auction scene also embeds, through Asase's act, a spiritual offering of divine redemption to Henri. The soul's recognition is crucial here as well. Henri's soul registers the divine within Asase, which is powering her to crawl across the ground to the tip of his boot. In this witnessing, he comes to see or feel the affinity between Asase's flames of torture and those that engulfed the Catholic martyr Joan of Arc, a revered figure within Henri's professed faith.

In this way, Asase's act of fierce courage offered the slaveowner a chance at salvation and rebirth, a chance to recognize her humanity and heal his broken soul and distorted consciousness. She, the enslaved flesh and the indomitable spirit, was offering the slaveowner a way to recognize his severe mental and spiritual enslavement. She was giving him the opportunity to become more human, to become freer—or to see the unfreedom unleashed by his current state of being and actions.

As Hannibal wrote in his journal, "God was not moving *at* him but *for* him as well."

Although this moving-for was incomprehensible to Henri's so-called conscious mind, it was felt and known—however partially and fleetingly—by his soul. Unfortunately, Henri did not take the offering for redemption and healing of his own enslavement. He continued to purchase humans as though they were objects, thus perpetuating his own spiritual imprisonment. Asase, at the very least, was able to remain living with her two children for a while.

Hannibal spoke of how Asase was illumined by the divine fire of her soul, by her conscious union with the Creator who dwelled within her. It was the same sacred fire that T-Bone Walker had spoken to him about when Hannibal was a teenager, cautioning him to never lose that fire or let anyone take it.

"Sometimes, when people see that fire, depending on where they are in their life, it can terrify them," Hannibal said. "When the plantation owner sees Asase crawling towards him, that was the fire. And it terrified him. And it should terrify him. It should terrify anyone who feels they have a right to buy another human being, to enslave another human being. See, so, to the tyrant, that fire is totally different."

"I see, because it's so bright that it illuminates the darkness?"

"There you go," he replied. "You can't hide from it."

For Henri, none of the ostensible comforts of his life could protect him from the terror and awe he felt in witnessing the divine fire in Asase.

"All of his trappings of life were not enough to keep him from shivering," Hannibal noted.

When Hannibal was completing the auction scene with Asase's crawling, he shared that he was drawing upon the feeling and information he received from the eyes of the great James Baldwin.

"I saw once in James Baldwin's eyes, I saw the look of someone who had concern for all beings, who saw their worth and their divinity. I just wrote that in Asase's part, in the opera. I wrote what I saw in James Baldwin's eyes, I wrote that. It goes from a d flat to a b flat."

I asked Hannibal if he also heard what he saw in Baldwin's eyes.

"Yes, of course."

"And you felt it and converted the feeling into notes?"

"Yes, of course."

After a pause, he added, "For anyone to feel that they're better than anyone else, it's such a state of ignorance. That is true enslavement, enslavement of the mind."

Hannibal explained how, in this mental enslavement, Henri was the true slave but completely blind to it. In turn, Asase—writhing on the ground with dust in her eyes—was free. She was moved by the soul fire of her inherent divinity and became one with the Creator.

One day, Hannibal texted the blank first page of Veil II of his then at-work opera, *The Jonah People* (veil is the word Hannibal uses for a movement or part in an opera that indicates a passing through the veils of consciousness as people make the journey of creating, witnessing, or listening to the work).[4] Veil II is titled "They Swallowed the Ocean for Me," and it addresses the Middle Passage.

"Were I able to explain the process of gathering thousands of tiny black dots and lines streaming in endless patterns of sound and emotion inside the ether of my existence, then I think that I would not have the ability to gather them, welcome them, and send them through the miraculous sieve of mind onto a blank sheet of paper so that they then could be shared with both the heavens and the Earth."

When Hannibal embarks on a new piece—a new creative journey that taps into the eternal realms of sounds—he often retreats into the forest, where he can be ensconced in the clarity, purity, and truth of human silence amid the tones of spirit as it runs through nature.

"In silence, I hear everything," Hannibal said.

Many do not know the healing powers of sleeping in the forest, the spiritual recharging that comes of it, and Hannibal finds this to be a very unfortunate thing.

"Those who have never done it, I wish they would try it. They deserve the healing it can give them."

When Hannibal retreats to his times alone in the forest, where he often sleeps for days on end alone in a sleeping bag or a tent, he submits to the work.

His composing is an act of deep spiritual communion, during which he co-creates with the ancestors, other spirits of the work, and the Creator in profound ways. He streams the presence of the Everlasting within his own spiritual presence. They work so intimately that they become one, and through this deep interlacing or fusion, Hannibal becomes the work itself.

One day, after conversing for a couple of years, I asked Hannibal what word he would use to describe the way in which he works with the ancestors and the Spirit in general.

"Would you say it's a form of deep connection that is a form of communing? Would you call it channeling? Would you call it tapping to the streams of the spirit with your spirit to run it through your human body, like a stream of consciousness or electricity or energy?" I asked. "What is the word you would use?"

"Becoming," he said. "And not only becoming, but realization. You see, you can't write what you don't become."

"You become the spirits of the work, and you realize this?"

"Yes, the realization is the coming to understand that you are them, and they are you," he explained. "You are one. And once you realize this, you become the work. And then you are able to write it, once you become it. You can't write something unless you become it."

This is where his retreats into solitude and silence become vital and integral to his composing and, by extension, his soul's journey in pursuit of its purpose.

"Sometimes that's why I have to go to the forest and just be quiet, because then I realize that I am them, and they are me," Hannibal said of the spirits. "I have to get away from all the voices, people talking, and especially my own voice, my own talking. And then in the silence, I can realize, and I can become the spirits and do the work. No one can truly do the work without becoming it. Ultimately, my goal is solitude. The peace of it. And in peace, you can learn a great deal. The things that I'm interested in learning, I access them much better in an environment of peace."

Hannibal once explained the concept of becoming the work with a counterintuitive and striking example after the final completion of *The Jonah People*. There is a horrendous, callous white captain who is at the helm of the ship whose voyage through the Middle Passage a portion of the opera chronicles.

"I've never been a white slave-trading captain on a ship, but I at least had to have something in me to be able to write that. I had to come to terms, at least in some way, with the capacity for destruction that is within me to be able to write that," Hannibal said.

It was one of the most difficult and taxing aspects of composing the opera, but it was essential to the whole. Hannibal said that we all should remain mindful that everyone has the capacity for destruction within them.

"We all must realize what is in us, including the destruction, or the potential for destruction. All humans have the potential to be all things, and it is very important to acknowledge this and be mindful of this."

If we avoid only condemning others and instead also look inside of ourselves to work on elements of destruction or negativity we may carry, sometimes in ways that are mostly hidden to ourselves, then we can learn to see ourselves in one another. We can then move into a unity of consciousness. What is more, this honesty with ourselves—as well as this compassion and mercy toward the misdeeds and failings of others—also serves as our best form of protection against any negativity or destruction within ourselves or that others may try to aim at us.

This radical practice of loving thy neighbor as thyself, and even loving thy enemy as thyself, also works to protect the clarity, intent, and spiritual integrity of the music and other artistic creations.

"That saying that was attributed to the great sage, Jesus, to love thy neighbor as thyself, that was some powerful stuff. And I think we would do well to take it even deeper than what is often taught in the churches. Loving thy neighbor as thyself is the strongest shield, the strongest protection, against evil. Because love is everything in this world, and when you love even those who attempt to break your soul or destroy you, they lose power over you. It is only when you respond to them with fear, hatred, or destruction that they have any power over you," Hannibal said.

He was quick to add that it was not only the Old and New Testament that taught things such as loving thy neighbor as thyself. It has been known and taught by sages throughout the ages, and it is ancient and timeless wisdom.

"Jesus, he spent a lot of time in Africa. And it shows," Hannibal said, acknowledging the many wisdom teachings from throughout the millennia in Africa that have taught these same truths.

Hannibal sees that many fear silence because of what they hear and see in themselves when silence surrounds them. There is a seeking for truth and honesty with oneself when a person seeks solitude and silence.

"The egotist is terrified of silence. In silence, we can more clearly hear in ourselves, the voice of God and of the Beast," he said.

Many people fear peace when it comes upon them for similar reasons.

"Some people have become so accustomed to chaos and to destruction that they feel uneasy or upset when they experience peace. They feel that something is wrong, because they have become so conditioned to the opposite of peace."

While he finds sanctuary in solitude for his traversing the spiritual soundscapes, and while he cherishes the silence and the absence of spoken language with himself and others during such times, he holds great reverence for words and for what they can do. His charge is to always use them mindfully. Words, even when spoken in seeming neutrality or monotone, can carry tonalities, intentions, positive or negative charges, and lifeforces. In the most direct sense, words can do things—and often do.

"Sometimes, the best thing in the world is a word. Sometimes, the worst thing in the world is a word," Hannibal said. "Nothing in the world is worse than a misplaced word."

During one of his many retreats from society during the composition of *The Jonah People*, Hannibal sent me this note:

> The requirements of this work at times render me both speechless and in a state of total silence. I have asked of the work that it reveal its very essence to me so that I might be accurate in my efforts to capture the soul of it in sound and share it with creation. This sincere asking does not come without requirements. As of

now I am but a vessel upon the ocean of mercy, waiting to be filled with what is needed to hear the spirit of my mother and my ancestors whisper into my soul the words, "Well done, son. Well done."

Becoming the work requires this asking that the essence be revealed, becoming one with it, as well as a near-total absorption with it as the mission of its manifestation and outward realization becomes complete.

For Hannibal, creating a composition is closely analogous to giving birth. The gestation process is long, consequential, and moving. What is more, composing can be a matter of life or death, as destructive forces that do not want the healing and liberating work to be completed will work through people, circumstances, and spaces. They will try to infiltrate Hannibal's headspace in order to halt the creation and abort the process. At times, Hannibal's own life will be imperiled. This has been the case throughout his career.

Hannibal had a telling dream in January 2023, following the full composition of *The Jonah People* yet in advance of its April premiere. He documented the dream in his journal, in an entry dated January 28, 2023: "The level of fatigue resulting from the sustained intensity of my work resulted in my dreaming last night that I was standing over my own grave, placing flowers upon it."

When Hannibal was a boy, he asked his deeply loving and light-filled mother, Ms. Peterson—otherworldly in her wisdom—what it was like to have a child.

"'Every time a woman gives birth, son, she puts her life on the line,' was the brilliant reply of my mother to my question, 'Mama, what is it like to have a baby?' About composing, I feel *exactly* the same," Hannibal said.

During one of the many trying times while composing *The Jonah People*, Hannibal's mother visited in a dream and gifted him strength and tones for the piece through the feeling she transmitted during her visitation. He remarked upon this in a journal entry dated February 5, 2021:

> Last night, Mom came to me. She looked so different as in her many visitations in the past. Her skin was a radiant brown reddish clay. Her eyes were timeless. Her words were few, life-altering. "Reet [her primary nickname for Hannibal], preserve and protect your health. The work you are doing is great. Your strength must be greater so that you can share the work with the world. I love you and will never leave you."
>
> There were tones in her eyes while speaking to me. I wrote them as half notes on page [worksheet 48] of the Overture. I assigned them to the cellos, trombones in F, clarinet 1, and flutes. In these tones and through those tones, she will give to all who hear them, what she in fact gave to and continues giving to me.

In the course of composing this opera, Hannibal asked that he be shown what his great-grandfather, Silas Burgess, had endured. His ancestor had been stolen from his home in West Africa, pushed through the door of no return on Bunce Island off the coast of Sierra Leone, and forced aboard a ship to be enslaved in the United States. Hannibal asked that he be shown the suffering and the horrors.

When Hannibal was in the early phases of composing the music, he said of his dreams: "I'm starting to see their eyes, and hear their cries and moans and chains, and I smell the stench of the womb of the ship."

The ancestors (and Creator) were showing him clearly, in dreams, what they had gone through. Hannibal is part of the spiritual continuum of Silas Burgess that was passed down through his daughter (Hannibal's grandmother) to her daughter (Hannibal's mother) and on through to Hannibal.

This shared continuum means that Hannibal, in many ways, is a reincarnation of Silas and that his spirit in this previous life had endured the horrors of the Middle Passage.

Hannibal said that Silas had no idea where he was going or what was going to happen to him when he was on the ship in chains.

As Hannibal worked on the piece, he would ask to be shown more of Silas's experiences so that he could become the work and make it as profoundly healing as possible. "Otherwise, it wouldn't be real. And the medicine wouldn't work."

While Hannibal was composing the Middle Passage scene, he spent a lot of time on his belly on the floor, mirroring the sensation of being chained inside a slave ship. It was an act of communing with those who have crossed over to spirit and a recognition of the generative gifts of Mother Earth. For Hannibal, such acts summon a feeling of oneness from which he composes.

"When I lie on my stomach, on the Earth, on the ground, I speak first to the people who are in the ground. And I see how the ground produces the food. I speak to all of the contents of the ground. Everything in the belly of the Earth, and all in the water, too."

"Do you feel like it's an acknowledgment of your union with all, of a oneness?" I asked.

"My existence, yes. It's the true definition of 'mine.' When I say 'my,' I'm saying people I've met, to the people that I know care for me. This whole separation concept is backwards. People have it backwards. It's totally backwards. And that's why you have tribes fighting tribes, and you have nations fighting nations, because they have no idea of what 'I' means, the essence of 'I.'"

He said that this more expansive concept of subjectivity, in which all is interconnected with everything else, is something that many humans have lost but that animals remember. He regularly taps into the oneness of Earth and the perfection and justice of nature's harmonies when he composes.

"If Earth is your mother, how can you not communicate with her? How can you not listen to her? How can she not instruct you? A mother will take care of you and form you, protect you. Let you know when the wind is getting ready to get high. That's why the birds, before an earthquake, or anything, they make a move—all the animals. We are the only ones who are dead to the language of the Earth, dead to the language of our mother."

While Hannibal was composing his opera, he endured a great deal of suffering. As he had asked to be shown the essence of the work, he had to pass through many of the experiences himself.

"I now see why I was spending so much time on my belly, on the cold concrete floor of my studio space. This is what would bring me closest to Silas's experience and to the experience of all of my brothers and sisters who passed through the womb of those ships," he explained. "I asked to be shown what he endured, and I did. I felt everything. I had to."

When Hannibal spiritually visited the space of a ship at sea in order to compose the soundscapes for the opera, he would endure many of the trials of that experience. To take one example, Hannibal heard the rhythmic sounds of the ship rising and falling on the waves of the sea. He said it could be received as a hypnotic rhythm or as a form of torture. The keel of the ship was orchestrated in the drum.

"At one point, I wanted the drum to go away, but my higher mind prevailed and said, 'It's not what you want. It's what was. And the truth is not what you want or what you wish, but what is, and what was.' And the truth is that [for the entire voyage], my great-grandfather heard that drum, which is representative of the keel, the ship going into the water. And he could not say to that drum stop," he said. "So, he had only two choices: to go insane or to let that drum become his heartbeat. It altered not only the mind, but it affected the systems of the body. You see, these Jonah People—there is a reason why Miles [Davis] is Miles, and Fannie Lou Hamer is Fannie Lou Hamer, and [my mother] Lillian Peterson is Lillian Peterson. There's a *reason*."

He then paused before continuing to explain.

"The orchestra drum is the keel of the slave ship crashing into the water. It becomes the heartbeat of the captives. It regulated their heart rate and became a metronome of life and of death for both their minds and their bodies. It was an incessant sound, which led to insanity for some and to hope for others, to the alchemization of a sound of horror to one of enduring."

Following the completion of a major work, it is always a significant transition back into the regular flow of life, or what Hannibal calls the realm of finite things.

After the arduous yet exultant process of composing an extensive oratorio piece, *Healing Tones*, which was premiered by the Philadelphia Orchestra in 2019, Hannibal wrote in his journal: "Reentering civilization gets to be more taxing with each journey away from it."

After putting in a full day of work, Hannibal enjoys the privilege of getting to clean his studio by sweeping the floor, washing the dishes, and arranging things.

"Cleaning after a long day with the music is my reward," he said. "And I have the opportunity to feel so grateful for the work and for all the things I have in my life."

This practice of mindful gratitude is central to his composing and also to his way of life. When he falls out of alignment with this gratitude, for example, if he becomes momentarily angry or upset, he aims to stop and become silent and then prays for forgiveness.

"I ask for forgiveness for being so selfish, and then I quickly get back to the work at hand," he said.

His cherished ancestors will also quickly remind him about the broader healing and liberating purposes of the work he does, and what he has been given to do with his creative gifts.

"If I ever start feeling sad or depressed, the ancestors quickly remind me that it is because I am thinking too much about myself. I am too focused on myself. They say, 'You have been given too much to do to waste time feeling this way. Get back to work.' And then I do. The work, the music, is the best medicine."

Hannibal rarely reads, and never really did read, critics' reviews of his work.

"Why waste juice on something like that? I don't pay much attention at all to critics and what they have to say. How are they supposed to get, in say forty-five minutes, what I have given my whole life to create?"

On rare occasions, he will look at reviews that friends send him, especially if he finds them amusing.

"Every once in a while, someone I know will send me something one of these critics or so-called music experts has written about one of my pieces. And I'll read them, if I have time—which is never," he said, laughing.

For Hannibal, it is part of his soul's purpose to keep moving forward with his creations always, and though he hopes that it will help heal and elevate the consciousness of people seeking that, it is not his purpose to pay attention to the reactions of humans.

"I've never followed humans," Hannibal said. "It's too confusing."

To worry about external human reactions to his work also will pull him from the central task at hand, which is to remain focused on the next work and on offering the sacred alchemy of the music to people.

"I don't choose to waste time or juice on such things. My real critics are the ones who tell me, 'It's not about you. Get out of the way,'" Hannibal stated, referring to the spirits with whom he co-creates in his works.

The human ego part of himself is not tasked to be directly involved in the musical creation process.

"The truth comes when the ego dies."

Once, while the Philadelphia Orchestra was rehearsing its premiere of Hannibal's oratorio *Healing Tones*, the conductor, Yannick Nézet-Séguin, asked Hannibal if he could share a few words about the piece with the orchestra.

Hannibal stood and said to all gathered for the rehearsal, "One more time, so the spirits come. If the spirits don't come, we're all wasting our time."

Hannibal recalled that Nézet-Séguin replied, "Perfect."

The rehearsal then proceeded, and the spirits indeed joined. Hannibal explained that when musicians have an open ear and mind, the deeper healing can happen.

"And when that's the case, everyone profits from that because the musicians then play to the fullest extent of their capabilities, especially to their emotional capabilities. And when that happens, then usually ancestors join the celebration, and the people are healed."

"When I compose, it is with the clear intent to impact the actions of all living matter. To function in this capacity is to be worthy of the gift," Hannibal proclaimed.

He was alluding to his overarching soul's purpose of transmuting the pain, suffering, and ignorance of the world to healing, beauty, and truth to help to advance enlightenment for all beings. He seeks to heal and transform the consciousness of humans while also mending the imbalances and pains that are within nature and the entirety of the created world. He intends to do so not only for the naturally seen and tangible physical world here on Earth, but for all of creation, including ancestors and others of the spirit realm who carry pain, suffering, sorrow, or who have forgotten their connection to the everlasting, to all that is.

Hannibal often receives his musical assignments from the Creator and the ancestors in dreams or waking visions, both while composing or in silent solitude in nature. He ordinarily will receive the next work from spirit while he is still in the

FIGURE 4.1 Hannibal reflecting on "the pain and the joy of doing the work" at his studio in Smithville, Texas, with background painting by Eternal Faith Lokumbe.

Photograph by Randy Kerr (2020).

FIGURE 4.2 Hannibal's Altar and *Jonah People* tapestry, created in his Smithville, Texas, studio.

Photograph by Haile Selassie Lokumbe (2022).

FIGURE 4.3 Hannibal with Giancarlo Guerrero, music director of the Nashville Symphony during the planning of the production, *The Jonah People: A Legacy of Struggle and Triumph*, commissioned by the Nashville Symphony and premiered in 2023.

Photograph by Bernadette Gildspinel (2022).

creative process of building another piece. After the assignment is revealed, he will receive spiritual transmissions of the work, including music, words, and various scenes, figures, and other visual representations. As he creates the work, what Hannibal calls the work's essence will reveal itself to him or emerge more fully in his consciousness through various layers, aspects, or dimensions. In the course of the work's revelation, Hannibal will surround himself in a studio with visual art that he has crafted for the gestation and birth of a piece. This art often will include large paper scrolls with, say, an opera's libretto, along with related photographs of those whose spirits are significantly inspiring the piece. He also paints various symbols or forms of sacred iconography that resonate with the spiritual concept of the piece.

Hannibal keeps an altar for ancestral remembrances in his current studio space in Smithville. He begins each day with expressions of gratitude to the Creator and to the ancestors for the love, guidance, protection, and wisdom that they continually give him. In particular, he regularly thanks his mother for his life and for all of her sacrifices. He keeps her wallet on his altar, to remind him of her selfless generosity, how she was always giving money to those in need even when she barely had enough money for herself. People still come up to Hannibal, all these years later, and tell him stories of how his mother, Ms. Lillian E. Peterson, gave them unasked-for gifts that were deeply needed at critical times. Hannibal tries to do the same whenever he can, especially when sharing the fruits of what he enjoys by virtue of his musical gift, which he said also comes with obligations to share what flows from this gift.

Often Hannibal receives the music in its totality first—every note of an orchestral piece (or nearly every note) in his spirit mind—before he writes it down. The words usually come after the music.

In his most recently completed opera, *The Jonah People*, the usual order was reversed: the libretto came first, and he completed it almost in totality, before composing most of the music.

"I don't care which comes first or how it comes, as long as the work continues to come," Hannibal said.

He often refers to the process of composing and receiving the gifts of music as receiving from within the womb of sound, or from the rivers of sound.

In a journal entry from December 26, 2019, Hannibal wrote:

> The music finds new tributaries into my soul. New awakenings, new worlds I discover with each note, each day. Something more alluring than the Blues. More astral than the whispering clouds. I thrive as never before in the ever-expanding womb of sound.

This spiritual communication of musical creations comes with a whole multisensorial suite. He can hear, taste, smell, feel, and see the spiritual revelations of the work—sometimes all at once. It is a part of his gift. This is similar to what some call synesthesia, though these creative capacities are multivalent and widely varied, and they can be found throughout time and space. They are not reducible to a word.

As Hannibal enlists a wide-ranging multisensorial suite in composing, playing, and otherwise emanating music from his soul—and the spiritual realms—he offers these perceptual encodings as access points or portals. His work is for the spirits of others who listen to or play the music, should their spirits choose to be open to receiving the music via their own multisensorial suites. Broadly, this can facilitate the healing, liberation, and perpetual expansion of humans in their bodies as well as their spirits. It also helps those who are solely in spirit and, ideally, works to elevate or positively transform all living consciousnesses that the music suffuses or travels through.

Another way to think of this is soul mirroring. Hannibal mirrors his light out from his soul self, through his music, and offers it to those who imbibe or play it, offering the opportunity to practice accessing and mirroring their own soul's light and truth in their own ways. This could be solely through internal soul work or through their human form into the exterior realm of things, fashioned as their own soul's work in the form of art such as sculpture, painting, poetry, symphonic music, or architectural creation. Through Hannibal's exercising of his own multisensorial spiritual capacities, and through his sharing these gifts through his outward creations and serving them as medicine or food for people to ingest if they wish, he helps to remind people of the divinity and unmeasurable capacity within themselves and all other beings.

"To put every drop of your being into the sound chamber of your life and send it hurtling out into every pore of existence is to be at one with the universe," Hannibal said.

For him, composing is also life—his way of life. He is never not composing. It is a ceaseless mode of existence.

"I'm always writing. I'm always composing. Even when I'm not just actively putting notes on the page, I'm always composing because I'm always experiencing. And I'm always seeing, and I'm always being shown things."

Hannibal also hears music all the time, no matter where he is. He could be in the middle of a conversation with someone, or in a train station or grocery store, or alone in the woods, and he will hear music. It is always streaming through his spirit mind, there for him to pay attention to or not, although it is sometimes hard not to tune into it even while doing something else.

The ancestors and the Creator always remind Hannibal that, as long as he remains pure in heart and true to the work, he will always have everything he needs. As he has followed his truth, they have never failed him. Everything has been provided for him on his journey. In essence, he seeks to discern and follow the truth of things, seeking to travel in resonance or harmony with the principles of nature. He knows the truth, the tempo, the resonance, and the way because of the feeling he receives in his heart, mind, and soul. This often far exceeds language, though some layers of it may register in conscious corporeal or discursive forms.[5]

During the composition of *The Jonah People*, Hannibal wrote in his journal on October 16, 2021:

> Like nature, I only want to record the truth. The ground holds the true history of creation and of the affairs of humans. It is the canvas upon which is painted each and every footprint and step taken by every being which ever walked upon it. It is the canvas of every color and hue. And it is the repository of both the wretched and the saint, the wealthy and the destitute, the virgin and the prostitute.
>
> It has always been my desire that like the ground, my music will hold all things and all people; that it will exclude nothing or no one. The land has taught me the meditative strength of patience. Its indelible influence upon my compositional direction is evident in most of my work. That patience often determines both my tempos and my choice of instrumental pairings. To deny the truth which lives in the voice of the land is to deny the truth of our bones, skin, blood, and deeds. Increasingly, the land rejects our greed and our misguided illusions of power, so masterfully outlined in the text and ingenious wisdom of Marvin Gaye [1939–1984] as was put forth in his brilliant composition entitled, "What's Going On."

Although the divine spirit in all is limitless, full access to the divine is not needed while a soul is inhabiting and working through a human vessel. At the same time, as Hannibal reminds people—especially children—all things are accessible through their divine spirit, their receptor in the base of the brain. Everyone has direct access to the divine themselves, despite what anyone else—even people who love them—might say to the contrary. However, not everything in existence needs to be accessed and understood by the physical form's existence.

"Some things are to be known by the spirit, not by the flesh. The body is the noble house of the soul and has its own unique language, yet it is governed by gravity and finality. True mind, pure mind, is in need of nothing."

At times, technical explanation of a process—say, his composing—can even get in the way of the creative gift or the deployment of its generative capacities.

Hannibal often spoke of the great stumbling blocks that technical training can pose to musicians. He experienced this when he was playing with jazz bands. It is not a matter of technical prowess for Hannibal, but more about the feeling with which one plays—whether the soul is speaking or it is a mechanical, technical act. These are two very different things.

"I'd much rather play with a musician who's playing music because it keeps them alive, and although they might not have technical prowess, I'd much rather play with them than play with someone with extraordinary musical technical training, but who played it as a hobby."

While in the throes of composing Veil II of his *Jonah People* opera, Hannibal explained that much of his struggle when composing comes from the need to clear the mind of distractions and be still.

"I struggle so hard to clear my mind, to step away from the world and all that it requires. The struggle for me is never a struggle of being in need of the [musical] information, but to clear my head so that I can get the information and hear the information and execute the information by way of composing tones," he said. "But at any rate, the first weaving [of the part he was then composing] starts with the cello, which is sound. And then the second weaving will start with the French horn, the brass, which is light. The third weaving will start with the strings. And then with the voices, with the choir, and the choir says, 'cord of light, of sound, of love, connected to the placenta of God. Now come once more to feed us the food of eternal life.' And when I played that on the piano, it made me get up!"

He said that music often pours into his head, or streams into his mind, and his task is to be still so that he can accurately grasp a portion of the notes and convert them to piano and then to parts of orchestral compositions. This is only a small part of the music that he receives from the spirits and the Creator that he can actually capture and translate into his works.

"This composing, it's like a sieve," Hannibal said, laughing. "It's a noble effort at replicating at least a portion of what I am hearing in my mind, what the spirits are bringing to me in unending streams."

When Hannibal reviews his compositions, or when he reads his libretto—in silence or aloud—it activates the music in his mind. Once, after a reading much of the libretto for *The Jonah People*, the music was instantly set off in his mind.

"I'm enjoying a full concert right now," he said. "It's like that hum that's four miles above the Earth that encircles the Earth. For me, in that hum, is the language of the ancestors. When you feel that inside. That's what's so remarkable about playing music because you can transfer it to people. That's what I love so much about the music: its ability to transfer things that could not be transferred in ways other than in music, maybe in a glance or a look or something like that."

He also emphasized that the struggle is more instructive than music that comes fluidly and easily, without struggle.

"I learn more from the notes I struggle to play and write than from the ones I play and write with ease."

In addition to all of the sheer physical and other human-based difficulties that attend the process of composing a major piece, Hannibal endures regular spiritual attacks from forces of negativity that do not want the healing or the sonic alchemy that his works offer to people to come to fruition.

In a journal entry dated December 30, 2019, Hannibal wrote:

> With this work, *The Jonah People—A Legacy of Struggle and Triumph*, I will come for my people as Moses came for his. Oh, the beast comes incessantly at me, for my health and my will. But to no avail, as my spirit moves with certainty towards its destiny. First, to point the eyes of a suffering people to a perfection just below their line of human consciousness. Second, to have that perfect gaze in ways never done before.
>
> The light of their existence, the light which is the truth of the people thrown aboard the abysmal wooden vessels of hell where they were dared to survive; where God spoke in a language later deciphered by those captive in chains, in vomit, in blood, in feces, in terror. They deciphered God's verse in prose, mortar, science, art, dance, and music. Music, music, music!!!!

Just as unrelenting struggle is part of composing, so too are the spiritual gifts of healing that the music and his creative processes provide. As a form of birth, it involves pain and suffering as well as great exaltation and beauty.

In a journal entry dated January 19, 2021, Hannibal wrote:

Clear pristine sound patterns are currently flowing through me. To be in the process of giving birth to this opera, at this time of human implosion, is to be given an infusion of the spirit.

In another entry, dated January 21, 2021, Hannibal wrote:

The relentless pace of weeks past caused my body to say enough. It could no longer keep pace with the waterfall of music information rushing from the tributaries of my mind. Hopefully, it will reboot sooner than later as I intend to move closer to completing the Overture by the end of the weekend. The sound of the overture rivals that of a thousand elephants running towards the last viable oasis of the season. The text shimmers in my soul.

5

THE MUSIC LIBERATION ORCHESTRA IN PRISONS AND SCHOOLS

In 2014, Hannibal witnessed one of the most powerful spiritual liberations he has ever seen. It happened in the Philadelphia Detention Center after he had been playing music and talking in a circle with a group of men who were incarcerated there. The gathering was part of a meeting of the Music Liberation Orchestra (MLO), which Hannibal founded in the 1970s. The MLO promotes music, genealogy, and journal writing with people in prisons and schools, especially with students who have been classified as at risk.

"I saw a resurrection happen within the confines of the prison in Philadelphia. The man's spirit rose out of his body, I felt it and I saw it, and it came back into his body, and he was weeping. It was a spiritual cleansing and liberation, and it happened within the physical walls of a prison," Hannibal said. "And the man was weeping, having been healed. And everyone was perfectly silent throughout the entire thing. It was as though everyone knew, in their hearts, in their spirits, what to do. Out of respect for the significance of what was happening, everyone remained silent."

Hannibal reflected upon the collective power they had generated. It had brought them to a different space and was the apex of what the MLO can achieve.

"I think the facilitator of it was created by our joint presence; what was created by all of us sitting in a circle with the purpose that we all have in mind, and that was of human and spiritual liberation. That was the pinnacle example of what the MLO was. That was the MLO in its fullest glory, that this brother just had a complete cleansing of his soul," Hannibal recalled. "His whole life, the very essence of who he was and wanted to become—and who he wanted to become was what he once was, before he was taken through his own particular door of no return, that door that caused him to be locked up and away from his daughters."

In tying this revelation and spiritual resurrection to his compositions, Hannibal turned to a pivotal moment in an orchestral piece. He drew upon what he witnessed in the prison for his writing and orchestration of a key movement.

"I was thinking of that particularly when I wrote the gamma ray burst," he said, referring to the blugue movement in his orchestral work *One Land, One River, One People*, which would premiere a year later with the Philadelphia Orchestra in 2015.

"The true fate of a nation is not measured by the amount of churches it has, but by the amount of prisons it has," he added. "I don't believe in kings and queens and social strata. It's a great way to waste your life, I think. 'Here comes your queen.' I think that diminishes the sense of the human worth of others when they worship somebody. It's a very dangerous thing to do. Nothing is more deserving of being worshipped than the truth. Nothing I know."

Hannibal established the MLO in the seventies when he began working with incarcerated men in Bethlehem Prison in Bethlehem, Pennsylvania, and later in the Holmesburg Prison in Philadelphia. The infamous Philadelphia facility, nicknamed "the Terrordome," was officially decommissioned in 1995.

FIGURE 5.1 Music Liberation Orchestra, Holmesburg Detention Center, Philadelphia, Pennsylvania.

Photograph by Zenovia Gallagher (ca. 2019).

More recently, Hannibal has worked with the MLO in the Philadelphia Detention Center and in a prison in Nashville, Tennessee. He has also worked with incarcerated people in Bastrop County Jail in Bastrop, Texas, and in the Orleans Parish Prison in New Orleans, Louisiana.

MLO activities involve the teaching and practicing of music, poetry, genealogy, and journal writing in schools and prisons. The MLO has four principles, and accepting them is the only requirement for membership: renounce violence, acknowledge the presence of the divine, keep a journal for yourselves and your children, and fall in love with forgiveness. There are no fees. There are no required pledges of allegiance to certain countries or names of God or communities of people. It is open to all humans.[1]

As soon as Hannibal arrives at a prison for MLO work, he tells the people, usually men, why he is there. When Hannibal goes to speak to kids in elementary and high schools to share some musical wisdom, he teaches the principles of the MLO as well.

"I say immediately why I'm there. I say, 'I'm here to remind you that the living God lives within you.' That's all I'm here for," Hannibal said. "There are no five hail Mary's, and no six jumps over the fence. No beating yourself with a chain. That's a different channel. And no 10 percent of whatever you earn is required. There's no Rolls Royce, jet, or mansion that needs to be paid off. No such measured things."

He said so many people visit prisons wanting to push something on them, while those in prison have usually already been through so much in life that they are skeptical of newcomers. They also tend to be skeptical of words like *God* or *love*, as many of them have been deeply wounded by people who claimed that they loved them or who wielded the name of God while inflicting traumas or engaging in deception.

"Some of them have been so victimized by people who say they love them and by using the word God that understandably, they look at me in disbelief," he said. "But none of those who initially doubted has not come to acknowledge the truth of what I said, the authenticity of my initial address."

He recalled one instance when a man who was initially angered by Hannibal's presence subsequently approached him to ask for his forgiveness.

"'I apologize that I did not acknowledge your sincerity. Brother, I ask for your forgiveness. When I look in your eyes, I see a new foundation,'" Hannibal recollected his having said.

Hannibal said that what is important to him is that the proverbial food is on the table. That he fulfills his sacred duty to offer the principles of the MLO. Whether people accept them and want to join is, of course, completely up to them.

"I say to them, 'What I am saying to you is on behalf of a power much greater than me. I'm not speaking to you as Hannibal. This is on behalf of the Everlasting.'"

He then begins every session with a song, followed by silence. In Philadelphia, he was even able to get the facility to store musical instruments that some of the men can play.

He shares with people in the prisons the reality of how music can liberate them and save their lives. And he testifies to the ways in which music has saved his life, both physically and spiritually.

"Music is what has kept me from succumbing to the Beast. It has saved me, throughout my life."

One of the most profound things that Hannibal has learned while working in prisons with the MLO is that people tend to go in one spiritual direction or the other while there.

"In those cages, it is not a neutral space. That's one thing I've learned from my brothers and sisters in the prisons," he related. "People either grow closer to the Creator or to the Beast. It's deep. It's the same with the slave ship."

Hannibal said he learns continuously from the people in the prisons, including about what it means to be free.

"I often tell the inmates that I know of more criminals in Washington, DC, than in the prisons they occupy. Not that I know a lot of politicians there, but I know enough about them to say that," he said, laughing. "If the cover were pulled off of many of them, they'd be serving nine life terms."

When I asked Hannibal what initially moved him to start the MLO in Bethlehem Prison in the seventies, he explained that it was part of the sacred obligation that was part of the gift that he had been given with music. He promised that, whenever he was someplace for an extended period, he would go inside the prisons to do spiritual liberation work.

"There are obligations that come with having been given a gift. You're not just given a gift without obligations," he explained. "And one that came with my gift of music was to share it with those who needed it most, those who have given up on themselves. You can't give up on yourself and remain in a situation where you're not destructive toward yourself and others, thereby landing in a cage. What kept me from the cage was not only my recognition of the gift but also that I owed sharing it with others. The gift is not just for me or for my own personal needs. First and foremost, it is to share with others. Just like the music in the cotton field saved my ancestors' lives, I know it has the power to save their lives."

While Hannibal was composer-in-residence at the Philadelphia Orchestra, he got some people from the orchestra to accompany him with the MLO. He would speak with them about the urgent importance of real community engagement and how that must include people who are locked away in prisons right there in the city.

"Rivers and rivers of people, particularly men of Jonah, flow through the prisons of Philadelphia."

Hannibal would speak to orchestra personnel at staff meetings that he attended as part of his appointment. He would use the opportunity to tell them that true racial and social justice efforts cannot end in the comfort of the orchestra's fancy buildings and that music is not just for those who can afford the tickets to the concert halls and have the freedom of movement to attend.

He was able to bring a string quartet into the Philadelphia Detention Center, which played "A Star for Anne" that Hannibal had written in honor of Anne Frank. It expresses some of the brutal, ashen horrors of Dachau during the Holocaust. He was able to have a recording made.

"My brothers in the MLO in the prison had put so much work into the study of the violin, the viola, the cello, and the bass, and then so much study into the Holocaust. So, we really do research. We go very deep," he said. "So, the [Orchestra] quartet came and, before we began, I said to the brothers, 'You know, on my way here, I was hearing you making this sound.' And without going into any time-consuming detail, at the end of this piece . . . the ashes from the crematoriums were so abundant that they covered the entire landscape of Dachau in the summertime. So, many of the people there thought that it—the children thought that—it was snowing in the summertime, but actually it was the ashes of the people they were burning. And so, at the end of the song, sister Kay will make this sound on her strings. And the other [musicians on the] cello and viola and violin will do the same. And that sound is to pay homage to all of those floating flakes of flesh. And the part that you have the right, by the virtue of what you have suffered, to make is the sound of rushing air, because the only friend, the only mercy that the flakes had was the air.'"

All of these orchestral instructions, with their accompanying concepts and gravity, were news to Kay, a violinist from the Philadelphia Orchestra, as well. Hannibal had not briefed her on any of the instrumentation in advance.

"So, I'm giving the instructions from the stage right before we began the piece. 'Just watch her, just watch her bow. And she'll tell you when to begin and when to end.' And when they did that, the sound that they were making with the strings . . ." he said in awe. "One of the brothers said, 'It's the first time I've been out of this cage in five years. It's the first time I felt free of this place.'"

The MLO work is full of deep and transformative experiences such as this. Hannibal shared that the profound knowledge and sustenance that he gets from his MLO prison experiences are immeasurable.

He introduced me one day to his friend Jamal Dickerson, a music teacher and band leader at the Creative Arts Morgan Village Academy in Camden, New Jersey. Jamal had accompanied Hannibal once with the MLO program in Philadelphia and found it to be a powerful experience. Hannibal also visits Jamal's music classes at school in Camden and shares his wisdom with the students.

The first time Jamal met Hannibal, he thought he was late. When Jamal arrived in a suit, he explained to Hannibal that one of his former students, who had recently graduated, had just passed away. He was delayed by the funeral and traffic.

Jamal recalled, speaking with me, that Hannibal had assured him that Jamal was not late, not at all. He was right on time. He was busy doing the work.

Hannibal has worked a lot with students in Camden, especially when in the Philadelphia area, as the two cities are not far from one another. He said he has the utmost respect for Jamal because he is someone who is doing the work of teaching music with everything he has. He does not just teach it technically, Hannibal said, but he uses it to teach students that music can be a tool of liberation and healing. It can save their lives, as Hannibal said it had saved his on many occasions. He shares this wisdom regularly with students.

Jamal said Hannibal's mere presence is a perpetual blessing.

"He's like a little angel. Every time he smiles at you, it's like a few years have been added to your life."

Hannibal will call spontaneously, out of the blue, whenever Jamal might most need to hear from him and lift his spirits.

And he'll say, "Hello, my brother," then share some words that are exactly what Jamal needed to hear.

"That's how he moves," Jamal said.

Hannibal often hears from the MLO members when they get out of prison. They will call him—and sometimes they will have their kids call him on Father's Day—to send him happy wishes of the day.

Not one person from the MLO has ever asked Hannibal for money.

"So much for this idea of criminals, these so-called criminals," Hannibal said. "Not one of them has ever asked me for a dime, over all these years."

Hannibal shared how some MLO members suggested that they all, as part of the MLO, should design a special MLO tattoo for those who are part of the organization.

"I told them that the real tattoo is the invisible one. You don't see it, and that's the one that goes with doing the work of liberation."

One day, Hannibal was driving in his truck in Smithville and called me out of the blue to share some thoughts about the MLO.

"I would always tell the brothers, 'That's why I'm here, because I want you to know that there's something beautiful about life. No matter how much terror, how much brutality you have experienced, how much apathy you have been fed, and if you get to the point where you see no beauty in life, then you are imprisoned in ways as severe as your being in this cage. There are many people who are in different kinds of cages. And so, you aren't the only ones who are imprisoned. Whoever fails to see any degree of beauty in life, then they are truly imprisoned,'" he said.

Hannibal also spoke to the illusions of freedom that come with amassing fortunes, or the imprisonment that flows from humanity's violations of Mother Earth and nature.

"The pursuit of the things that people consider success keeps them from seeing the things that are truly beautiful. That you don't have to be a king or a millionaire, you don't have to be wealthy to see them, because they only require that you look. And it's impossible to see beauty in the nature and not see beauty in the humans. But if you think that the nature is yours to control and to own, then you will see humans the same way, that they are to be controlled and owned," he said, drawing a breath. "So, that's why we have the unending saga of slavery and brutality, because people fail to see the true beauty of life, and they don't think about it until they can no longer take a breath or until they struggle to breathe, or they lose what can't be replaced. And that's my sermon for today, looking at these extraordinary cumulus clouds steady talking to us with a powder blue background."

Hannibal often says that looking at the sky is an important spiritual practice for him, a vital element of his religion. He proposed having a "National Look at the Sky Day" to remind people of its generosity and its healing properties.

I asked whether some people in the prisons where he works can see the sky from inside.

"Seldom, and that's one of the things I always plead, I plead my case. I say to the warden, 'So, if the concept of prisons is to restore, how can a person be restored if they can't see the sky?' Because all you've got to do is look at the sky, and the sky will let you know clearly that people should be free," Hannibal explained. "But if someone can't see the sky, that's just like saying, 'Don't drink water. Sky is of the same family as the water. It's nature. And why is it there? To generate life.' So, many times that works, I don't have to go through a whole thing, 'If you want to destroy people, cut them off from the nature.' Which is what they do in the prisons, right? Often, if they have access to nature, it's to do some forced labor that is unpaid or far below minimum wage."

"Right. I was in Holmesburg, and the chaplain grew to trust me. He was about to retire, and one session, we were there, he said, 'Hannibal, I want to show you something, but we have to be very quick.' And I said, 'mmm,' that part of me that always says, 'that sounds like something I want to check out.' Another part of me is knowing right away that there might be a price to pay for it," he continued, laughing lightly. "Sometimes, there's a price to pay for beauty just like there's a price to pay for terror, for experiencing beauty. So, we started walking down the hall, and he said, 'Follow me.' We started walking in a direction I had not walked before, and we came up to this door. Now, this is inside the prison. We came up to this area, I mean, when I think about it. Well, at any rate, I was there long enough to see a section hidden the prison, like it was hidden inside away from the general population, and the lighting sources were neon lights. . . . They were cut off from the rest of the population. I can't describe it. I can't describe what I felt, what I saw. It was macabre. You know when this cat, Dante, was explaining hell? It was worse than that. It's like where you keep people whom you've given up on, where you've basically just said, 'You know, all we're doing is just feeding them.' It's worse than that. I can't describe it."

He had mentioned something about their eyes, what he saw in them. I asked him if he could elaborate.

"There was no life in their eyes is what I'm trying to say. They were the living dead. They were like zombies. And when a guard saw me there, they rang a bell the way they do for a lockdown, because I wasn't supposed to be there. And then it made sense to me; the chaplain was retiring, so all the years I had known him and had gone there, he never mentioned that place.

But since he was retiring, they couldn't fire him for doing that. So, he said to them, 'Oh, it's my fault, it's my fault, it's my fault.' I mean, they surrounded me, man. But what I saw, I'll never forget. Nobody ever has to talk about hell or try to make me see hell or anything of that kind, because there's not a day in my life that I'm not affected by that image."

Hannibal said these people do not really get to go outside.

"It's like their own city within the prison."

Just as Hannibal was never able to know about this group within the prison (until the retiring chaplain introduced him), these people of course were never able to join the MLO.

In MLO gatherings, the group often discusses ways of healing through coming to know themselves.

"I always tell my brothers and sisters in the prisons, we're all a work in progress. All of us. It is through doing the work that we become free, and our work is what makes us immortal," he said. "I also tell them that most of the people walking the halls of so-called power in Washington, DC, are more imprisoned than they are within the walls of the prison. The mental enslavement among those who are drunk on delusions of power is so great that the people themselves cannot even see their own enslavement for what it is. Mental and spiritual enslavement."

The journey of self-knowing is one way in which the journals are so instructive. As people materialize their feelings, memories, emotions, and imaginations onto the page, they begin to disclose themselves—to themselves—in a new way. It is a process that can be difficult and also tremendously restorative and rewarding. They discuss discovering themselves truly so that they can harness the power of their minds and spirits, which no one can ever truly take from them.

Hannibal recalled learning this truth early in life through the wise instruction of his mother. How to not let people tell him what he could or could not do when it came to the power of his mind, gift, and spiritual freedom.

"There was a certain kind of weapon I always had. This weapon was my thoughts. And that's what Mama always told me. Nobody can take your mind, your spirit. That's why you have to be mindful about that. That's the meaning of that line in the Bible, 'Don't cast your pearl before the swine,'" he said. "When someone refuses your doing the work, you never have to worry about there being a way shown to you of how to do the work, because this place that the work comes from, this source that the work comes from—and you're recognizing that—that is what determines whether or not you are able to complete the work. And if you don't complete the work, then you become something other than yourself. You become things that are strange, or you become a stranger to yourself, and the most destructive thing in the world is boxing yourself, shadowboxing yourself. Fighting against yourself."

He shared how often this arises in his MLO work. They talk about fighting themselves, without even realizing it, and then coming to realize that this had been happening—sometimes, for their entire lives, unbeknownst to them.

"I see that a lot with the brothers in the prisons. When we finish our circle, especially after we've wept a lot, we've healed by tears, then they say, 'Man, brother Hannibal, now I realize all these years I've been fighting myself. I thought I was fighting the system or fighting somebody else, but I've been fighting myself.' And that's what the madness of all of this will do. It will cause you to fight yourself, to destroy yourself, because when you destroy yourself, then you become a slave," he explained. "My great-grandfather was never a slave. He was *enslaved*. Big difference. He was never a slave. That's why he lived how he lived and left the treasures that he left. That ain't nothing a slave would leave. You've got this thing you seek—and anytime that brilliant, unknown appears in the form of a painting or a novel or a social documentation of the life of people in a community—as was done by [W. E. B.] Du Bois [1868–1963] in Philadelphia—anytime that kind of thing comes up and flourishes in the mind—whew!"

Even with all of this creative genius and fortitude in the face of systemic racism and societal oppression, Hannibal noted that the Jonah People of course are still fighting—and he feels they will always have to fight to be recognized in their fullest light, for the incredible beings that they are.

"Like Mrs. [Rosa] Parks said, the fight is eternal. It's going to be forever."

In the 1970s, Hannibal had an unforgettable experience at Bethlehem Prison in Pennsylvania. He went to play trumpet for six hundred incarcerated men.

"I played something that I still don't know what I played. But when I finished, those that weren't screaming were weeping."

Hannibal was so moved that the trumpet had had such an effect. Someone in the prison, Hannibal's guide, told him he would never be allowed back in the place.

"I'll never forget when the brother who was my guide took me to the iron bars, the gate, he said to me, 'Brother, I hate to tell you this, but you'll never come back here.' And I said, 'Why, brother? Was it something I did? Is it something I said?' He said, 'It was something you did.'"

Hannibal asked the guide to please let him know what he did that would cause him to be effectively banned from returning to the place.

"You made us feel free. And no matter all these other things they do, there are these iron gates—and you made us feel free.... And they're afraid of that."

Hannibal called the prison five or six times, asking if he could return. The prison officials thanked him for his emotionally moving playing but said each time that they had other things scheduled. The guide's clear foresight was accurate. Hannibal was never able to get back inside Bethlehem Prison to play again.

CONCLUSION
"Pure Mind Has No Time"

When Hannibal plays music or composes, he transcends the illusions of time that are part and parcel of the finite realm here on Earth. It has been like this for him since he first picked up the trumpet, and the depth, texture, and vastness of the music have only grown since. Similar to many who possess extraordinary musical gifts, through sound, he experiences an expansion far beyond his finite existence as the human, Hannibal.

While playing, he taps into the limitless spiritual potential in what he refers to as the base of the brain.

"The base of the brain is like a spiritual Rosetta stone," Hannibal said. "And it's there to be deciphered. And to decipher it, you don't need a degree in archaeology or forensic science. Wovoka [ca. 1858–1932] [a Paiute spiritual leader and innovator in the Ghost Dance movement] understood it. Chief Crazy Horse understood it. It doesn't require any kind of intense reflection. All you have to do is just take a deep breath and let go of all the things we've been burdened with. All of the isms."[1]

From that place, he can travel anywhere and everywhere. He accesses and experiences the interconnectedness of all things and, from that place, flows forth from the divine that resides within him—and everyone—and traverses many aspects of the earthly and spiritual worlds.

"The base of the brain becomes completely open, and you realize that everything is there. Wherever you want to go, you've already been. You have full access to anywhere and at any time—fifteenth century, thirtieth century, the present century. It doesn't matter."[2]

It is in these movements of music, with the multisensorial and affectively porous states of expanding and contracting consciousness, that the essential features of spiritual soundscapes become clearest and truest for Hannibal. Yet such spiritual soundscapes run throughout our everyday lives and our collective existence as humans. Music is a unifying thread, or web of connectivity, while it is also a living consciousness and a conduit for the transmission of other forms of spirit and consciousness. If done with the intent of spiritual liberation and healing, music can remind people of their inner powers and awaken them to the sacred interconnectedness that is the truth of all things.

"The music is how my grandmother and grandfather could be in 105-degree weather in the cotton field and come to not even need the water I had brought for them. My grandfather would throw it up in the air. They would be singing in the most beautiful voices I have ever heard, to this day. The music took them someplace else, to a place not of bondage."

When Hannibal was touring with his band and other jazz ensembles, he would sometimes play double sets, perhaps six or seven hours straight.

"It doesn't hurt until you come back," Hannibal said, referring to the end of the final set when the outward playing of music stops. "The farther you go in exhilaration, the more painful it is to return."

Hannibal said the difficulty of returning to regular reality on Earth is what leads so many to the bottle or drugs, as a way of continuing the feeling or as a way of easing the pain of coming down from the exhilaration. However, because Hannibal, on instruction of his mother and ancestors, forswears drugs and alcohol, he has found different ways of managing this transition.

"If I was near the ocean, I would leave the show and drive, sometimes hours, to the ocean. The ocean was my dope."

"What do you think it was about the ocean?"

"The tonalities, of course. You can hear everything in the ocean."

With these intentions and this sacred wisdom, Hannibal seeks to give to others all that he can through his music and educational work. Whether in schools, prisons, concert halls, grocery stores, gas stations, churches, or the open expanses of fields, woods, gardens, parks, and farms, Hannibal works to shine the striking light of his musical gifts.

The lifelong paths of his creative journey demonstrate an unwavering devotion to serving his spiritual purpose through continual creation. The nature of all of his creative works attests to his steadfast commitment to remain true to the cause of spiritual liberation, awakening consciousness, and authentic justice for all beings.

As I was finishing much of the first version of this book manuscript in the summer of 2022, Hannibal had just completed the entire composition for his opera *The Jonah People: A Legacy of Struggle and Triumph*. He dedicated the piece to the women of Jonah and noted that "they have known suffering like no other people."[3]

On the day of the opera's completion (June 6, 2022), Hannibal wrote in his journal:

> At 3:30 P.M. I finished the opera. My emotions are as varied as the work itself. I suspect a more verbal expression of my elation will come as some days pass, allowing me to restore my strength.

Several days later, he said to me that he felt reborn: "I feel like the first man or woman whose flesh has yet to rot. I feel the truth of the immortality of the spirit. I feel, for the first time, in a way that I never have before, the knowledge that all things and all beings are connected."

He also said that all of his experiences and all of the people in his entire life had gone into this work.

"Now that the opera is finished, I can say that every single person I have ever known has gone into this piece. Every sorrow and every joy. I am as grateful for the moments of suffering as I am for the moments of elation. And I am as grateful to those who tried to break my soul as I am to those who helped to nourish it."

He also shared a photograph of a painting that his daughter Eternal Faith Lokumbe had recently finished. He said it was a perfect visual representation of how he was feeling, having completed *The Jonah People* opera.

One day in the fall of 2022, Hannibal sent me a photograph of his presenting the bound score and libretto of *The Jonah People* to the spirit of Ms. Miranda Griffin. He had placed the score before her gravestone and wrote "homage," as an accompanying explanation for the photograph he had shared. Ms. Griffin, a woman of Jonah, was the midwife whose hands had welcomed him onto Earth as he was born. He routinely visits Ms. Griffin's grave to pay respects, give thanks, and ask for her guidance and blessings.

While at her grave, Hannibal wrote to me: "A line in the opera goes, 'I sing the blues of the elders, their blood still warm in the sand.' Ethereal to read such words standing above her sacral bones."

Hannibal then sent a photograph of his shadow extending over her grave. He was in clear outline against the grass, the granite gravestone, and the rod iron fence behind it. In his shadow, he appeared to be holding the bound opera score in his hand.

FIGURE C.1 *Time*, painting by Eternal Faith Lokumbe, Houston, Texas. Photograph by Eternal Faith Lokumbe (2023).

Once, after he had delivered a reading of the opera's libretto, Hannibal shared that he kept seeing a vision from his childhood with his grandmother, on whose farm he had lived until he was five.

"I keep seeing my grandmother. I keep seeing how we would walk to the mailbox, and she would look at me, and I asked her, 'Grandma, are you okay? Did I do something wrong?' She'd just smile and say, 'No, baby, I just can't wait to see what you're going to be when you grow up and be a man.' So, I saw that and I felt that, when we walked to the mailbox, she'd say these things to me that I'm now living. It's extraordinary how her father [Silas] passed that story [told in *The Jonah People*] to her, and she passed it to her daughter, my aunt, who passed it to me. And now the whole world will hear that story that this sacred lady poured into me. She told her daughter. She didn't tell me the story. But in a way, that's what she was saying to me. She was telling me the story anyway. My aunt told it to me verbatim. My grandmother told it to me by her spirit. It's her father *of whom* I'm speaking [as Boukman in the opera], and *his mother*, of whom I'm speaking [as Asase in the opera]."

On another occasion, when he was heading to Nashville for a symphony board event and a full read-through of the opera, Hannibal said, "I feel like the most grateful person in the world right now. There might be someone more grateful, but I don't know them."

He had prepared some remarks for the Nashville event that spoke to the opera, his creative process, and the meaning of *The Jonah People* as a concept. He also included a very direct statement about how he easily could have died during the composition of the opera, if not for the existence of the Creator.

Greetings!

The sky is not big enough to hold the suffering of our people, and it could never be big enough to hold my love for you. This is the mantra given to be spoken by The Jonah People upon meeting each other and when parting from each other. The Jonah People are those and the descendants of those taken from Africa and shipped to all parts of the world to be slaves forever. The Jonah

People are those born of three wombs. The womb of the Creator, the womb of a mother, and the womb of a slave ship.

There is no race known as black or white. There is but one race, the human race. All people come from tribes and from nations, including those stolen from Africa. To effectively enslave them and their descendants, knowledge of their tribe or nation had to be completely erased from their memory.

The most egregious and effective erasure of all was the erasure of their names, for in the name lies the cultural and spiritual soul of a being, the very tap root of who and what they are. Music was the only divine inheritance which could not be taken from those who were cast into the floating wooden dungeons of death, suffering, and rebirth.

In the music, the presence of the Creator is evident. Without this presence, none would have survived the hideous passage. Without this presence, the blood of Crispus Attucks would not have been the first to fall into the chalice known as America.

Without this presence, the Chairwoman of the board of this remarkable institution, which bears the name of the Nashville Symphony would not be a woman of Jonah.

And finally, if not for this presence, the composer of this work, *The Jonah People: A Legacy of Struggle and Triumph*, would have been found lying dead in a pool of blood upon the floor of his studio, long before he completed writing it.

Thy will be done.

The sky is not big enough to hold the suffering of our people, and it could never be big enough to hold my love for you.

Many Blessings,

Hannibal Lokumbe
Man of Jonah
Chief Musician, The Tribe of Jonah

Later, I asked Hannibal if he would like to share anything for this book about his brushes with death during the composition. He replied with an expression of gratitude for the work.

"I don't know anything that makes me appreciative of living more than having something for which I would gladly die. And you see, it's not just *The Jonah People*, it's *Children of the Fire*," he continued, referring to his early composition from the late 1970s, the tribute to Dr. Kim Phúc Phan Thị ("the girl in the picture," running in terror from a napalm bombing). "It's all the same. They all introduced me to each other."

In the time I have known him, and throughout his decades of voluminous and intricate journals that he has shared with me, Hannibal has always emphasized the beauty and truth of the music he is given. He views the attacks by the Beast, or evil, as an inevitable part of the journey.

"The Beast does not want healing."

The Beast will approach Hannibal through spiritual and human forms.

"Those people who have lost their own strength or their own power as a human will seek to destroy that same power in others. They try to take it from others, but if they can't take it, they just destroy it."

And these forces of destruction have approached him during all of his time working, during every assignment and piece throughout his life. In fact, they have approached him ever since he was five years old, when he first encountered the force of sheer negativity coming through the eyes and voice of a woman working in the soda shop who told him he could not eat his ice cream at the counter on account of his skin. It was his fifth birthday, and his mother had taken him into town in Bastrop, Texas, for the first time. They were going to get ice cream to celebrate. His mother encountered an acquaintance and started talking. Hannibal ran ahead and jumped up to sit at the counter, not knowing he was not allowed to do this on account of his race. The woman then berated him with the force of destruction.

"It was the first time I ever realized that the Beast could be inside of a human," Hannibal remembered. "I went and told my mother I wanted to go straight to the river, instead of getting the ice cream. She asked me what was wrong. I told her I just wanted to go to the river. I always felt better at the river."

It was not only what this woman said, Hannibal recalled, but also the evil that coursed through her as she said it. He instantaneously felt it, and he shook in terror that such a force existed. It has never stopped trying to approach him since and often tries through many mechanisms and people to interrupt and thwart his musical creations.

"It's because everything I've ever written has carried the same intent and purpose," he said, referring to his central aims of healing and spiritual liberation in all he does. "I think that, when I write music, my greatest desire is that I can give people that place to go when they need to go and have their existence be affirmed. I want to give them a space, a place, where they can go and feel whole and not feel condemned or judged. That's really what it is."

Hannibal added that he wishes for his music to serve as a portal through which people's spirit can travel to the eternal garden that he knows from his co-residence in spirit. This is the medicinal and liberating capacity of his spiritual soundscapes, which he offers as sonic meals in all of his musical works.

"I want everyone to find their garden. I want my music to provide a garden, to be that place by the river, the mountaintop, or wherever they need to go to get respite."

For Hannibal, heaven and hell are ever-present in all spaces on Earth and in all so-called times.

"Hell is the absence of and the perpetual longing for peace."

At times, some ancestral spirits communicate various forms of nostalgia, wistfulness, or things that they miss from their lives as humans in physical forms.

"What is it that some of the spirits miss?" I once asked Hannibal, referring to a discussion we had had about his ancestors and other spirits sharing that they miss parts of the lives they lived when human.

"If you're doing the work, there's nothing to miss," he replied.

"Because those spirits who are doing the work are still involved in the so-called living beings in the physical realm?"

"Right. It's the ones [the spirits] who are not doing the work or who have not completed the work that they were given that are doing the missing."

Hannibal then reflected again upon the immortal and divine nature of the work of Ms. Sparks, the regal and healing elder in the community of the projects in Texas City where he grew up.

"Ms. Sparks was never known to go to or be affiliated with any church. Given that the church was the social heartbeat of the Jonah People, her not actively being part of it added to her unique standing in the community. She did her work, the work, which is the liberation of souls. And in doing such work, she, like the work, remains immortal. She simply, as John [T. Scott] loved to say, passed it on to me and to others," Hannibal said. "The work of spiritual liberation is a living entity. Unlike monuments of marble, brick, or stone, it is not governed by wind, rain, gravity, or time. The Ms. Sparks of the world did not do the work for adulation or popularity. This work is done because you understand that you, in fact, are the work. The immortal paradigm lies in the work, not in the people who do it. They are but the vessels who carry and share it. The work is the God of us. When we complete doing the work in this realm, there is no need to miss those and aspects of those left in this realm because we are still connected by virtue of the work."

Hannibal shared that one of the most perfect things that Coltrane had said was that he, Coltrane, would never be the musician that he had wanted to be.

"That is one of the most beautiful things that could come from someone who wrote *A Love Supreme*. And what he meant was that there is no ending; there is always more expansion of the work."

"Do you feel that way as well, that you'll never be the musician you want to be? Like Coltrane?"

"I already am. And he already is, too."

Hannibal explained that, in acknowledging that truth about the work and its unending nature, one realizes that one already has become part of the unending work of the music.

"Here, then, is my perception of the meaning of never being what you strive to be, or in Trane's monumental statement of, 'I will never become the musician I want to be': to seek the infinitum, is to be the infinitum," Hannibal said.

While conversations for this book were coming to a close in September 2022, Pharoah Sanders (1940–2022) transcended to spirit.

Hannibal recalled Sanders's fearlessness and complete devotion on the altar of the bandstand.

"On the bandstand, for us it's the altar, and in Montreal one night, we were playing, and I looked over, and there were strands of saliva coming out on each side of his mouthpiece. I looked over and saw that, and I said, 'Yeah, you've got to be willing to die on the altar.'"

Hannibal also said, in the wake of Sanders's passing, "It is very important to bare your soul on the altar with those who are not afraid to die."

When I asked him how he has managed to identify and avoid destructive or evil forces, so that they cannot infiltrate or tamper with the spiritual resolve of his art, he replied that he knows them by the feeling. Even when the evil tries to masquerade as something else, he almost always can feel it immediately because of the awareness he senses.

"The feeling. I've always known it by the feeling. Always go with the feeling," Hannibal said.

He seeks not to judge others, even when they appear to have diametrically opposed understandings and intents.

"I always see many different strata of things. I don't see one layer of things. I see many layers of things. That's why I've never been argumentative. I try to never be judgmental or critical of others, how they see things. I'm accepting of other people's perspective of things. But not at the expense of the erasure of my own opinion of things, and my own way to see and to live. It's important to be open. It's certainly still important to have connection to who you are in the universe. That prevents you from becoming enslaved."

He also maintained that a state of universal love can always overcome negativity. Hannibal often recites a mantra by which he has long sought to live his life: "The highest law is life, the highest life is knowledge, and the highest knowledge is love."

He said he would gladly give his life if it would mean that no children were starving. For Hannibal, it is an absurdity of human life on Earth that any child would not have the food they needed.

"If I had a guarantee that I could exchange my life in the elimination of hunger for children, if I knew my life would end the hunger for children, I would readily give it," he explained. "The idea of a child on this verdant orb, without access to food, more food than we could ever need; the idea of a child starving, being hungry, is, I think, the gravest of all human characteristics. It's the most painful condemnation of humanity that I know of. The starvation of a child on the planet Earth."

For Hannibal, every human deserves and requires not only food and water but a deep source of replenishment for their soul. That is part of what he seeks to remind and provide people with through the spiritual soundscapes of his music.

"Everyone should find their own well from which they can drink and be restored. Music is my deepest well. Another is Clearview Cemetery where the bones of my ancestors lie. I have many wells. The sky. Memories of people I adore. But I think the deepest well of all is to share, the sharing of my wells that I actually love. I can never remember being fuller than that, wishing that all people could be full. I never remember having joy, and not wishing that all people could have joy. And that's truly the understanding of what 'I' really means, which is everyone and everything. 'I' is everyone and everything. That's the true meaning of 'I.'"

I asked Hannibal whether he taps into the essence of the oneness or the interconnectedness of all things with these wells.

"I think it came from a very natural awareness that I didn't live on this Earth by myself. And that all that I knew and was able to accomplish—and better than accomplish, but to understand—was the restoration of many people that I knew and didn't know. I am my great-grandfather. I am the spirit of him, who is my grandmother, who is my mother. That's why that lineage is so important. It gives you more than a foundation. It gives you a root. It gives you more than the root of a tree. It is a spiritual root."

He also said that this recognition of the interconnectedness across the generations and across the worlds—physical and spiritual—means that he can traverse many different domains in the here and now, in the power of the present, and that "the present is the future." These are just things many humans understand to be the afterlife in spirit.

"It means that I can live heaven on Earth and hell on Earth. I can see them both," he explained. "But most of all, I can understand the magnificent beauty of nature. I like the variation in the nature, and of the sermons of nature. Sometimes the wind, sometimes the rain. And it's never condemning and condescending. And you don't have to pay part of your hard-earned money to be a member of this church either."

Hannibal attributes much of his capacity to discern between authentic love and the pretenses of destructive intents in people and spirits to the unconditional love he experienced from his mother, his grandmother, his grandfather, and other family members and ancestral spirits since he was a young child.

"I always had that gift that they gave to me, the greatest gift. I knew absolute love through them, and that has been my foundation and has given me the strength to continue. For many people who have never experienced that degree of love, it is much harder to not to succumb to destruction."

He feels that his completion of the monumental *The Jonah People* opera has paid a significant homage to what these figures of love and liberation have taught him.

"I might never be able to repay—the way I want to—my mother and Sojourner Truth (c. 1797–1883) and Harriet Tubman (1822–1913) and Mrs. Till [Emmett Till's mother]. I might never be able to repay them for what they have given. But with this opera, I can stop worrying about it," he said, laughing.

After Hannibal had finished *The Jonah People* for its April 2023 premiere, Hannibal quickly embarked upon his next journey of composition—a commission from the Oklahoma City Philharmonic to write a piece titled *Trials, Tears, Transcendence:*

The Journey of (Clara Luper, 1923–2011). It premiered in May 2023 and was part of a centennial commemoration concert.

The Creator has given Hannibal another new work as well, with the title *Once a Place Called Earth*. When I asked if the work would be a tribute in honor of someone or something, he replied, "It's a tribute to humanity."

"I'm fascinated now with the imposition that the nature is. It's like the ultimate example of reaping what you sow," he explained. "I don't want to say it will be the culmination of my work, but it will really be something. It's not going to be the biggest fish, but it's going to be tasty."

The revelation of this assignment from the Creator came in the midst of his lamenting the humans' maltreatment of Mother Earth.

"Well, one of the things that causes me to seek the depths of my creative abilities, composing playing the trumpet, I think of what it cost from the Earth to make my trumpet. So, I figured the least I could do is play it as best as I can. When we destroy the nature, it will try to restore itself, and in that restoration, we are forced to realize what we've given to her and what we've taken from her. The only thing that she would need from us is the only thing that we should give to her, and that's respect and honor. But we have chosen to see her as an oyster and not our mother. Too many of us have come to see her as our oyster and not our mother, and that's why we are coming to find out that we're not the star of the show."[4]

Once a Place Called Earth includes a poignant movement, part of which he already has completed, called "Lamentations of the Sun."

"Even a being so magnificent as the sun laments doing what it was created to do and has to do," he said, explaining this concept. "The sun shines its brilliant rays, and because of humans' arrogance and greed and egotistical destruction of Mother Earth, these rays burn the Earth and the humans."

After a pause, he added, "All that we are required to do is what we are given to do by the Creator. It is all we are required to do, and it is all we can do."

At the time of this book's completion, Hannibal shared the part of the libretto he had already written for *Once a Place Called Earth*, saying: "Best make a way for a new beginning. Lamentations of the sun."

ONCE A PLACE CALLED EARTH

The water falling from your eyes and the water falling from the mountains are the same.

It is the same dance of life.

Each drop, an affirmation of being part of the Everlasting.

The fear of the people grew stronger than the storms of both sea and sky. And they bought more weapons than they did seed, and shouted more loudly, and more often than they prayed.

The momentum of their hatred redirected the path of the wind and made the rain a stranger to the land.

The perfect painting of nature began to fade. Its radiant colors were soon covered by the oceans of blood, from the blade of tyranny made.

They uprooted more than they planted. The land became their oyster and ceased to be their mother. Again and again, they raped her with spade, dynamite, and greed. Into her bowels they bored and blasted searching for ancient stones which glowed like stars and for metals the color of the sun and the moon.

Even the sun lamented what was next to come. It had no choice but to send its final glow which then turned all that lived upon the once verdant orb, into a memory of stone and dust, thus preparing the way for the new beginning.

Reflecting upon it all, Hannibal shared that he feels that he is planting more deeply than he ever has before, planting so that winds cannot blow the seeds away, as his grandfather taught him to do long ago when he was a boy living on his grandparents' farm in Upton, Texas.

"And I never plant alone, just like in that field. My grandfather, my grandmother, my mother, all of these noble people are there with me, more than if they were sitting next to me in flesh and bones. I'm saying all of that to say that, no matter how difficult my task in the coming years, I'll never complain because I'm too honored to have been given what I prayed to be given. So, if I have two days, or two weeks, two months, two years, twenty years—no matter how much time I have on this physical clock, there could not possibly be another human being more grateful than me. I can't imagine it. There might be, but I can't imagine it."

CODA
The Living Temples

After this book went under review with the press, the spiritual soundscapes of Hannibal's creations continued to flourish and take new shapes. Following the great success of the premiere of *The Jonah People* in April 2023, Hannibal turned his full focus to his next opera, *Once a Place Called Earth*. In fact, he received many of the ancient tones that further illumined the path of the piece after he performed a ceremony of gratitude to the ancestors for the gift of the fruition of *The Jonah People*.

Once a Place Called Earth, still now in the works, presently consists of four veils—titled earth, air, water, and fire—each appearing in different languages from around the world that contain spiritual and symbolic significance. The opera covers the last living human, Khoisan, who chronicles the history of humans as told to him by two birds, black crows. The birds have been watching humans and passing down their history over the course of humanity's existence. Khoisan inscribes the history on the wall of a cave, to be discovered by other beings who may arrive in the future to read the traces.

One central theme of the libretto is the lamentation of humans' having turned away from the living temples, from the divine within them and in the nature around them, and instead focusing on outer, invisible forms to worship.

"It will come to be known that humans are in fact the gods they seek to worship and praise and the demons they seek to curse and fear," Hannibal said.

Humans forgot their true essence, including the everlasting within them and the everlasting that runs throughout nature all around them. In the course of this forgetting, humans also have taken to destroying the nature and, ultimately in the opera, themselves as a living species.

Khoisan imparts the wisdom of lost oneness. It is at once ancient and futuristic, collapsing time:

> Once the Beings and the water were one. The Beings knew the language of the water, and the water knew the language of the Beings. Upon the Earth, they lived as one.
>
> Once the Beings knew the language of the land, and the land knew the language of the Beings. Upon the Earth, they lived as one.
>
> Once the Beings knew the language of the air, and the air knew the language of the Beings. Upon the Earth they lived as one.
>
> Once the Beings knew the language of the fire, and the fire knew the language of the Beings. Upon the Earth they lived as one.

In veil four, in the final text of the opera's libretto, Pheta, the Aura/Fire, a figure in the piece, having been betrayed by the humans, calls out to the Beings:

> Can you no longer see me? Your soul is now blind to the sight of me.

We spoke of things immortal.

Into your hands, I placed the keys to the true heaven, the heaven of peace and of knowing. Still, you found need to create gods, demons, a place of heaven, and a place of hell.

And to the gods and demons you could not see, you built temples of wood, marble, and stone.

And slowly you began to turn from the temples which you could see. The living temples. The temples of the ocean, the soil from which came your bread and fruit. The temple of air caressing your lungs. The sacred fire surrounding your body. These temples of life, you no longer chose to praise. And in your spiritual blindness, you could no longer see the living temples of yourselves. Then, came the dying.

Soon Being, you will come to know that you are the God and the Gods you seek to worship and praise, and you are the devil and the demons you fear and curse. And in you lies the power to choose which you will be. And as you have chosen, so shall you be.

THE SHADOW

I am only the thought of twilight, in the world's
Movement from night to day.
For bounty rendered unto that timeless
   space,
      I can only extend my shadow.

It is not for me to conquer the shadow,
     but to seek its span.
There is not one of breath that breathes
beyond his shadow.

Your shadow once ordained becomes your soul's
testimonial to the orders of life.

—HANNIBAL LOKUMBE, 1976[1]

ACKNOWLEDGMENTS

LAUREN COYLE ROSEN'S ACKNOWLEDGMENTS

I am grateful to so many that it would be impossible to name everyone. I wish to express deep gratitude to my family, interlocutors, friends, and spirit guides. I also, of course, am so grateful to Hannibal for opening his remarkable journey for this collaboration, as well as to his family, colleagues, friends, supporters, and ancestors.

Among the human spirits, I especially want to thank the cultural icon Bernadette Gildspinel, who is also Hannibal's amazing manager, for her incredible vision and her commitment to helping this book come to its full fruition. Among many other contributions, she read the book multiple times and provided invaluable feedback and edits. I would like to thank Kirsten Keels, for her wonderful background research in the summer of 2020, before the conversations and work with Hannibal started in earnest. I also am so grateful to Guillermo Javier Bisbal Cabrera, for his insightful background research assistance, and to Peter Letzelter-Smith for his excellent copyediting work. I also am grateful for the very strong and illuminating anonymous reviews for the press, as well as for the marvelous guidance of Eric Schwartz, Alyssa M. Napier, Zachary Friedman, Meredith Howard, Ben Kolstad and their fantastic colleagues at Columbia University Press. Much gratitude is also due to the visionary leadership of all editors involved in the pathbreaking new series, *Black Lives in the Diaspora: Past/Present/Future*, a recent partnership of Howard University and Columbia University Press.

The first draft of this book was written while I was on the faculty at Princeton University, where I benefited from several sources. For grants, awards, or other support, I am grateful to the Princeton University Center for Human Values; Princeton Humanities Council; Magic Grant for Innovation; Princeton Institute for International and Regional Studies; Program in African Studies; University Council on Research in the Humanities and Social Sciences; and Center for Culture, Society, and Religion.

Beyond the university, I am grateful for the support of the Athenaeum, the W. E. B. Du Bois Research Institute in the Hutchins Center at Harvard, and the Institute on the Formation of Knowledge at the University of Chicago.

As ever, I am especially grateful to Jeffrey Rosen, a great blessing, brilliant mind, inspired creator, and beacon of light in this world. He is also my beloved husband. This book would not have been possible without him, quite literally, as it was Jeff who first introduced me to Hannibal after they met at a mutual friend's place in Philadelphia, where Hannibal was in the throes of composing a major piece for the Philadelphia Orchestra during his most recent residency there.

HANNIBAL LOKUMBE'S ACKNOWLEDGMENTS

FIGURE A.1 *My Family—My Cocoon*, Hannibal, Sumai, Haile, Nile, Eternal, Krystal, Shawn, Carter, Morning Star, Yohan. Photograph from the world premiere of *The Jonah People: A Legacy of Struggle and Triumph*, Nashville Symphony, Nashville, Tennessee.

Photograph courtesy of Hannibal Lokumbe (2023).

NOTES

INTRODUCTION: MUSICAL ALCHEMY AND SPIRITUAL LIBERATION

1. This definition of spiritatorio can be found on the "Projects" page of Hannibal's website at https://www.hanniballokumbe.com/projects.
2. For a powerful articulation of the need to add language, discourse, particular epistemologies, and new media forms to understanding the sensorial and embodied knowledges, including in musical and other sonic forms, see Thomas Porcello, Louise Meintjes, Ana Maria Ochoa, and David W. Samuels, "The Reorganization of the Sensory World," *Annual Review of Anthropology* 39 (2010): 51–66.
3. As Vincane Despret evocatively writes of the so-called dead, or the ancestors, anthropological work done in certain registers actually can restore a sense of consciousness to people about the ways in which the so-called dead, or those who have crossed over to spirit, actively participate as co-creating forces in the lives of those still left in human form on Earth. For example, Despret writes, "This [process of re-membering the dead] is the same as what is done discursively with funeral orations. In an article on the relations between the living and the dead, Molinié asks what it is that is fabricated in these ceremonies. Her response is all the more interesting in that it avoids the fairly accepted analysis we see in functionalist theories, which generally explain rituals with the assumption that they help people carry out their mourning, or that they reinforce collective relations, etc. A very asymmetrical kind of analysis,

furthermore, since the dead are only there as support act for the living. Molinié proposes a pragmatic hypothesis, another coming, once again, 'through the milieu,' to the extent that, to understand the tributes, what they do and what they make happen, she makes sure she follows the beings, dead and alive, in what is holding them together. The tributes work away at 'keeping things going' [*faire tenir*]; they begin a process of instauration. She notes that during the ceremonies, each comes to speak of the dead person. And everyone who starts to speak tells either an anecdote, or talks of something that left its mark, or speaks of their humor, their wisdom, or their generosity, sometimes even of a flaw, but one that people now are clearly prepared to find interesting. Here people are cultivating the art of versions, that is to say, the art of the coexistence of heterogeneous stories. And each of those left behind thus discovers something about the defunct that they didn't know. Death thickens with all these stories, these accounts that compose it in a new person, more complete, more important, denser, better linked up, unified in the heterogeneity of the versions of the self, more surprising: a person with a richer personality than she had during her life for each person present. The departed becomes more important, and more important for and with each of us, in the sense that she imports more, and in new ways. Tributes are processes of amplification of existence. The dead person acquires more reality here. He can therefore prolong the effects that he had as a live person in the lives of those who at present are going to inherit from him and make him live differently: to be multiple and with multiple effects, and therefore more present in his new mode of existence. The tribute stories intensify the presence; they are vectors of vitality. These ceremonies transform all involved and create new relations, as in new ways of relating oneself to others. It is a 'becoming with' in the future anterior; from now on, he will have been. And thus, a real becoming for the future. *We recompose the departed in order to be able, in the future and for a long time, to compose with them, at least we hope so.*" Vinciane Despret, *Our Grateful Dead: Stories of Those Left Behind*, trans. Stephen Muecke (Minneapolis: University of Minnesota Press, 2021), 49–50 (emphasis added). For a concise discussion of the affective turn in anthropology and related disciplines, please see Kathleen Stewart, "In the World That Affect Proposed," *Cultural Anthropology* 32, no. 2 (2017): 192–98.

4. Conceptual and theoretical touchstones for the uses of soundscapes here include, for example, Michael Veal's work on soundscapes in Jamaican reggae, Charles Hirschkind's work on ethical soundscapes in the Islamic Revival in cities across the Middle East, and Steven Feld's work on soundscapes in his writings on jazz in Accra and elsewhere. Michael E. Veal, *Dub: Soundscapes and Shattered Songs in Jamaican Reggae* (Middletown, CT: Wesleyan University Press, 2007); Charles Hirschkind, *The Ethical Soundscape: Cassette Sermons and Islamic Counterpublics* (New York: Columbia University Press, 2006); and Steven Feld, *Jazz Cosmopolitanism in Accra: Five Musical Years in Ghana* (Durham, NC: Duke University Press, 2012), 5, 249. In this use of soundscapes, I also draw upon the works of many others. See, for example, David W. Samuels, Louise Meintjes, Ana Maria Ochoa, and Thomas Porcello, "Soundscapes: Toward a Sounded Anthropology," *Annual Review of Anthropology* 39 (2010): 329–45; Louise Meintjes. *Dust of the Zulu: Ngoma Aesthetics After Apartheid* (Durham, NC: Duke University Press, 2017); Charles Hirschkind, *The Feeling of History: Islam, Romanticism, and Andalusia* (Chicago: University of Chicago Press, 2020); Gavin Steingo and Jim Sykes, eds., *Remapping Sound Studies* (Durham, NC: Duke University Press, 2019); David Abram, *The Spell of the Sensuous: Perception and Language in a More-Than-Human World* (New York: Vintage, 2012); Steven Feld, *Sound and Sentiment: Birds, Weeping, Poetics, and Song in Kaluli Expression* (1982; reprinted, Durham, NC: Duke University Press, 2012); Steven Feld, "Waterfalls of Song: An Acoustemology of Place Resounding in Bosavi, Papua New Guinea," in *Senses of Place*, ed. Steven Feld and Keith Basso (Santa Fe, NM: School of American Research Press, 1996), 91–135; Steven Feld, "A Sweet Lullaby for World Music," *Public Culture* 12, no. 1 (2000): 145–71; Feld, *Jazz Cosmopolitanism in Accra*; Steven Feld and Keith H. Basso, eds., *Senses of Place* (Santa Fe, NM: School for Advanced Research Press, 1996); Eitan Wilf, "Sincerity Versus Self-Expression: Modern Creative Agency and the Materiality of Semiotic Forms," *Cultural Anthropology* 26, no. 3 (2011): 462–84; Eitan Wilf, "Rituals of Creativity: Tradition, Modernity, and the 'Acoustic Unconscious' in a U.S. Collegiate Jazz Music Program," *American Anthropologist* 114, no. 1 (2012): 32–44; Eitan Wilf, "Semiotic Dimensions of Creativity," *Annual Review of Anthropology* 43 (2014): 397–412; Stefan Helmrich, "An Anthropologist Under

Water: Immersive Soundscapes, Submarine Cyborgs, and Transductive Ethnography," *American Anthropologist* 34, no. 4 (2007): 621–41; Matt Sakakeeny, "'Under the Bridge': An Orientation to Soundscapes in New Orleans," *Ethnomusicology* 54, no. 1 (2010): 1–27; Matt Sakakeeny, "New Orleans Music as a Circulatory System," *Black Music Research Journal* 31, no. 2 (2011): 291–325; C. Nadia Seremetakis, ed., *The Senses Still: Perception and Memory as Material Culture in Modernity* (Boulder, CO: Westview, 1994); Brian Larkin, *Signal and Noise: Media, Infrastructure, and Urban Culture in Nigeria* (Durham, NC: Duke University Press, 2008); R. Murray Schafer, *The Soundscape: Our Sonic Environment and the Tuning of the World* (Merrimac, MA: Destiny Books, 1993); Charles Hirschkind, Maria José de Abreu, and Carlo Caduff, "New Media, New Publics? An Introduction to Supplement 15," *Current Anthropology* 58, no. S15 (2017): S3–S12; David Howes, ed., *The Varieties of Sensory Experience: A Sourcebook in the Anthropology of the Sense* (Toronto, Ontario: University of Toronto Press, 1991); Michael Jackson, *The Varieties of Temporal Experience: Travels in Philosophical, Historical, and Ethnographic Time* (New York: Columbia University Press, 2018); Brian Larkin, *Signal and Noise: Media, Infrastructure, and Urban Culture in Nigeria* (Durham, NC: Duke University Press, 2008); Jesse Weaver Shipley, *Living the Hiplife: Celebrity and Entrepreneurship in Ghanaian Popular Music* (Durham, NC: Duke University Press, 2013); Jennifer Lynn Stoever, *The Sonic Color Line: Race and the Cultural Politics of Listening* (New York: NYU Press, 2016); Alessandro Duranti, Jason Throop, and Matthew McCoy, "Jazz Etiquette: Between Aesthetics and Ethics," in *The Oxford Handbook of the Phenomenology of Music Cultures*, ed. Harris M. Berger, Friedlind Riedel, and David VanderHamm (New York: Oxford University Press, 2018); R. Anderson Sutton, "Interpreting Electronic Sound Technology in the Contemporary Javanese Soundscape," *Ethnomusicology* 40, no. 2 (1996): 249–68; Salomé Voegelin, *Sonic Possible Worlds: Hearing the Continuum of Sound* (London: Bloomsbury Academic, 2014); and Salomé Voegelin, *The Political Possibility of Sound: Fragments of Listening* (London: Bloomsbury Academic, 2018). Steven Feld has been one of the central innovators of soundscapes in anthropology, and in his recent book, *Jazz Cosmopolitanism*, he elaborates ways in which his ethnography of the Nima area of Ghana's capital taught him "a great deal about everyday listening to sonic stratigraphy," and how "[t]his sonic stratigraphy is the topic of my ambient soundscape composition of dawn in this community, *Waking in Nima*, CD, VoxLox, 2010. There you hear a multiplicity of acoustic coexistences, intentionally or unintentionally layered interactions, in figure and ground, variously cooperative, competitive, planned or unplanned, related or unrelated, opportunistic or idiosyncratic. The sound sources, recorded from roofs and treetops from five to seven in the morning where I wake in Nima, include a close and distant mosque, a close and distant evangelical Pentecostal church, song birds, roosters, car alarms, trains, and instrumental and vocal sounds of men and women waking and working." Feld, *Jazz Cosmopolitanism in Accra*, 5, 249.

5. For my mobilization of anthropologies of affect and the affective registers or archives as key aspects of sonic soundscapes and knowledge about them, I draw upon multiple recent works on affect and affective ways of knowing, including Kathleen Stewart, *Ordinary Affects* (Durham, NC: Duke University Press, 2007); Stewart, "In the World That Affect Proposed"; Aimee Meredith Cox, *Shapeshifters: Black Girls and the Choreography of Citizenship* (Durham, NC: Duke University Press, 2015); Kamari Maxine Clarke, *Affective Justice: The International Criminal Court and the Pan-Africanist Pushback* (Durham, NC: Duke University Press, 2019); Deborah Thomas, *Political Life in the Wake of the Plantation: Sovereignty, Witnessing, Repair* (Durham, NC: Duke University Press, 2019); Nina Sun Eidsheim, *Sensing Sound: Singing and Listening as Vibrational Practice* (Durham, NC: Duke University Press, 2015); Nina Sun Eidsheim, *The Race of Sound: Listening, Timbre, and Vocality in African American Music* (Durham, NC: Duke University Press, 2019); and David Scott, *Stuart Hall's Voice: Intimations of an Ethics of Receptive Generosity* (Durham, NC: Duke University Press, 2017).

6. Arturo Escobar, *Pluriversal Politics: The Real and the Possible* (Durham, NC: Duke University Press, 2020). Arturo Escobar gives the following proposition, in his visionary work on pluriversal politics: "that realities are plural and always in the making, and that this has profound political consequences," and "another world is possible because another real and another possible are possible. That other world is a world where many worlds fit, or the pluriverse. By breaking with conventional premises of the real and the possible, the essays locate politics at this very level." In

Charles Hirschkind's study of ethical soundscapes in the emergence of the cassette sermon and its multivalent effects for urban life across many cities in the Middle East, he argues that "the contribution of this aural media [of the cassette sermon] to shaping the contemporary moral and political landscape of the Middle East lies not simply in its capacity to disseminate ideas or instill religious ideologies but in its effect on the human sensorium, on the affects, sensibilities, and perceptual habits of its vast audience. The soundscape produced through the circulation of this medium animates and sustains the substrate of sensory knowledges and embodied aptitudes undergirding a broad revival movement within contemporary Islam. From its inception in the twentieth century, this movement has centered on a critique of the existing structures of religious and secular authority. For those who participate in the movement, the moral and political direction of contemporary Muslim societies cannot be left to politicians, religious scholars, or militant activists but must be decided upon and enacted collectively by ordinary Muslims in the course of their normal daily activities. The notions of individual and collective responsibility that this movement has given rise to have come to be embodied in a wide array of institutions, media forms, and practices of public sociability. In doing so, they have changed the political geography of the Middle East in ways that have vast implications for the future of the region. . . . Although the listening practices I explore inhabit a counterhistory—counter to the modernist formations of politics and religion and the ideologies that sustain and legitimate them—this history nonetheless exerts forcible claims on the contemporary, and thus on the futures imaginable from its shores." Hirschkind, *The Ethical Soundscape*, 122–33. For recent, groundbreaking work on cosmopolitics, see Marisol de la Cadena, "Indigenous Cosmopolitics in the Andes: Conceptual Reflections Beyond 'Politics,'" *Cultural Anthropology* 25, no. 2 (2010): 334–70, and Marisol de la Cadena, *Earth Beings: Ecologies of Practice Across Andean Worlds* (Durham, NC: Duke University Press, 2015). For pathbreaking new work on theopolitics, see Carlota McAllister and Valentina Napolitano, "Political Theology/Theopolitics: The Thresholds and Vulnerabilities of Sovereignty," *Annual Review of Anthropology* 50 (2021): 7.1–7.16; Carlota McAllister and Valentina Napolitano, "Incarnate Politics Beyond the Cross and the Sword," *Social Analysis* 64, no. 4 (2020): 1–20; Carlota McAllister, "No One Can Hold It Back:

The Theopolitics of Water and Life in Chilean Patagonia Without Dams," *Social Analysis* 64, no. 4 (2020): 121–39; Valentina Napolitano, "On the Touch-Event: Theopolitical Encounters," *Social Analysis* 64, no. 4 (2020): 81–99. For visionary recent work on the pluriverse and pluriversal politics, see Arturo Escobar, *Designs for the Pluriverse: Radical Interdependence, Autonomy, and the Making of Worlds* (Durham, NC: Duke University Press, 2018), and Escobar, *Pluriversal Politics*.

7. Yannick Nézet-Séguin, backstage at the Philadelphia Orchestra in 2019 for an interview with WRTI 90.1, a classical and jazz station, and available at https://www.wrti.org/wrti-spotlight/2019-09-10/the-philadelphia-orchestra-in-concert-on-wrti-hannibals-healing-tones-sibelius-symphony-no-2.

8. Hannibal's three volumes of poetry are *The Ripest of My Fruits* (1976); *Trilogy: Freedom Dance Cycle* (2014); and *Love Poems to God* (2002). A writer at the *Amsterdam News* newspaper compared *The Ripest of My Fruits* to Kahlil Gibran's *The Prophet* (which Hannibal appreciated, as he enjoys Gibran's work). However, Hannibal does not identify as a prophet, shaman, or anything of that sort. "Everyone is sacred," he said when I asked directly if he identified as any of these things. Although his poetry is admired by many, he had a critical reaction from one potential publisher in the 1970s, who told him that the poems were "very incendiary," a word he found to be deeply irritating and missing the point. "The publisher said, 'Well, the poems are very powerful and imaginative and blah, blah, blah,' and then at the end, they said, 'but very incendiary,'" Hannibal recalled. "I said, 'What's more incendiary than the Bible?' See, I've been having to put up with these things ever since I've been here. . . . And you know what I regret most of all? That I wasted the time, the minutes, and the hours, if you add them all up, I could've written a string quartet in the time I wasted talking to these cowards. If you don't like it, if you just say, 'Well, you know, it's not really up to literary standards,' I could respect that. But don't tell me things are incendiary. That's what this place needs, some incendiary stuff."

9. These accolades include, among others, a Bessie Award, a Joyce Award, and the Detroit Symphony Orchestra's Lifetime Achievement Award. He also has held many fellowships and residencies, including from the United States Artist Award in Music, the National Endowment for the Arts, and Americans for the Arts.

1. THE PASSAGES OF YOUTH IN TEXAS

1. Hannibal's mother's grandfather was named George Wilson, and her grandmother was named Candace Burgess.

2. NEW YORK CITY AND THE JAZZ YEARS

1. This book, though narrative and dialogical, is deeply informed by the profound work of many scholars in music studies, and free jazz studies in specific, who have written remarkable and illuminating texts on the genre, on improvisation, on tonality, on musical innovation, and on their own theories of soundscapes, including spiritual ones. We have kept these citations and discussions largely to the endnotes, so as not to disrupt the narrative flow of the book or detract from the focus on Hannibal's journey (and so as to reach as broad a readership as possible), but we wish to acknowledge the pathbreaking work that powerfully informs the writing, conceptualizing, and theorizing in this book. We hope that this book will resonate as being in dialogue with these rich, long-running interdisciplinary conversations and debates. These foundational and groundbreaking works include, but are certainly not limited to, George E. Lewis, *A Power Stronger Than Itself: The AACM and American Experimental Music* (Chicago: University of Chicago Press, 2009); George E. Lewis and Benjamin Piekut, eds., *The Oxford Handbook of Critical Improvisation Studies, Volume 1* (Oxford: Oxford University Press, 2016); George E. Lewis and Benjamin Piekut, eds., *The Oxford Handbook of Critical Improvisation Studies, Volume 2* (Oxford: Oxford University Press, 2016); Paul Steinbeck, *Sound Experiments: The Music of the AACM* (Chicago: University of Chicago Press, 2022); Paul Steinbeck, *Message to Our Folks: The Art Ensemble of Chicago* (Chicago: University of Chicago Press, 2017); John Szwed, *So What: The Life of Miles Davis* (New York: Simon & Schuster, 2004); John Szwed, *Billie Holiday: The Musician and the Myth* (New York: Penguin, 2016); John Szwed, *Space Is the Place: The Lives and Times of Sun Ra* (Durham, NC: Duke University Press, 2020); Paul Youngquist, *A Pure Solar World: Sun Ra and the Birth of Afrofuturism* (Austin: University of Texas Press, 2016); Fred Moten, *In the Break: The Aesthetics of the Black Radical Tradition* (Minneapolis: University of Minnesota Press, 2003); Fred Moten,

Black and Blur (consent not to be a single being) (Durham, NC: Duke University Press, 2017); Howard Mandel, *Miles, Ornette, Cecil: Jazz Beyond Jazz* (New York: Routledge, 2010); Maria Golia, *Ornette Coleman: The Territory and the Adventure* (London: Reaktion, 2020); Stephen Rush, *Free Jazz, Harmolodics, and Ornette Coleman* (New York: Routledge, 2016); Henry Threadgill and Brent Hayes Edwards, *Easily Slip into Another World: A Life in Music* (New York: Knopf, 2023); Nicolas Fils, *Don Cherry: Le Petit Prince du Free* (Marseille, France: Mot et le Reste, 2023); and Cisco Bradley, *Universal Tonality: The Life and Music of William Parker* (Durham, NC: Duke University Press, 2021).

2. For discussions of the emergences of these styles, see Kathleen Cornell Berman, *Birth of the Cool: How Jazz Great Miles Davis Found His Sound* (Essex, MA: Page Street, 2019); Steven Cerra, "Gil Evans: The Arranger as Re-composer—Part 1 & 2," *JazzProfiles*, May 10, 2011, https://jazzprofiles.blogspot.com/2017/10/gil-evans-arranger-as-re-composer-parts.html; David Hajdu, "The Gorgeous, Quirky, Uncategorizable Music of Gil Evans," *The New Republic*, October 1, 2010, http://www.newrepublic.com/blog/the-famous-door/78088/the-gorgeous-quirky-uncategorizable-music-gil-evans#; Larry Hicock, *Castles Made of Sound: The Story of Gil Evans* (London: Hachette, 2002); Stephanie Stein Crease, *Gil Evans: Out of the Cool: His Life and Music* (Chicago: Chicago Review Press, 2003); and Steve Lajoie, *Gil Evans & Miles Davis: Historic Collaborations: An Analysis of Selected Gil Evans Works, 1957–1962* (Mainz, Germany: Advance Music, 2003).

3. Miles Davis with Quincy Troupe, *Miles: The Autobiography* (New York: Simon & Schuster, 1989).

4. Although Miles Davis shared in his autobiography that he was spiritual, he said he was not a follower of any organized religion, and he was skeptical of religious institutions. Toward the end of his book, he wrote: "I don't like throwing God up into anybody's face and I don't like it thrown in mine. But if I have a religious preference, I think it would be Islam, and that I would be a Muslim. But I don't know about that, or any organized religion. I've never been into that, using religion as a crutch. Because I personally don't like a lot of things that are happening in organized religion. It don't seem too spiritual to me, but more about money and power, and I can't go for that." Davis with Troupe, *Miles*, 411. Davis also powerfully wrote in a direct way about his spirituality and

his interrelation with spirits. "But I do believe in being spiritual and do believe in spirits. I always have. I believe my mother and father come to visit me. I believe all the musicians that I have known who are now dead do, too. When you work with great musicians, they are always a part of you—people like Max Roach, Sonny Rollins, John Coltrane, Bird, Diz, Jack DeJohnette, Philly Joe. The ones that are dead I miss a lot, especially as I grow older: Monk, Mingus, Freddie Webster, and Fat Girl. When I think about the ones who are dead it makes me mad, so I try not to think about it. But their spirits are walking around in me, so they're still here and passing it on to others. It's some spiritual shit and part of what I am today is them. It's all in me, the things I learned to do from them. Music is about the spirit and the spiritual, and about feeling, I believe their music is still around somewhere, you know. The shit that we played together has to be somewhere around in the air because we blew it there and that shit was magical, was spiritual." Davis with Troupe, *Miles*, 411. Likewise, he wrote about dreams and visions he would have with spirits of loved ones. "I used to have these dreams where I thought I could see things, see some other stuff, like smoke or clouds, and my mind would make pictures of them. I do that now when I wake up in the morning and want to see my mother or father or Trane or Gil or Philly, or whoever. I just say to myself, 'I want to see them,' and they're there and I'm talking to them. Sometimes now when I look in the mirror I see my father there. This has been happening since he died and wrote that letter. I definitely believe in the spirit, but I don't think about death; there's too much for me to do to worry about that." Davis with Troupe, *Miles*, 411. He also wrote about his unyielding creative drive with the music, how it would rush into and through him, compelling him to play and to write it. He ended his autobiography with words to this effect: "For me, the urgency to play and create music today is worse than when I started. It's more intense. Its like a curse. Man, the music I forget now drives me nuts trying to remember it. I'm driven to it—go to bed thinking about it and wake up thinking about it. It's always there. And I love that it hasn't abandoned me; I feel really blessed. . . . I feel good, because I have never felt this creative. I feel the best is yet to come. Like Prince says when he's talking about hitting the beat and getting to the music and the rhythm, I'm going to keep 'getting up on the one,' brother, I'm just going to try to keep my music getting up on the one, getting up on the one every day I play. Getting up on the one. Later." Davis with Troupe, *Miles*, 411–12. See also Marc Antomattei, *Miles: The Companion Guide to the Miles Davis Autobiography* (Raleigh, NC: Marc Antomattei Press, 2011) and Franck Bergerot, *We Want Miles: Miles Davis* (New York: Rizzoli International, 2010). Prince also wrote, in his posthumously edited and published autobiography, that he would sense that everything was coded with levels of meaning since he was a child, and he would see faces in things. He wrote of how his brain had always been overactive, and he would have blackouts from this when he was young. "I used to stare and stare at everything in the house until I was fried. Maybe a lot of kids do it. I'd see faces in everything. Faces talking to faces. I'd stare at the marble until I saw faces in it. I thought, this house is coded for me. I'd lose myself in every object. Good thing there was music. You can compare it to the Bible, where everything seems coded. Place names, especially. There's something there, something sacred being guarded. Levels of meaning. And once you get down deep, you can't read them any other way." Prince, *The Beautiful Ones*, ed. Dan Piepenbring (New York: One World, Random House, 2019), 94.

5. Film footage of two of their live performances of the song "Hannibal" can be found at https://www.youtube.com/watch?v=Ek7Bunt6GP4 (1990, Montreux Jazz Festival) and https://www.youtube.com/watch?v=UAqWeoEwez8 (1991, Vienne Jazz Festival).

6. For more on Miles Evans's music and growing up with Gil Evans as his father, see Melanie Futorian, "Miles Evans: Two-Part Harmony," AllAboutJazz, August 9, 2012, http://www.allaboutjazz.com/php/article.php?id=42498&pg=1.

7. Leslie Kandell, "On the Towns: Music; How the Voices of One Continent Influenced the Culture of Another," *New York Times*, November 8, 1998, https://www.nytimes.com/1998/11/08/nyregion/towns-music-voices-one-continent-influenced-culture-another.html.

8. For work on Coltrane's musical innovations, pieces, and spirituality, see Leonard Brown, ed., *John Coltrane and Black America's Quest for Freedom: Spirituality and the Music* (London: Oxford University Press, 2010); Chris DeVito, *Coltrane on Coltrane: The John Coltrane Interviews* (Chicago: Chicago Review Press, 2012); Arun Nevader, "John Coltrane: Music and Metaphysics," *The Threepenny Review*, no. 10 (1982): 26–27;

Gary Golio, *Spirit Seeker: John Coltrane's Musical Journey* (New York: Clarion, 2012); Ashley Kahn, *A Love Supreme: The Story of John Coltrane's Signature Album* (New York: Penguin, 2003); Peter Jan Margry and Daniel Wojcik, "A Saxophone Divine: The Transformative Power of Saint John Coltrane's Jazz Music in San Francisco's Fillmore District," in *Spiritualizing the City: Agency and Resilience of the Urban and Urbanesque Habitat*, ed. V. Hegner and P. J. Margry (Oxfordshire, UK: Routledge, 2017), 169–94; and Carl Woideck, *The John Coltrane Companion* (New York: Schirmer, 1988).

9. In Hannibal, *Love Poems to God* (New Orleans, LA: Hannibal Lokumbe Music, 2002), 53.
10. For details on Ornette Coleman's many ingenious varieties of composition, politics, and life, see Rush, *Free Jazz, Harmolodics, and Ornette Coleman*; Golia, *Ornette Coleman*; Michael Stephans, *Experiencing Ornette Coleman: A Listener's Companion* (Lanham, MD: Rowman & Littlefield, 2017); and Mandel, *Miles, Ornette, Cecil*.
11. "Around the World on the Phonograph (1888)," *The Public Doman Review*, n.d., https://publicdomainreview.org/collection/around-the-world-on-the-phonograph-1888.
12. This resonates with the wisdom of many other great Black artists. To take one example, Prince was famous for adamantly declaring, in the face of huge music industry pushback: "If you don't own your masters, your masters own you." For related discussions, see Prince, *The Beautiful Ones*, 17.
13. https://www.amazon.com/Carnegie-Hall-Millennium-Piano-Book/dp/B00009W8PV.

3. COMPOSING THE SPIRITATORIOS

1. Hannibal has searched for the language in which Lokumbe originates, but he has been unable to locate it. He knows the meaning of Lokumbe because he received the name's significance directly from the spirit of his great-grandmother, Cora, who revealed the name to him and gave him permission to use it in public.
2. These acts of love, respect, and remembrance continually remind Hannibal and the ancestral spirits of their close kinship, their continuing interrelations, their proximity, and their co-presence at all times.

3. COMPOSING THE SPIRITATORIOS

Hannibal's morning rituals are akin to many acts of giving offerings to ancestors on altars, at grave sites, or at other sacred locations. It is often less what precisely is given that matters than the respect that such giving connotes. Writing of offering gold dust to spirits among some Akan people in Ghana and beyond, philosopher Kwame Anthony Appiah set forth a more generalizable scheme for the symbolic repertoires of ritual acts, which are also actual acts—they are symbolic in that they take symbolic form, not in that they are not authentic phenomena in the world or worlds. "Many symbolic ritual acts have this character. They are not arbitrary signs, like words or salutes; they are acts that draw their meaning from the nonritual significance of relevantly similar performances. What makes them symbolic is the recognition by the agents that these acts in ritual contexts do not work in the standard way. The spirit comes not because we have given it some money but because we have done something that shows respect, and giving the gold dust shows respect because outside these ritual contexts the giving of gold dust is standardly accompanied by respect. I have spent some time discussing the role of this symbol in this ritual because to many it has seemed that it is the distinguishing character of these religious acts that they are symbolic. Clifford Geertz has famously remarked that religion is 'a system of symbols.' Now it is, of course, an impressive fact about many religious practices and beliefs that they have symbolic elements: the Eucharist is loaded with symbolism, and so is the Passover meal. But I want to argue that the symbolism arises out of the fundamental nature of religious beliefs, and that these fundamental beliefs are not themselves symbolic. All my life, I have seen and heard ceremonies like the one with which I began. This public, ritual appeal to unseen spirits on a ceremonial occasion is part of a form of life in which such appeals are regularly made in private. When a man opens a bottle of gin, he will pour a little on the earth, asking his ancestors to drink a little and to protect the family and its doings. This act is without ceremony, without the excitement of the public installation of an *Obosom* [Twi for an exalted spirit or saintly spirit, a messenger for the Creator] in a new shrine, yet it inhabits the same world. Indeed, it is tempting to say that, just as the public installation of a spirit is like the public installation of a chief, the private libation is like the private pouring of a drink for a relative. The element of ceremonial is not what is essential; what is essential is the ontology of invisible beings. So that in the wider context of Asante life it seems absurd to claim that what was happening, when my father casually poured a few drops from the top of a newly opened bottle of Scotch onto the carpet, involved anything other than a literal belief in the ancestors. The pouring of the drink may have been symbolic: there is no general assumption in Asante that the dead like whiskey. But for the gesture of offering them a portion of a valued drink to make sense, the ancestors who are thus symbolically acknowledged must exist." Kwame Anthony Appiah, *In My Father's House: Africa in the Philosophy of Culture* (New York: Oxford University Press, 1993), 112–13; citing to, Clifford Geertz, *The Interpretation of Cultures* (New York: Basic Books, 1973). See also Kwame Anthony Appiah, *Cosmopolitanism: Ethics in a World of Strangers* (New York: W.W. Norton), 2006.

3. For a sample of Martin Payton's recent "Broken Time" exhibit (2017–2018), see the Louisiana State University Museum of Art's website at https://www.lsumoa.org/martin-payton. For more information on Ron Bechet's paintings, drawings, and philosophies, see the Xavier University of Louisiana's "Art Collections and Gallery" website at https://xulagallery.com/our-team/ron-bechet/. For more information on the work of John T. Scott, see Richard J. Powell, *Circle Dance: The Art of John T. Scott* (New Orleans: New Orleans Museum of Art; Jackson: University Press of Mississippi, 2005).

4. Paul Robeson's son has assembled a fascinating book that draws upon the family's archives and covers Robeson's politics, as well as many other things: Paul Robeson, Jr., *The Undiscovered Paul Robeson: An Artist's Journey, 1898–1939* (Hoboken, NJ: Wiley, 2008). See also Paul Robeson, *Here I Stand* (1958; Reprint, Boston: Beacon, 1998); Paul Robeson, Jr., *Paul Robeson: Tributes and Selected Writings* (Forest Park, IL: Paul Robeson Archives, 1976); Paul Robeson, *Paul Robeson Speaks: Writings, Speeches, and Interviews, a Centennial Celebration*, ed. Philip Sheldon and Henry Foner (New York: Citadel Press, 1978); Murali Balaji, *The Professor and the Pupil: The Politics and Friendship of W.E.B Du Bois and Paul Robeson* (New York: Nation Books, 2019); Lloyd L. Brown, *The Young Paul Robeson: On My Journey Now* (New York: Basic Books, 1997); Jordan Goodman, *Paul Robeson: A Watched Man* (London: Verso, 2013); Jeffrey Stewart, ed., *Paul Robeson: Artist and Citizen* (New Brunswick, NJ: Rutgers University Press, 1998); Lindsey R. Swindall, *Paul Robeson:*

A Life of Activism and Art (Washington, DC: Rowman & Littlefield, 2013); and Gerald Horne, *Paul Robeson: The Artist as Revolutionary* (London: Pluto, 2016).

5. Ralph Ellison directly wrote about his love and devotion to jazz and to music writ large. In John F. Callahan's introduction to a collection of Ellison's essays, he recounts how an interviewer asked whether Ellison's desire for composing what is conventionally called classical music was somehow a disavowal of his culture. Ellison very quickly addressed the false premise of the question. As Callahan writes, "Asked much later if his 'desire to be a symphony composer rather than a jazz instrumentalist [stood] for a sort of denial of [his] own cultural situation,' he changed the questioner's frequency without hesitation: 'No, no. You see, what is often misunderstood nowadays is that there wasn't always this division between the ambitions of jazz musicians and the standards of classical music; the idea was to master both traditions.'" For Hannibal, of course, no such division needs to exist between jazz and classical music at all, and Hannibal finds that the most classical music is jazz music. Ralph Ellison, *The Collected Essays of Ralph Ellison* (New York: Random House, 1995), Kindle location 217. See also Ralph Ellison, *Living with Music: Ralph Ellison's Jazz Writings*, ed. Robert O'Meally (New York: Modern Library, 2002).

6. A historian, Timothy Tyson, obtained a copy of Bryant Donham's unpublished memoir while interviewing her for research in 2008. He provided a copy of it to the Associated Press on Thursday, July 14, 2022. For recent coverage, see Associated Press, "Woman Who Accused Emmett Till Says She Didn't Want Him Dead in Memoir," *The Guardian*, July 14, 2022, https://www.theguardian.com/us-news/2022/jul/14/emmett-till-accuser-harm-memoir. For fuller accounts of the murder, see Devery S. Anderson, *Emmett Till: The Murder That Shocked the World and Propelled the Civil Rights Movement* (Jackson: University Press of Mississippi, 2015); Minrose C. Gwin, *Remembering Medgar Evers: Writing the Long Civil Rights Movement* (Athens: University of Georgia Press, 2013); Elliott J. Gorn, *Let the People See: The Story of Emmett Till* (Oxford: Oxford University Press, 2018); Timothy B. Tyson, *The Blood of Emmett Till* (New York: Simon & Schuster, 2017); and Dave Tell, *Remembering Emmett Till* (Chicago: University of Chicago Press, 2019).

7. A collection of Evers's writings can be found in Medgar Wiley Evers, *The Autobiography of Medgar Evers: A Hero's Life and Legacy Revealed Through His Writings, Letters, and Speeches*, ed. Myrlie Evers-Williams and Manning Marable (New York: Civitas, 2006).

4. THE JONAH PEOPLE AND BECOMING THE WORK

1. Hannibal has published a full statement on the meaning of the Jonah People name and the significance of the Jonah People symbol on a Tribe of Jonah website that he launched in 2020 at https://www.tribeofjonah.com.
2. See, for example, Jean Casimir, *The Haitians: A Decolonial History*, trans. Laurent Dubois (Chapel Hill: University of North Carolina Press, 2020); Laurent Dubois and Richard Lee Turtis, *Freedom Roots: Histories from the Caribbean* (Chapel Hill: University of North Carolina Press, 2019); Laurent Dubois, *A Colony of Citizens: Revolution and Slave Emancipation in the French Caribbean, 1787–1804* (Chapel Hill: University of North Carolina Press, 2004); John Henry Gonzalez, *Maroon Nation: A History of Revolutionary Haiti* (New Haven, CT: Yale University Press, 2019); Laurent Dubois, *Haiti: The Aftershocks of History* (New York: Metropolitan, 2012); Laurent Dubois, "The Citizen's Trance: The Haitian Revolution and the Motor of History," in *Magic and Modernity: Interfaces of Revelation and Concealment*, ed. Birgit Meyer and Peter Pels (Stanford, CA: Stanford University Press, 2003), 103–28; Kate Ramsey, *The Spirits and the Law: Vodou and Power in Haiti* (Chicago: University of Chicago Press, 2011); and Kate Ramsey, "Vodou, History, and New Narratives," *Transition* 111 (2013): 31–41.
3. Hannibal explained that the name Boukman is a tribute to Dutty Boukman, an early leader of the Haitian Revolution. Boukman was born in Senegambia before being stolen and enslaved, brought to Jamaica, and then later Haiti. He was a leader of the revolutionary Maroons and a Vodou priest (called an *oungan* or *houngan*). See, for example, Ramsey, *The Spirits and the Law*; Zora Neale Hurston, *Tell My Horse: Voodoo and Life in Haiti and Jamaica* (1938; Reprint, New York: HarperCollins, 2008); Deborah A. Thomas, *Political Life in the Wake of the Plantation: Sovereignty, Witnessing, Repair* (Durham, NC: Duke University Press,

2019); Deborah A. Thomas, "Time and the Otherwise: Plantations, Garrisons, and Being Human in the Caribbean," *Anthropological Theory* 16, no. 2–3 (2016): 177–200; Andrew Apter, "On African Origins: Creolization and *Connaissance* in Haitian Vodou," *American Ethnologist* 29, no. 2 (2002): 233–60; Orlando Patterson, *Slavery and Social Death: A Comparative Study* (Cambridge, MA: Harvard University Press, 2018); and Laurent Dubois, "The Citizen's Trance: The Haitian Revolution and the Motor of History," in *Magic and Modernity: Interfaces of Revelation and Concealment*, ed. Birgit Meyer and Peter Pels (Stanford, CA: Stanford University Press, 2003), 103–28.

4. Imani Perry has drawn a beautiful parallel between Sun Ra's work and the Veil concept in the work of W. E. B. Du Bois: "Sun Ra, that eccentric jazz master who walked the same blocks, once told us what he wanted to do with the Du Boisian veil, that persistently pitch-perfect metaphor of the color line, the divider not just of the nation but, in Du Bois's estimation, of the world. He wanted to pull aside the veil, to reach to a deeper truth, to see it not as a dividing line but as a portal into something new." Imani Perry, *South to America: A Journey Below the Mason-Dixon to Understand the Soul of a Nation* (New York: Ecco, 2022), 382. See also John Szwed, *Space Is the Place: The Lives and Times of Sun Ra* (Durham, NC: Duke University Press, 2020); William Sites, *Sun Ra's Chicago: Afrofuturism and the City* (Chicago: University of Chicago Press, 2021); W. E. B. Du Bois, "The Princess Steel," *PMLA* 130, no. 3 (2015): 819–29; W. E. B. Du Bois, *Darkwater: Voices from Within the Veil* (1920; Reprint, London: Verso, 2021); and Paul Youngquist, *A Pure Solar World: Sun Ra and the Birth of Afrofuturism* (Austin: University of Texas Press, 2016).

5. Language itself is of course rife with porousness, gaps, and indeterminacies of meanings, just as are perceptual suites and sonic resonances. David Abram writes: "Every attempt to definitively say what language is is subject to a curious limitation. For the only medium with which we can define language is language itself. We are therefore unable to circumscribe the whole of language within our definition. It may be best, then, to leave language undefined, and to thus acknowledge its open-endedness, its mysteriousness. Nevertheless, by paying attention to this mystery we may develop a conscious familiarity with it, a sense of its texture, its habits, its sources of sustenance. [Maurice]

Merleau-Ponty . . . spent much of his life demonstrating that the event of perception unfolds as a reciprocal exchange between the living body and the animate world that surrounds it. He showed, as well, that this exchange, for all its openness and indeterminacy, is nevertheless highly articulate. (Although it confounds the causal logic that we attempt to impose upon it, perceptual experience has its own coherent structure; it seems to embody an open-ended logos that we enact from within rather than the abstract logic we deploy from without.) The disclosure that preverbal perception is already an exchange, and the recognition that this exchange has its own coherence and articulation, together suggested that perception, this ongoing reciprocity, is the very soil and support of that more conscious exchange we call language." So it is also with sonic and other multisensorial suites that are part and parcel of the spiritual soundscapes through which Hannibal and the spirits co-create and interrelate throughout the worlds, on Earth and in spirit. David Abram, *The Spell of the Sensuous: Perception and Language in a More-Than-Human World* (New York: Vintage, 2012), Kindle locator 1392–1400. See also Maurice Merleau-Ponty, *Phenomenology of Perception*, trans. Colin Smith (1945; Reprint, London: Routledge, 1962).

5. THE MUSIC LIBERATION ORCHESTRA IN PRISONS AND SCHOOLS

1. A moving piece about a Music Liberation Orchestra session in Philadelphia, "Music Liberation Orchestra: The First Meeting," by Zenovia Campell (June 10, 2014) can be found on Hannibal's website: https://www.hanniballokumbe.com/music-liberation-orchestra.

CONCLUSION: "PURE MIND HAS NO TIME"

1. For more on the Wovoka Ghost Dance phenomenon and the life of Wovoka, see, Michael Hittman, *Wovoka and the Ghost Dance*, ed. Don Lynch (1990; Reprint, Lincoln: University of Nebraska Press, 1997 [exp. ed.]). For more on Chief Crazy Horse and the Lakota, see Joseph M. Marshall, III, *The Journey of Crazy Horse: A Lakota History* (New York: Penguin, 2005).

2. Others with extraordinary musical gifts have remarked upon similar experiences when they play or create, with the sensation of—or the actuality of—accessing all that existed, exists, or will exist all at once, or traversing great soundscapes while they play or write. For example, Prince said: "When I'm onstage, I'm out of body. That's what the rehearsals, the practicing, the playing is for. You work to a place where you're all out of body. And that's when something happens. You reach a plane of creativity and inspiration. A plane where every song that has ever existed and every song that will exist in the future is right there in front of you. And you just go with it for as long as it takes." Prince, *The Beautiful Ones*, ed. Dan Piepenbring (New York: One World, Random House, 2019), 250 [quoting from a piece published in *Essence*, 2014]. David Bowie also powerfully wrote about the mysteries of time, memory, language, and expression: "Time, one of the most complex expressions / Memory made manifest / It's something that straddles past and future without ever quite being present / Or rather, it at first seems indifferent to the present / There's a tension of a most unfathomable nature / The word desires to be understood, to have meaning / But you somehow feel that it's not you yourself that the word is addressing / It washes over you / Holding a dialogue with something arcane / That's maybe not mortal / And you feel intrigued, captured even / You're aware of a deeper existence / Maybe a temporary reassurance that indeed there is no beginning, no end / And all at once, the outward appearance of meaning is transcended / And you find yourself struggling to comprehend a deep and formidable mystery / All is transient / Does it matter? / Do I bother?" From the first track, spoken, "Time . . . One of the most complex expressions . . ." on a posthumously released soundtrack to a 2022 retrospective cinematic voyage through David Bowie's creative and spiritual life, *Moonage Daydream*, directed by Brett Morgen, https://www.moonagedaydream.film.

3. There is a vast and powerful literature on the suffering and the freedom fighters of Black American women, within music scenes and in society at large. For just a few examples of this broad literature, see Angela Y. Davis, *Blues Legacies and Black Feminism: Gertrude Ma Rainey, Bessie Smith, and Billie Holiday* (New York: Knopf Doubleday, 2011); Angela Y. Davis, *Women, Race, and Class* (New York: Knopf Doubleday, 2011);

Monica Hairston-O'Connell, "Gender, Jazz, and the Popular Front," in *Big Ears: Listening for Gender in Jazz Studies*, ed. Sherrie Tucker and Nichole Rustin (Durham, NC: Duke University Press, 2007), 64–89; Farah Jasmine Griffin, *If You Can't Be Free, Be a Mystery: In Search of Billie Holiday* (New York: One World, 2002); Farah Jasmine Griffin, *Harlem Nocturne: Women Artists and Progressive Politics During World War II* (New York: Civitas, 2013); Etta James and David Ritz, *Rage to Survive: The Etta James Story* (New York: Hachette, 2003); Keisha N. Blain, *Until I Am Free: Fannie Lou Hamer's Enduring Message to America* (Boston: Beacon Press, 2021); Fannie Lou Hamer, *The Speeches of Fannie Lou Hamer: To Tell It Like It Is*, ed. Maegan Parker Brooks and Davis W. Houck (Jackson: University Press of Mississippi, 2013); Saidiya Hartman, *Wayward Lives, Beautiful Experiments: Intimate Histories of Riotous Black Girls, Troublesome Women, and Queer Radicals* (New York: Norton, 2019); Saidiya Hartman, *Lose Your Mother: A Journey Along the Atlantic Slave Route* (New York: Farrar, Straus, and Giroux, 2008); Elizabeth Peréz, *Religion in the Kitchen: Cooking, Talking, and the Making of Black Atlantic Traditions* (New York: NYU Press, 2016); Julia Blackburn, *With Billie: A New Look at the Unforgettable Lady Day* (New York: Vintage, 2006); and Janell Hobson, "Everybody's Protest Song: Music as Social Protest in the Performances of Marian Anderson and Billie Holiday," *Signs* 33, no. 2 (2008): 443–48.

4. Hannibal's sentiments about the maltreatment of Mother Earth and humans' mental and spiritual enslavement that largely blind people to the depth of this violence done to the Earth resonate with those about which Arturo Escobar writes, concerning the Nasa Indigenous movement (Colombia) and its philosophy that humans will only truly be free when the Earth is free: "We are all thrust into the liberation of Mother Earth from whichever place and position we happen to occupy, for as long as Earth is enslaved, as the Nasa argue, so are all living beings." Arturo Escobar, *Pluriversal Politics: The Real and the Possible* (Durham, NC: Duke University Press, 2020), xvii. Marisol de la Cadena and Mario Blaser, in their introduction to *A World of Many Worlds*, also similarly write with great power and force about the violence and epistemic colonialism that occurs in how nature is discussed in much of academic literature or popular consciousness, as a separate or inert or inanimate "thing," as opposed to a vital, dynamic, and more-than-human realm of

interrelation with humans and many other entities: "Environmentalists claim that accelerated extraction destroys nature; investors claim that it develops backward regions. We hold that what is currently being destroyed is also other-than-human persons because what extractivist and environmentalist practices enact as nature may be, also, other than such. This is one of the things we (the editors) have learned from a mountain in the Andes of Peru that is also a being and from forest animals in Paraguay that are also spirit masters of their world. We have also learned that their destruction, perhaps unlike the destruction of nature, is hard for analysts to grasp. Similarly, making public these kinds of other-than-humans is difficult for those who live with them; translating their destruction into a political issue is often impossible and even disempowering. After all, hegemonic opinion is that nature is—publicly—only nature; to think otherwise, to think that mountains or animals are other-than-human persons is a cultural belief." Mario Blaser and Marisol de la Cadena, "Introduction: Pluriverse: Proposals for a World of Many Worlds," in *A World of Many Worlds*, ed. Marisol de la Cadena and Mario Blaser (Durham, NC: Duke University Press, 2018), 2.

THE SHADOW

1. In Hannibal Lokumbe, *The Ripest of My Fruits* (New York: Sunrise Orchestra Music, 1976), 41.

BIBLIOGRAPHY

Abram, David. *The Spell of the Sensuous: Perception and Language in a More-Than-Human World*. New York: Vintage, 2012.

Ake, David. *Jazz Cultures*. Oakland: University of California Press, 2002.

Anderson, Devery S. *Emmett Till: The Murder That Shocked the World and Propelled the Civil Rights Movement*. Jackson: University Press of Mississippi, 2015.

Antomattei, Marc. *Miles: The Companion Guide to the Miles Davis Autobiography*. Raleigh, NC: Marc Antomattei, 2011.

Appiah, Kwame Anthony. *In My Father's House: Africa in the Philosophy of Culture*. New York: Oxford University Press, 1993.

Appiah, Kwame Anthony. *Cosmopolitanism: Ethics in a World of Strangers*. New York: Norton, 2006.

Appiah, Kwame Anthony. *Experiments in Ethics*. Cambridge, MA: Harvard University Press, 2008.

Apter, Andrew. "On African Origins: Creolization and *Connaissance* in Haitian Vodou." *American Ethnologist* 29, no. 2 (2002): 233–60.

Apter, Andrew. *Beyond Words: Discourse and Critical Agency in Africa*. Chicago: University of Chicago Press, 2007.

Armstrong, Louis. *Satchmo: My Life in New Orleans*. 1954. Reprint, Boston: Da Capo, 1986.

Armstrong, Louis. *Louis Armstrong, in His Own Words: Selected Writings*, ed. Thomas Brothers. Oxford: Oxford University Press, 2001.

Bacigalupo, Ana Mariella. *Thunder Shaman: Making History with Mapuche Spirits in Chile and Patagonia*. Austin: University of Texas Press, 2016.

Bailey, Derek. *Improvisation: Its Nature and Practice in Music*. Ashbourne, UK: Moorland Publishing, 1980.

Baker, David. *Jazz Improvisation: A Comprehensive Method of Study for All Players*. Chicago: Maher Publications, 1969.

Balaji, Murali. *The Professor and the Pupil: The Politics and Friendship of W.E.B. Du Bois and Paul Robeson*. New York: Nation, 2019.

Baldwin, James. *The Cross of Redemption: Uncollected Writings*. New York: Vintage, 2010.

Baldwin, James. *The Fire Next Time*. 1963. Reprint, New York: Modern Library, 2021.

Barker, Danny. *A Life in Jazz*. Oxford: Oxford University Press, 1988.

Beckert, Sven. *Empire of Cotton: A Global History*. New York: Knopf Doubleday, 2014.

Benjamin, Ruha. *Captivating Technology: Race, Carceral Technoscience, and Liberatory Imagination in Everyday Life*. Durham, NC: Duke University Press, 2019.

Bennett, Jane. *The Enchantment of Modern Life: Attachments, Crossings, and Ethics*. Princeton, NJ: Princeton University Press, 2016.

Bergerot, Franck. *We Want Miles: Miles Davis*. New York: Rizzoli 2010.

Berliner, Paul F. *Thinking in Jazz: The Infinite Art of Improvisation*. Chicago: University of Chicago Press, 1994.

Berman, Kathleen Cornell. *Birth of the Cool: How Jazz Great Miles Davis Found His Sound*. Essex, MA: Page Street, 2019.

Bindman, David, Suzanne Blier, and Vera Ingrid Grant, ed. *The Art of Jazz: Form/Performance/Notes*. Cambridge, MA: Harvard University Press, 2017.

Black, Steven P. "Creativity and Learning Jazz: The Practice of 'Listening.'" *Mind, Culture, and Activity* 15 (2008): 1–17.

Blackburn, Julia. *With Billie: A New Look at the Unforgettable Lady Day*. New York: Vintage, 2006.

Blain, Keisha N. *Until I Am Free: Fannie Lou Hamer's Enduring Message to America*. Boston: Beacon, 2021.

Blaser, Mario, and Marisol de la Cadena. "Introduction: Pluriverse: Proposals for a World of Many Worlds." In *A World of Many Worlds*, ed. Marisol de la Cadena and Mario Blaser. Durham, NC: Duke University Press, 2018.

Bliek, Rob van der, ed. *The Thelonious Monk Reader*. Oxford: Oxford University Press, 2001.

Bowen, José A. "The History of Remembered Innovation: Tradition and Its Role in the Relationship Between Musical Works and Their Performances." *Journal of Musicology* 11, no. 2 (1993): 139–73.

Bowie, David. *Moonage Daydream: The Life and Times of Ziggy Stardust*. London: Genesis, 2022.

Bowie, David. *Moonage Daydream*. Soundtrack to film. Directed by Brett Morgen. Los Angeles: Rhino Records, 2022.

Bradley, Cisco. *Universal Tonality: The Life and Music of William Parker*. Durham, NC: Duke University Press, 2021.

Brinkley, Douglas. *Rosa Parks: A Life*. London: Penguin, 2005.

Brothers, Thomas. "Solo and Cycle in African-American Jazz." *The Musical Quarterly* 78, no. 3 (1994): 479–509.

Brothers, Thomas. *Louis Armstrong, Master of Modernism*. New York: Norton, 2014.

Brothers, Thomas. *Help! The Beatles, Duke Ellington, and the Magic of Collaboration*. New York: Norton, 2018.

Brown, Leonard, ed. *John Coltrane and Black America's Quest for Freedom: Spirituality and the Music*. London: Oxford University Press, 2010.

Brown, Lloyd L. *The Young Paul Robeson: On My Journey Now*. New York: Basic Books, 1997.

Carby, Hazel V. "On the Threshold of Woman's Era: Lynching, Empire, and Sexuality in Black Feminist Theory." In *"Race," Writing and Difference*, ed. H. L. Gates, Jr., 301–16. Chicago: University of Chicago Press, 1986.

Carby, Hazel V. "It Just Be's That Way Some Time: The Sexual Politics of Women's Blues." In *The Jazz Cadence of American Culture*, ed. Robert O'Meally, 470–83. New York: Columbia University Press, 1998.

Carson, Clayborne. *The Autobiography of Martin Luther King, Jr.* New York: Grand Central, 2001.

Carson, Susan, Stewart Burns, Ralph E. Luker, Martin Luther King, Jr., Penny A. Russell, Clayborne Carson, and Pete Holloran. *The Papers of Martin Luther King, Jr., Volume III: Birth of a New Age*. Oakland: University of California Press, 1992.

Carson, Susan, Martin Luther King, Jr., Peter Holloran, Penny A. Russell, Tenisha Hart Armstrong, Clayborne Carson, Stewart Burns, and Luker E. Ralph. *The Papers of Martin Luther King, Jr., Volume V: Threshold of a New Decade*. Oakland: University of California Press, 1992.

Carson, Susan, Martin Luther King, Jr., Ralph E. Luker, Penny A. Russell, Stewart Burns, Clayborne Carson, and Peter Holloran. *The Papers of Martin Luther King, Jr., Volume IV: Symbol of the Movement*. Oakland: University of California Press, 1992.

Carson, Clayborne, Ralph E. Luker, Peter Holloran, Martin Luther King, Jr., and Penny A. Russell. *The Papers of Martin Luther King, Jr., Volume VII: To Save the Soul of America*. Oakland: University of California Press, 1992.

Carson, Clayborne, Penny A. Russell, Ralph E. Luker, Pete Holloran, and Martin Luther King, Jr. *The Papers of Martin Luther King, Jr., Volume II: Rediscovering Precious Values*. Oakland: University of California Press, 1992.

Casanova, José. *Public Religions in the Modern World*. Chicago: University of Chicago Press, 1993.

Cassidy, Donna M. *Painting the Musical City: Jazz and Cultural Identity in American Art, 1910–1940*. Washington, DC: Smithsonian Institution Press, 1997.

Castor, N. Fadeke. *Spiritual Citizenship: Transnational Pathways from Black Power to Ifá in Trinidad*. Durham, NC: Duke University Press, 2017.

Cerra, Steven. "Gil Evans: The Arranger as Re-composer—Part 1 & 2." Jazz Profiles. May 10, 2011. https://jazzprofiles.blogspot.com/2017/10/gil-evans-arranger-as-re-composer-parts.html.

Césaire, Aimé. *Discourse on Colonialism*, trans. Joan Pinkham. 1955. Reprint, New York: Monthly Review Press, 2000.

Chakrabarty, Dipesh. *Provincializing Europe: Postcolonial Thought and Historical Difference*. Princeton, NJ: Princeton University Press, 2000.

Chambers, Leland H. "Improvising and Mythmaking in Eudora Welty's 'Powerhouse.'" In *Representing Jazz*, ed. Krin Gabbard, 54–69. Durham, NC: Duke University Press, 1995.

Chevigny, Paul. *Gigs: Jazz and the Cabaret Laws in New York City*. New York: Routledge, 1991.

Clarke, Kamari Maxine. *Mapping Yoruba Networks: Power and Agency in the Making of Transnational Communities*. Durham, NC: Duke University Press, 2004.

Clarke, Kamari Maxine. *Affective Justice: The International Criminal Court and the Pan-Africanist Pushback*. Durham, NC: Duke University Press, 2019.

Clay, Adrienne, Susan Carson, Penny A. Russell, Martin Luther King, Jr., Louis R. Harlan, Dana L. H. Powell, Peter Holloran, Tenisha Armstrong,

Clayborne Carson, Stewart Burns, and Ralph E. Luker. *The Papers of Martin Luther King, Jr., Volume I: Called to Serve.* Oakland: University of California Press, 1992.

Cohen, Leonard. *Stranger Music: Selected Poems and Songs.* New York: Vintage, 1994.

Cole, Teju. *Black Paper: Writing in a Dark Time.* Chicago: University of Chicago Press, 2021.

Collier, James Lincoln. *Louis Armstrong: An American Genius.* Oxford: Oxford University Press, 1985.

Collins, Edmund John. "Jazz Feedback to Africa." *American Music* 5 (1987): 176–93.

Cook, Richard. *It's About That Time: Miles Davis On and Off Record.* Oxford: Oxford University Press, 2007.

Cooke, Mervyn. "Jazz Among the Classics, and the Case of Duke Ellington." In *The Cambridge Companion to Jazz*, ed. Mervyn Cooke and David Horn, 153–73. Cambridge: Cambridge University Press, 2003.

Cooke, Mervyn, and David Horn, eds. *The Cambridge Companion to Jazz.* Cambridge: Cambridge University Press, 2003.

Corbett, John. *Microgroove: Forays into Other Music.* Durham, NC: Duke University Press, 2015.

Corbett, John. *A Listener's Guide to Free Improvisation.* Chicago: University of Chicago Press, 2016.

Costin, Cathy Lynne, and Michael C. Ennis-McMillan. "Creativity and Innovation: Anthropological Perspectives." *Open Anthropology* 9, no. 2 (2021).

Cox, Aimee Meredith. "In the Dunham Way: Sewing (Sowing) the Seams of Dance, Anthropology, and Youth Arts Activism." In *Katherine Dunham: Recovering an Anthropological Legacy, Choreographing Ethnographic Futures*, ed. Elizabeth Chin, 127–44. Santa Fe, NM: SAR Press, 2015.

Cox, Aimee Meredith. *Shapeshifters: Black Girls and the Choreography of Citizenship.* Durham, NC: Duke University Press, 2015.

Coyle Rosen, Lauren. *Fires of Gold: Law, Spirit, and Sacrificial Labor in Ghana.* Berkeley: University of California Press, 2020.

Coyle Rosen, Lauren. *At the Altar of the Winds (Smokeless Mirrors, Vol. 1).* Washington, DC: Seven Lighthouses, 2023.

Coyle Rosen, Lauren. *A Thousand Lit Streams (Smokeless Mirrors, Vol. 2).* Washington, DC: Seven Lighthouses, 2023.

Coyle Rosen, Lauren. *Storms of Silent Wings (Smokeless Mirrors, Vol. 3)*. Washington, DC: Seven Lighthouses, 2023.

Coyle Rosen, Lauren. *Sky Ensouled (Prisms, Vol. 1)*. Washington, DC: Seven Lighthouses, 2023.

Coyle Rosen, Lauren. *Seven Tones of Time (Prisms, Vol. 2)*. Washington, DC: Seven Lighthouses, 2023.

Coyle Rosen, Lauren. *Veils of Apollo (Prisms, Vol. 3)*. Washington, DC: Seven Lighthouses, 2024.

Coyle Rosen, Lauren. *Law in Light: Priestesses, Priests, and the Revitalization of Akan Spirituality in the United States and Ghana*. Berkeley: University of California Press, 2024.

Crapanzano, Vincent. *Imaginative Horizons: An Essay in Literary-Philosophical Anthropology*. Chicago: University of Chicago Press, 2010.

Crosson, J. Brent. *Experiments with Power: Obeah and the Remaking of Religion in Trinidad*. Chicago: University of Chicago Press, 2020.

Crouch, Stanley. *Kansas City Lighting: The Rise and Times of Charlie Parker*. New York: Harper, 2013.

Dance, Helen Oakley. *Stormy Monday: The T-Bone Walker Story*. Baton Rouge: Louisiana State University Press, 1987.

Dance, Stanley. *The World of Duke Ellington*. Boston: Da Capo, 2000.

Daniel, Yvonne. *Dancing Wisdom: Embodied Knowledge in Haitian Vodou, Cuban Yoruba, and Bahian Candomblé*. Champaign: University of Illinois Press, 2005.

Das, Joanna Dee. *Katherine Dunham: Dance and the African Diaspora*. New York: Oxford University Press, 2017.

Davis, Angela Y. *Blues Legacies and Black Feminism: Gertrude Ma Rainey, Bessie Smith, and Billie Holiday*. New York: Knopf Doubleday, 2011.

Davis, Angela Y. *Women, Race, & Class*. New York: Knopf Doubleday, 2011.

Davis, Miles, with Quincy Troupe. *Miles: The Autobiography*. New York: Simon & Schuster, 1989.

Davis, Thulani. *The Emancipation Circuit: Black Activism Forging a Culture of Freedom*. Durham, NC: Duke University Press, 2022.

Dawdy, Shannon Lee. *American Afterlives: Reinventing Death in the Twenty-First Century*. Princeton, NJ: Princeton University Press, 2021.

de la Cadena, Marisol. "Indigenous Cosmopolitics in the Andes: Conceptual Reflections Beyond 'Politics.'" *Cultural Anthropology* 25, no. 2 (2010): 334–70.

de la Cadena, Marisol. *Earth Beings: Ecologies of Practice Across Andean Worlds*. Durham, NC: Duke University Press, 2015.

Dean, Roger T. *New Structures in Jazz and Improvised Music Since 1960*. Milton Keynes, UK: Open University Press, 1992.

Deren, Maya. *Divine Horsemen: The Living Gods of Haiti*. Kingston, NY: McPherson, 1983.

Despret, Vinciane. *Our Grateful Dead: Stories of Those Left Behind*, trans. Stephen Muecke. Minneapolis: University of Minnesota Press, 2021.

DeVito, Chris. *Coltrane on Coltrane: The John Coltrane Interviews*. Chicago: Chicago Review Press, 2012.

Di Franco, Ani, and Lauren Coyle Rosen. *The Spirit of Ani*. Manuscript on file with authors.

Douglas, Tony. *Jackie Wilson: Lonely Teardrops*. Oxfordshire, UK: Taylor & Francis, 2016.

Drabinski, John. *Glissant and the Middle Passage: Philosophy, Beginning, Abyss*. Minneapolis: University of Minnesota Press, 2019.

Du Bois, W. E. B. *The World and Africa, and Color and Democracy*, ed. Henry Louis Gates, Jr. Oxford: Oxford University Press, 2007.

Du Bois, W. E. B. "The Princess Steel." *PMLA* 130, no. 3 (2015): 819–29.

Du Bois, W. E. B. *Darkwater: Voices from Within the Veil*. 1920. Reprint, London: Verso. 2021.

Dubois, Laurent. "The Citizen's Trance: The Haitian Revolution and the Motor of History." In *Magic and Modernity: Interfaces of Revelation and Concealment*, ed. Birgit Meyer and Peter Pels, 103–28. Stanford, CA: Stanford University Press, 2003.

Dubois, Laurent. *A Colony of Citizens: Revolution and Slave Emancipation in the French Caribbean, 1787–1804*. Chapel Hill: University of North Carolina Press, 2004.

Dubois, Laurent. *Haiti: The Aftershocks of History*. New York: Metropolitan, 2012.

Dubois, Laurent, and Richard Lee Turtis. *Freedom Roots: Histories from the Caribbean*. Chapel Hill: University of North Carolina Press, 2019.

Dunham, Katherine. *Island Possessed*. 1969. Reprint, New York: Doubleday, 2012.

Dunham, Katherine. *Journey to Accompong*. 1946. Reprint, Whitefish, MT: Literary Licensing, 2013.

Duranti, Alessandro, and Kenny Burrell. "Jazz Improvisation: A Search for Hidden Harmonies and a Unique Self." *Richerche di Psiocologia* 3 (2004): 71–101.

Duranti, Alessandro, and Nicco A. La Mattina. "The Semiotics of Cooperation." *Annual Review of Anthropology* 51 (2022): 85–101.

Duranti, Alessandro, Jason Throop, and Matthew McCoy. "Jazz Etiquette: Between Aesthetics and Ethics." In *The Oxford Handbook of the Phenomenology of Music Cultures*, ed. Harris M. Berger, Friedlind Riedel, and David VanderHamm. New York: Oxford University Press, 2018.

Edwards, Brent Hayes. *The Practice of Diaspora: Literature, Translation, and the Rise of Black Internationalism*. Cambridge, MA: Harvard University Press, 2003.

Edwards, Brent Hayes. *Epistrophies: Jazz and the Literary Imagination*. Cambridge, MA: Harvard University Press, 2017.

Eidsheim, Nina Sun. *Sensing Sound: Singing and Listening as Vibrational Practice*. Durham, NC: Duke University Press, 2015.

Eidsheim, Nina Sun. *The Race of Sound: Listening, Timbre, and Vocality in African American Music*. Durham, NC: Duke University Press, 2019.

Ellison, Ralph. *The Collected Essays of Ralph Ellison*. New York: Random House, 1995.

Ellison, Ralph. *Living with Music: Ralph Ellison's Jazz Writings*, ed. Robert O'Meally. New York: Modern Library, 2002.

Engelke, Matthew. *A Problem of Presence: Beyond Scripture in an African Church*. Berkeley: University of California Press, 2007.

Epstein, Dena J. *Sinful Tunes and Spirituals*. Champaign: University of Illinois Press, 1977.

Escobar, Arturo. *Designs for the Pluriverse: Radical Interdependence, Autonomy, and the Making of Worlds*. Durham, NC: Duke University Press, 2018.

Escobar, Arturo. *Pluriversal Politics: The Real and the Possible*. Durham, NC: Duke University Press, 2020.

Etinde-Crompton, Charlotte, and Samuel Willard Crompton. *Miles Davis: Jazz Musician and Composer*. Berkeley Heights, NJ: Enslow, 2019.

Evers, Medgar Wiley. *The Autobiography of Medgar Evers: A Hero's Life and Legacy Revealed Through His Writings, Letters, and Speeches*, ed. Myrlie Evers-Williams and Manning Marable. New York: Civitas, 2006.

Ewell, Philip. "Music Theory and the White Racial Frame." *Music Theory Online* 26, no. 2 (2020): 324–29.

Ewell, Philip. *On Music Theory, and Making Music More Welcoming for Everyone*. Ann Arbor: University of Michigan Press, 2023.

Feld, Steven. *Sound and Sentiment: Birds, Weeping, Poetics, and Song in Kaluli Expression*. 1982. Reprint, Durham, NC: Duke University Press, 1982.

Feld, Steven. "Waterfalls of Song: An Acoustemology of Place Resounding in Bosavi, Papua New Guinea." In *Senses of Place*, ed. Steven Feld and Keith Basso, 91–135. Santa Fe, NM: School of American Research Press, 1996.

Feld, Steven. "A Sweet Lullaby for World Music." *Public Culture* 12, no. 1 (2000): 145–71.

Feld, Steven. *Jazz Cosmopolitanism in Accra: Five Musical Years in Ghana*. Durham, NC: Duke University Press, 2012.

Feld, Steven, and Keith H. Basso, eds. *Senses of Place*. Santa Fe, NM: School for Advanced Research Press, 1996.

Fils, Nicolas. *Don Cherry: Le Petit Prince du Free*. Marseille, France: Mot et le Reste, 2023.

Fischlin, Daniel, and Eric Porter, eds. *Sound Changes: Improvisation and Transcultural Difference*. Ann Arbor: University of Michigan Press, 2021.

Foner, Eric. *Reconstruction Updated Edition: America's Unfinished Revolution, 1863–1877*. New York: Harper Perennial Modern Classics, 2014.

Futorian, Melanie. "Miles Evans: Two-Part Harmony." All About Jazz. August 9, 2012. http://www.allaboutjazz.com/php/article.php?id=42498&pg=1.

Gabbard, Krin, ed. *Jazz Among the Discourses*. Durham, NC: Duke University Press, 1995.

Gabbard, Krin, ed. *Representing Jazz*. Durham, NC: Duke University Press, 1995.

Gabbard, Krin. "The Word Jazz." In *The Cambridge Companion to Jazz*, ed. Mervyn Cooke and David Horn, 1–6. Cambridge: Cambridge University Press, 2003.

Gardner, Thomas, and Salomé Voegelin. "Editorial: Historical Continuum, Mimetic Fissures." *Organised Sound* 20, no. 2 (2015): 141–47.

Gerard, Charley. *Jazz in Black and White: Race, Culture, and Identity in the Jazz Community*. Westport, CT: Praeger, 1998.

Gibran, Kahlil. *The Prophet*. New York: Alfred A. Knopf, 1923.

Giddins, Gary. *Satchmo: The Genius of Louis Armstrong*. New York: Hachette, 2009.

Giddins, Gary. *Celebrating Bird: The Triumph of Charlie Parker*. Minneapolis: University of Minnesota Press, 2013.

Gillespie, Dizzy, with Al Fraser. *Dizzy: To Be or Not to Bop: The Autobiography of Dizzy Gillespie*. London: Quartet, 1982.

Gilroy, Paul. *The Black Atlantic: Modernity and Double Consciousness*. London: Verso, 1993.

Gilroy, Paul. *After Empire: Multiculture or Postcolonial Melancholia*. London: Routledge, 2004.

Gilroy, Paul. *Postcolonial Melancholia*. New York: Columbia University Press, 2005.

Glaude, Jr., Eddie S. *Begin Again: James Baldwin's America and Its Urgent Lessons for Our Own*. New York: Crown, 2020.

Globus, Gordon G. "Some Philosophical Implications of Dream Existence." *Anthropology of Consciousness* 5, no. 3 (1994): 24–27.

Golia, Maria. *Ornette Coleman: The Territory and the Adventure*. London: Reaktion, 2020.

Gonzalez, John Henry. *Maroon Nation: A History of Revolutionary Haiti*. New Haven, CT: Yale University Press, 2019.

Goodman, Jordan. *Paul Robeson: A Watched Man*. London: Verso, 2013.

Gorn, Elliott J. *Let the People See: The Story of Emmett Till*. Oxford: Oxford University Press, 2018.

Gourse, Leslie. *Dizzy Gillespie and the Birth of Bebop*. New York: Atheneum, 1995.

Gourse, Leslie. *Straight, No Chaser: The Life and Genius of Thelonious Monk*. New York: Schirmer Books, 1997.

Govenar, Alan. *Lightnin' Hopkins: His Life and Blues*. Chicago: Chicago Review Press, 2010.

Greene, Paul D., and Thomas Porcello, eds. *Wired for Sound: Engineering and Technologies in Sonic Cultures*. Middletown, CT: Wesleyan University Press, 2004.

Griffin, Farah Jasmine. *If You Can't Be Free, Be a Mystery: In Search of Billie Holiday*. New York: One World, 2002.

Griffin, Farah Jasmine. *Harlem Nocturne: Women Artists and Progressive Politics During World War II*. New York: Civitas, 2013.

Griffin, Farah Jasmine. *Read Until You Understand: The Profound Wisdom of Black Life and Literature*. New York: Norton, 2021.

Gwin, Minrose C. *Remembering Medgar Evers: Writing the Long Civil Rights Movement*. Athens: University of Georgia Press, 2013.

Haddix, Chuck. *Bird: The Life and Music of Charlie Parker*. Champaign: University of Illinois Press, 2013.

Hairston-O'Connell, Monica. "Gender, Jazz, and the Popular Front." In *Big Ears: Listening for Gender in Jazz Studies*, ed. Sherrie Tucker and Nichole Rustin, 64–89. Durham, NC: Duke University Press, 2007.

Hajdu, David. "The Gorgeous, Quirky, Uncategorizable Music of Gil Evans." *The New Republic*. October 1, 2010. http://www.newrepublic.com/blog/the-famous-door/78088/the-gorgeous-quirky-uncategorizable-music-gil-evans#.

Hamer, Fannie Lou. *The Speeches of Fannie Lou Hamer: To Tell It Like It Is*, ed. Maegan Parker Brooks and Davis W. Houck. Jackson: University Press of Mississippi, 2013.

Hartman, Saidiya. *Scenes of Subjection: Terror, Slavery, and Self-Making in Nineteenth-Century America*. New York: Oxford University Press, 1997.

Hartman, Saidiya. "The Time of Slavery," *South Atlantic Quarterly* 101, no. 4 (2002): 757–77.

Hartman, Saidiya. *Lose Your Mother: A Journey Along the Atlantic Slave Route*. New York: Farrar, Straus, and Giroux, 2008.

Hartman, Saidiya. *Wayward Lives, Beautiful Experiments: Intimate Histories of Riotous Black Girls, Troublesome Women, and Queer Radicals*. New York: Norton, 2019.

Heble, Ajay. *Landing on the Wrong Note: Jazz, Dissonance, and Critical Practice*. New York: Routledge, 2000.

Heble, Ajay, and Daniel Fischlin, eds. *The Other Side of Nowhere: Jazz, Improvisation, and Communities in Dialogue*. Middletown, CT: Wesleyan University Press, 2004.

Helmrich, Stefan. "An Anthropologist under Water: Immersive Soundscapes, Submarine Cyborgs, and Transductive Ethnography." *American Anthropologist* 34, no. 4 (2007): 621–41.

Heo, Angie. "The Divine Touchability of Dreams." In *Sensational Religion: Sensory Cultures in Material Practice*, ed. Sally M. Promey, 435–40. New Haven, CT: Yale University Press, 2014.

Hicock, Larry. *Castles Made of Sound: The Story of Gil Evans*. London: Hachette, 2002.

Hirschkind, Charles. *The Ethical Soundscape: Cassette Sermons and Islamic Counterpublics*. New York: Columbia University Press, 2006.

Hirschkind, Charles. *The Feeling of History: Islam, Romanticism, and Andalusia*. Chicago: University of Chicago Press, 2020.

Hirschkind, Charles, Maria José de Abreu, and Carlo Caduff. "New Media, New Publics? An Introduction to Supplement 15," *Current Anthropology* 58, no. S15 (2017): S3–S12.

Hittman, Michael. *Wavoka and the Ghost Dance*, ed. Don Lynch, 1990. Lincoln: University of Nebraska Press, 1997 (expanded edition).

Hobson, Janell. "Everybody's Protest Song: Music as Social Protest in the Performances of Marian Anderson and Billie Holiday," *Signs* 33, no. 2 (2008): 443–48.

Holiday, Billie. *Lady Sings the Blues*. New York: Crown, 2006.

Holiday, Billie. *Billie Holiday: The Last Interview: and Other Conversations*. New York: Melville House, 2019.

Hord, Fred Lee, and Jonathan Scott Lee, eds. *I Am Because We Are: Readings in Africana Philosophy*. Amherst: University of Massachusetts Press, 2016.

Horne, Gerald. *Paul Robeson: The Artist as Revolutionary*. London: Pluto, 2016.

Howes, David, ed. *The Varieties of Sensory Experience: A Sourcebook in the Anthropology of the Sense*. Toronto, Canada: University of Toronto Press, 1991.

Hurston, Zora Neale. *Tell My Horse: Voodoo and Life in Haiti and Jamaica*. New York: Harper Collins, 2008.

Iyer, Vijay. "Improvisation, Action Understanding, and Music Cognition with and Without Bodies." In *The Oxford Handbook of Critical Improvisation Studies*, ed. George E. Lewis and Benjamin Piekut, 74–90. New York: Oxford University Press, 2014.

Iyer, Vijay. "Beneath Improvisation." In *The Oxford Handbook of Critical Concepts in Music Theory*, ed. Alexander Rehding and Steven Rings. New York: Oxford University Press, 2019.

Jackson, Travis. "Jazz Performance as Ritual: The Blues Aesthetic and the African Diaspora." In *The African Diaspora: A Musical Perspective*, ed. Ingrid Monson, 21–82. New York: Routledge, 2003.

Jackson, Travis. *Blowin' the Blues Away: Performance and Meaning on the New York Jazz Scene*. Oakland: University of California Press, 2012.

Jaji, Tsitsi Ella. *Africa in Stereo: Modernism, Music, and Pan-African Solidarity*. New York: Oxford University Press, 2014.

James, Etta, and David Ritz. *Rage to Survive: The Etta James Story*. New York: Hachette, 2003.

Jarvis, Jeff. "The Improvised Jazz Solo: An Endangered Species." *Jazz Educators Journal* 22, no. 4 (Spring 1990): 70–74.

Johnson, Bruce. "Hear Me Talkin' To Ya: Problems of Jazz Discourse." *Popular Music* 12, no. 1 (January 1993): 1–12.

Johnson, Bruce. "Resituating Improvisation." *Journal of Improvisational Practice* 2, no. 1 (1996): 6–11.

Johnson, Paul Christopher. *Diaspora Conversions: Black Carib Religion and the Recovery of Africa*. Berkley: University of California Press, 2007.

Johnson, Walter. *River of Dark Dreams: Slavery and Empire in the Cotton Kingdom*. Cambridge, MA: Harvard University Press, 2013.

José de Abreu, Maria. *The Charismatic Gymnasium: Breath, Media, and Religious Revivalism in Contemporary Brazil*. Durham, NC: Duke University Press, 2021.

Kahn, Ashley. *A Love Supreme: The Story of John Coltrane's Signature Album*. New York: Penguin, 2003.

Kandell, Leslie. "On the Towns: Music; How the Voices of One Continent Influenced the Culture of Another." *New York Times*. November 8, 1998. https://www.nytimes.com/1998/11/08/nyregion/towns-music-voices-one-continent-influenced-culture-another.html.

Kandinsky, Wassily. *Concerning the Spiritual in Art*, trans. M. T. H. Sadler. Mineola, NY: Dover Publications, 1977.

Keane, Webb. *Ethical Life: Its Natural and Social Histories*. Princeton, NJ: Princeton University Press, 2016.

Kelley, Robin D. G. *Freedom Dreams: The Black Radical Imagination*. Boston: Beacon, 2002.

Kelley, Robin D. G. *Thelonious Monk: The Life and Times of an American Original*. New York: Free Press, 2009.

Kelley, Robin D. G., Lenny White, Greg Tate, and Clark Terry. *Miles Davis: The Complete Illustrated History*. Beverly, MA: Voyageur Press, 2012.

Kennedy, Randall. "Martin Luther King's Constitution: A Legal History of the Montgomery Bus Boycott." *The Yale Law Journal* 98, no. 6 (1989): 999–1067.

King, Jr., Martin Luther. *The Trumpet of Conscience.* New York: Harper & Row, 1968.
King, Jr., Martin Luther. *Strength to Love.* Glasgow, UK: Fontana, 1969.
King, Jr., Martin Luther. *A Call to Conscience: The Landmark Speeches of Dr. Martin Luther King, Jr.* New York: Grand Central, 2002.
King, Jr., Martin Luther. *I Have a Dream: Writings and Speeches That Changed the World, Special 75th Anniversary Edition.* San Francisco: HarperOne, 2003.
King, Jr., Martin Luther. *Stride Toward Freedom; The Montgomery Story.* Boston: Beacon Press, 2010.
King, Jr., Martin Luther. *Martin Luther King, Jr.: The Last Interview: And Other Conversations.* New York: Melville House, 2017.
King Jr., Martin Luther, and Vincent Harding. *Where Do We Go from Here: Chaos or Community?* Boston: Beacon Press, 2010.
Klima, Alan. *Ethnography #9.* Durham, NC: Duke University Press, 2019.
Kohn, Eduardo. *How Forests Think: Toward an Anthropology Beyond the Human.* Berkeley: University of California Press, 2013.
Kolin, Philip C. "Haunting America: Emmett Till in Music and Song." *Southern Cultures* 15, no. 3 (2009): 115–38.
Kruth, John. *Bright Moments: The Life and Legacy of Rahsaan Roland Kirk.* New York: Welcome Rain, 2000.
Lajoie, Steve. *Gil Evans & Miles Davis: Historic Collaborations: An Analysis of Selected Gil Evans Works, 1957–1962.* Mainz, Germany: Advance Music, 2003.
Larson, Kate Clifford. *Walk with Me: A Biography of Fannie Lou Hamer.* Oxford: Oxford University Press, 2021.
Lennon, John. *In His Own Write.* 1964. Reprint, New York: Simon & Schuster, 2010.
Lennon, John. *Skywriting by Word of Mouth.* 1986. Reprint, New York: It Books, 2010.
Lewis, George E. *A Power Stronger Than Itself: The AACM and American Experimental Music.* Chicago: University of Chicago Press, 2009.
Lewis, George E., and Benjamin Piekut, eds. *The Oxford Handbook of Critical Improvisation Studies, Volume 1.* Oxford: Oxford University Press, 2016.
Lewis, George E., and Benjamin Piekut, eds. *The Oxford Handbook of Critical Improvisation Studies, Volume 2.* Oxford: Oxford University Press, 2016.
Lieb, Sandra R. *Mother of the Blues: A Study of Ma Rainey.* Amherst, MA: University of Massachusetts Press, 1983.

Lokumbe, Hannibal (under his former name, Marvin Peterson). *The Ripest of My Fruits*. New York: Sunrise Orchestra Music, 1976.

Lokumbe, Hannibal. *Love Poems to God*. New Orleans, LA: Hannibal Lokumbe Music, 2002.

Lokumbe, Hannibal. *Trilogy: Freedom Dance Cycle*. Smithville, TX: Hannibal Lokumbe Music, 2014.

Maggin, Donald L. *Dizzy: The Life and Times of John Birks Gillespie*. New York: HarperCollins, 2006.

Maher Jr., Paul, and Michael K. Dorr, eds. *Miles on Miles: Interviews and Encounters with Miles Davis*. New York: Lawrence Hill, 2008.

Mandel, Howard. *Miles, Ornette, Cecil: Jazz Beyond Jazz*. New York: Routledge, 2010.

Margry, Peter Jan, and Daniel Wojcik. "A Saxophone Divine: The Transformative Power of Saint John Coltrane's Jazz Music in San Francisco's Fillmore District." In *Spiritualizing the City: Agency and Resilience of the Urban and Urbanesque Habitat*, ed. V. Hegner and P. J. Margry, 169–94. Oxfordshire, UK: Routledge, 2017.

Marshall, III, Joseph M. *The Journey of Crazy Horse: A Lakota History*. New York: Penguin, 2005.

Martin, Henry. *Charlie Parker, Composer*. New York: Oxford University Press, 2020.

McAllister, Carlota. "No One Can Hold It Back: The Theopolitics of Water and Life in Chilean Patagonia Without Dams." *Social Analysis* 64, no. 4 (2020): 121–39.

McAllister, Carlota, and Valentina Napolitano. "Incarnate Politics Beyond the Cross and the Sword." *Social Analysis* 64, no. 4 (2020): 1–20.

McAllister, Carlota, and Valentina Napolitano. "Political Theology/Theopolitics: The Thresholds and Vulnerabilities of Sovereignty." *Annual Review of Anthropology* 50 (2021): 7.1–7.16.

Meintjes, Louise. *Sound of Africa!: Making Music Zulu in a South African Studio*. Durham, NC: Duke University Press, 2003.

Meintjes, Louise. *Dust of the Zulu: Ngoma Aesthetics After Apartheid*. Durham, NC: Duke University Press, 2017.

Meintjes, Louise. "Hi-Fi Sociality, Lo-Fi Sound: Affect and Precarity in an Independent South African Recording Studio." In *State and Culture in Postcolonial Africa: Enchantings*, ed. Tejumola Olaniyan, 207–23. Bloomington: Indiana University Press, 2017.

Merleau-Ponty, Maurice. *Phenomenology of Perception*, trans. Colin Smith. 1945. Reprinted, London: Routledge, 1962.

Mittermaier, Amira. "The Book of Visions: Dreams, Poetry, and Prophecy in Contemporary Egypt." *International Journal of Middle East Studies* 39, no. 2 (2007): 229–47.

Mollin, David, and Salomé Voegelin. "During the Night the Crops Will Still Grow (Unless the Player Sleeps)." *Journal of Interdisciplinary Voice Studies* 1, no. 1 (2016): 85–93.

Monson, Ingrid. "Doubleness and Jazz Improvisation: Irony, Parody, and Ethnomusicology." *Critical Inquiry* 20, no. 2 (1994): 283–313.

Monson, Ingrid. *Saying Something: Jazz Improvisation and Interaction*. Chicago: University of Chicago Press, 1996.

Morris, Rosalind. "The Ancestors Call from the Future: Genealogy, Ancestrality, Judgment." *Comparative Literature Studies* 60, no. 1 (2023): 31–72.

Morrison, Toni. "Foreword." In *The Harlem Book of the Dead*. James Van Der Zee, Owen Dodson, and Camille Billops. Dobbs Ferry, NY: Morgan & Morgan, 1978.

Moten, Fred. *In the Break: The Aesthetics of the Black Radical Tradition*. Minneapolis: University of Minnesota Press, 2003.

Moten, Fred. *Black and Blur (Consent Not to Be a Single Being)*. Durham, NC: Duke University Press, 2017.

Napolitano, Valentina. "On the Touch-Event: Theopolitical Encounters." *Social Analysis* 64, no. 4 (2020): 81–99.

Neal, Mark Anthony. *Songs in the Key of Black Life: A Rhythm and Blues Nation*. New York: Routledge, 2003.

Neal, Mark Anthony. *Black Ephemera: The Crisis and Challenge of the Musical Archive*. New York: NYU Press, 2022.

Nettl, Bruno. "Thoughts on Improvisation." *The Musical Quarterly* 60, no. 1 (1974): 1–19.

Nettl, Bruno, and Melinda Russell, eds. *In the Course of Performance: Studies in the World of Musical Improvisation*. Chicago: University of Chicago Press, 1998.

Nevader, Arun. "John Coltrane: Music and Metaphysics." *The Threepenny Review*, no. 10 (1982): 26–27.

O'Brien, Timothy J. *Sam Lightnin' Hopkins: Houston Bluesman, 1912–1960*. Houston: University of Houston Press, 2006.

O'Brien, Timothy J., and David Ensminger. *Mojo Hand: The Life and Music of Lightnin' Hopkins*. Austin: University of Texas Press, 2013.

Ochoa Gautier, Ana M. *Aurality: Listening and Knowledge in Nineteenth-Century Colombia*. Durham, NC: Duke University Press, 2014.

Ogren, Kathy. *The Jazz Revolution: Twenties America and the Meaning of Jazz*. Oxford: Oxford University Press, 1989.

Olaniyan, Tejumola, and Ato Quayson, eds. *African Literature: An Anthology of Criticism and Theory*. Malden, MA: Blackwell, 2007.

Olaniyan, Tejumola, and James H. Sweet, eds. *The African Diaspora and the Disciplines*. Bloomington: Indiana University Press, 2010.

O'Meally, Robert, ed. *The Jazz Cadence of American Culture*. New York: Columbia University Press, 1998.

Palmié, Stephan. "Africanisms." *African Diaspora* 11 (2018): 17–34.

Patterson, Orlando. *Slavery and Social Death: A Comparative Study*. Cambridge, MA: Harvard University Press, 2018.

Peréz, Elizabeth. *Religion in the Kitchen: Cooking, Talking, and the Making of Black Atlantic Traditions*. New York: NYU Press, 2016.

Perry, Imani. *South to America: A Journey Below the Mason-Dixon to Understand the Soul of a Nation*. New York: Ecco, 2022.

Picker, John M. *Victorian Soundscapes*. Oxford: Oxford University Press, 2003.

Porcello, Thomas, Louise Meintjes, Ana Maria Ochoa, and David W. Samuels. "The Reorganization of the Sensory World." *Annual Review of Anthropology* 39 (2010): 51–66.

Porter, Eric. *What Is This Thing Called Jazz?: African American Musicians as Artists, Critics, and Activists*. Oakland: University of California Press, 2002.

Powell, Richard J. *Circle Dance: The Art of John T. Scott*. Jackson: University Press of Mississippi, 2005.

Pressing, Jeff. "Improvisation: Methods and Models." In *Generative Processes in Music: The Psychology of Performance, Improvisation, and Composition*, ed. John Sloboda, 129–78. Oxford: Oxford University Press, 1987.

Prince. *The Beautiful Ones*, ed. Dan Piepenbring. New York: One World, Random House, 2019.

Puett, Michael. "Ritual Disjunctions: Ghosts, Anthropology, and Philosophy." In *The Ground Between: Anthropologists Engage Philosophy*, ed. Veena Das, Michael Jackson, Arthur Kleinman, and Bhrigupati Singh, 218–33. Durham, NC: Duke University Press, 2014.

Puett, Michael, and Christine Gross-Loh. *The Path: What Chinese Philosophers Can Teach Us About the Good Life*. New York: Simon & Schuster, 2016.

Quayson, Ato. *Tragedy and Postcolonial Literature*. Cambridge: Cambridge University Press, 2021.

Raboteau, Albert J. *A Fire in the Bones: Reflections on African-American Religious History*. Boston: Beacon, 1996.

Raboteau, Albert J. *Canaan Land: A Religious History of African Americans*. Oxford: Oxford University Press, 2001.

Raboteau, Albert J. *Slave Religion: The "Invisible Institution" in the Antebellum South*. Oxford: Oxford University Press, 2004.

Radano, Ronald M. *Lying Up a Nation: Race and Black Music*. Chicago: University of Chicago Press, 2003.

Radano, Ronald M., and Philip V. Bohlman, eds. *Music and the Racial Imagination*. Chicago: University of Chicago Press, 2001.

Radano, Ronald, and Tejumola Olaniyan, eds. *Audible Empire: Music, Global Politics, Critique*. Durham, NC: Duke University Press, 2016.

Ramsey, Jr., Guthrie P. *Race Music: Black Cultures from Bebop to Hip-Hop*. Berkley: University of California Press, 2004.

Ramsey, Jr., Guthrie P. *The Amazing Bud Powell: Black Genius, Jazz History, and the Challenge of Bebop*. Berkeley: University of California Press, 2013.

Ramsey, Kate. *The Spirits and the Law: Vodou and Power in Haiti*. Chicago: University of Chicago Press, 2011.

Ramsey, Kate. "Vodou, History, and New Narratives." *Transition* 111 (2013): 31–41.

Ramsey, Kate. "Katherine Dunham and the Folklore Performance Movement in Post-US Occupation Haiti." In *Katherine Dunham: Recovering an Anthropological Legacy, Choreographing Ethnographic Futures*, ed. Elizabeth Chin, 51–72. Santa Fe, NM: SAR Press, 2015.

Richland, Justin. *Cooperation Without Submission: Indigenous Jurisdictions in Native Nation-U.S. Engagements*. Chicago: University of Chicago Press, 2021.

Ricoeur, Paul. *Figuring the Sacred: Religion, Narrative, and Imagination*, trans. David Pellauer. Minneapolis, MI: Fortress, 1995.

Rilke, Rainer Maria. *The Dark Interval: Letters on Loss, Grief, and Transformation*, trans. and ed. Ulrich Baer. New York: Modern Library, 2018.

Roberts, Donna, and Donna Read, dirs. *Yemanjá: Wisdom from the African Heart of Brazil*. Project Zula, 2015. 53 min. https://vimeo.com/ondemand/yemanja.

Robeson, Paul. *Paul Robeson Speaks: Writings, Speeches, and Interviews, a Centennial Celebration*, ed. Philip Sheldon and Henry Foner. New York: Citadel, 1978.

Robeson, Paul. *Here I Stand*. 1958. Reprint, Boston: Beacon, 1998.

Robeson, Jr., Paul. *Paul Robeson: Tributes and Selected Writings*. Forest Park, IL: Paul Robeson Archives, 1976.

Robeson, Jr., Paul. *The Undiscovered Paul Robeson: An Artist's Journey, 1898–1939*. Hoboken, NJ: Wiley, 2008.

Robinson, Cedric J. *On Racial Capitalism, Black Internationalism, and Cultures of Resistance*, ed. H. L. T. Quan. London: Pluto, 2019.

Robotham, Donald Keith. "Transnationalism in the Caribbean: Formal and Informal." *American Ethnologist* 25, no. 2 (1998): 307–21.

Rodney, Walter. "African History in the Service of the Black Liberation." *Small Axe* 10 (2001): 66–80.

Rosenberg, Martin E. "The Gift of Silence: Towards an Anthropology of Jazz Improvisation as Neuro-resistance." In *Play and Democracy: Philosophical Perspectives*, ed. Alice Koubová, Petr Urban, Wendy Russell, and Malcolm MacLean. London: Routledge, 2022.

Rush, Stephen. *Free Jazz, Harmolodics, and Ornette Coleman*. New York: Routledge, 2016.

Sakakeeny, Matt. " 'Under the Bridge': An Orientation to Soundscapes in New Orleans." *Ethnomusicology* 54, no. 1 (2010): 1–27.

Sakakeeny, Matt. "New Orleans Music as a Circulatory System." *Black Music Research Journal* 31, no. 2 (2011): 291–325.

Samuels, David W. *Putting a Song on Top of It: Expression and Identity on the San Carlos Apache Reservation*. Tucson: University of Arizona Press, 2006.

Samuels, David W. "Music's Role in Language Revitalization—Some Questions from Recent Literature." *Journal of Linguistic Anthropology* 25, no. 3 (2015): 346–55.

Samuels, David W., Louise Meintjes, Ana Maria Ochoa, and Thomas Porcello. "Soundscapes: Toward a Sounded Anthropology." *Annual Review of Anthropology* 39 (2010): 329–45.

Santo, Diana Espirito. "Making Dreams: Spirits, Visions, and the Ontological Effects of Dream Knowledge in Cuban *Espiritismo*." *Suomen Antropologi* 34, no. 3 (2009): 6–24.

Sarr, Felwine. *Afrotopia*, trans. Drew S. Burk and Sarah Jones-Boardman. Minneapolis: University of Minnesota Press, 2020.

Savage, Barbara Dianne. *Your Spirits Walk Beside Us: The Politics of Black Religion*. Cambridge, MA: Belknap Press of Harvard University Press, 2008.

Sawyer, R. Keith. *Group Creativity: Music, Theater, Collaboration*. Sussex, UK: Psychology Press, 2003.

Schafer, R. Murray. *The Soundscape: Our Sonic Environment and the Tuning of the World*. Merrimac, MA: Destiny Books, 1993.

Schwartz, Peggy, and Murray Schwartz. *The Dance Claimed Me: A Biography of Pearl Primus*. New Haven, CT: Yale University Press, 2012.

Scott, David. *Stuart Hall's Voice: Intimations of an Ethics of Receptive Generosity*. Durham, NC: Duke University Press, 2017.

Segrest, James, and Mark Hoffman. *Moanin' at Midnight: The Life and Times of Howlin' Wolf*. Boston: Da Capo, 2005.

Seremetakis, C. Nadia, ed. *The Senses Still: Perception and Memory as Material Culture in Modernity*. Boulder, CO: Westview, 1994.

Sharpe, Christina. *In the Wake: On Blackness and Being*. Durham, NC: Duke University Press, 2016.

Shaw, Rosalind. *Memories of the Slave Trade: Ritual and the Historical Imagination in Sierra Leone*. Chicago: University of Chicago Press, 2002.

Shelby, Tommie, and Brandon Terry M., eds. *To Shape a New World: Essays on the Political Philosophy of Martin Luther King, Jr.* Cambridge, MA: Harvard University Press, 2018.

Shipton, Alyn. *Groovin' High: The Life of Dizzy Gillespie*. New York: Oxford University Press, 1999.

Simone, AbdouMaliq. *Improvised Lives: Rhythms of Endurance in an Urban South*. New York: Polity, 2018.

Sites, William. *Sun Ra's Chicago: Afrofuturism and the City*. Chicago: University of Chicago Press, 2021.

Sloboda, John A., ed. *Generative Processes in Music: The Psychology of Performance, Improvisation, and Composition*. Oxford: Clarendon Press, 1988.

Solis, Gabriel. *Monk's Music: Thelonious Monk and Jazz History in the Making*. Oakland: University of California Press, 2007.

Stein Crease, Stephanie. *Gil Evans: Out of the Cool: His Life and Music*. Chicago: Chicago Review Press, 2003.

Steinbeck, Paul. *Message to Our Folks: The Art Ensemble of Chicago*. Chicago: University of Chicago Press, 2017.

Steinbeck, Paul. *Sound Experiments: The Music of the AACM*. Chicago: University of Chicago Press, 2022.

Steingo, Gavin, and Jim Sykes, eds. *Remapping Sound Studies*. Durham, NC: Duke University Press, 2019.
Stephans, Michael. *Experiencing Jazz: A Listener's Companion*. Lanham, MD: Scarecrow Press, 2013.
Stephans, Michael. *Experiencing Ornette Coleman: A Listener's Companion*. Lanham, MD: Rowman & Littlefield, 2017.
Stewart, Charles. *Dreaming and Historical Consciousness in Island Greece*. Chicago: University of Chicago Press, 2017.
Stewart, Jeffrey, ed. *Paul Robeson: Artist and Citizen*. New Brunswick, NJ: Rutgers University Press, 1998.
Stewart, Kathleen. *Ordinary Affects*. Durham, NC: Duke University Press, 2007.
Stewart, Kathleen. "In the World that Affect Proposed." *Cultural Anthropology* 32, no. 2 (2017): 192–98.
Stoever, Jennifer Lynn. *The Sonic Color Line: Race and the Cultural Politics of Listening*. New York: NYU Press, 2016.
Strange, Stuart E. "The Dialogical Collective: Mediumship, Pain, and the Interactive Creation of Ndyuka Maroon Subjectivity." *Journal of the Royal Anthropological Institute* 22, no. 3 (2016): 516–33.
Stryker, Mark. *Jazz from Detroit*. Ann Arbor: University of Michigan Press, 2019.
Sutton, R. Anderson. "Interpreting Electronic Sound Technology in the Contemporary Javanese Soundscape." *Ethnomusicology* 40, no. 2 (1996): 249–68.
Sweet, James. *Recreating Africa: Culture, Kinship, and Religion in the African-Portuguese World, 1441–1770*. Chapel Hill: University of North Carolina Press, 2004.
Sweet, James. *Domingos Álvares, African Healing, and the Intellectual History of the Atlantic World*. Chapel Hill: University of North Carolina Press, 2011.
Swindall, Lindsey R. *Paul Robeson: A Life of Activism and Art*. Washington, DC: Rowman & Littlefield, 2013.
Szwed, John. *So What: The Life of Miles Davis*. New York: Simon & Schuster, 2004.
Szwed, John. *Billie Holiday: The Musician and the Myth*. New York: Penguin, 2016.
Szwed, John. *Space Is the Place: The Lives and Times of Sun Ra*. Durham, NC: Duke University Press, 2020.

Tell, Dave. *Remembering Emmett Till*. Chicago: University of Chicago Press, 2019.

Thomas, Deborah A. *Political Life in the Wake of the Plantation: Sovereignty, Witnessing, Repair*. Durham, NC: Duke University Press, 2019.

Threadgill, Henry, and Brent Hayes Edwards. *Easily Slip into Another World: A Life in Music*. New York: Knopf, 2023.

Toop, David. *Ocean of Sound: Ambient Sound and Radical Listening in the Age of Communication*. Mineola, NY: Dover Publications, 2018.

Trouillot, Michel-Rolph. *Silencing the Past: Power and the Production of History*. Boston: Beacon, 1995.

Troupe, Quincy. "Up Close and Personal: Miles Davis and Me." *Conjunctions*, no. 16 (1991): 76–93.

Troupe, Quincy. *Miles and Me*. Oakland: University of California Press, 2002.

Ture, Kwame, and Charles V. Hamilton. *Black Power: Politics of Liberation in America*. New York: Vintage, 2011.

Tyson, Timothy B. *The Blood of Emmett Till*. New York: Simon & Schuster, 2017.

Veal, Michael E. *Dub: Soundscapes and Shattered Songs in Jamaican Reggae*. Middletown, CT: Wesleyan University Press, 2007,

Voegelin, Salomé. *Listening to Noise and Silence: Toward a Philosophy of Sound Art*. London: Continuum, 2010.

Voegelin, Salomé. *Sonic Possible Worlds: Hearing the Continuum of Sound*. London: Bloomsbury Academic, 2014.

Voegelin, Salomé. "Music as Public Art." *Essay for the Donauschinger Musiktage 2016*. Commissioned by radio SWR2, Donaueschingen, Germany, October 13–16, 2016.

Voegelin, Salomé. "Sound Words and Sonic Fictions: Writing the Ephemeral." *The Routledge Companion to Sounding Art*, ed. Marcel Cobussen, Vincent Meelberg and Barry Truax. Oxfordshire, UK: Routledge, 2017.

Voegelin, Salomé. *The Political Possibility of Sound: Fragments of Listening*. London: Bloomsbury Academic, 2018.

Voegelin, Salomé, and Thomas Gardner, eds. *Colloquium: Sound Art and Music*. London: Zero Books, 2016.

Walker, Alice. *We Are the Ones We Have Been Waiting For: Inner Light in a Time of Darkness*. New York: The New Press, 2021.

Weidman, Amanda. "Anthropology and Voice." *Annual Review of Anthropology* 43 (2014): 37–51.

West, Cornel, and Christa Buschendorf. *Black Prophetic Fire*. Boston: Beacon, 2014.

Wilf, Eitan. "Sincerity Versus Self-Expression: Modern Creative Agency and the Materiality of Semiotic Forms." *Cultural Anthropology* 26, no. 3 (2011): 462–84.

Wilf, Eitan. "Rituals of Creativity: Tradition, Modernity, and the 'Acoustic Unconscious' in a U.S. Collegiate Jazz Music Program." *American Anthropologist* 114, no. 1 (2012): 32–44.

Wilf, Eitan. "Semiotic Dimensions of Creativity." *Annual Review of Anthropology* 43 (2014): 397–412.

Woideck, Carl. *Charlie Parker: His Music and Life*. Ann Arbor: University of Michigan Press, 1998.

Youngquist, Paul. *A Pure Solar World: Sun Ra and the Birth of Afrofuturism*. Austin: University of Texas Press, 2016.

GPSR Authorized Representative: Easy Access System Europe, Mustamäe tee 50, 10621 Tallinn, Estonia, gpsr.requests@easproject.com

www.ingramcontent.com/pod-product-compliance
Lightning Source LLC
Chambersburg PA
CBHW031238290426
44109CB00012B/353